Ex Auditu

An International Journal of Theological Interpretation of Scripture

Volume 5 1989

Ex Auditu is published annually by Pickwick Publications, 4137 Timberlane Drive, Allison Park, Pennsylvania, 15101-2932, U.S.A.

Subscriptions:
- Individuals:
  - U.S.A. - $15.00
  - Canada - $12.00 (in U.S. Funds)
  - All other countries - $15.00 (in U.S. Funds)
  - Students - $10.00
- Institutions:
  - U.S.A. - $25.00
  - Canada - $20.00
  - All other countries - $25.00 (in U.S. Funds)

Indexed in *Religion Index One: Periodicals*, published by the American Theological Library Association, Chicago, Illinois, available online in the ATLA Religion Database through BRS Information Technologies (Latham, New York); DIALOGUE Information Services (Palo Alto, California); *Internationale Zeitschriftenschau für Bibelwissenschaft und Grenzgebeite*; *Religion and Theological Abstracts*.

Please address all subscription correspondence and change of address information to Pickwick Publications.

ISSN 08883-0053

EX AUDITU

An International Journal of Theological Interpretation of Scripture

THE EDITORIAL BOARD MEMBERS AND CONSULTANTS represent various disciplines and denominations. Theological Interpretation of Scripture is a task to be taken seriously by scholars who are committed to the Christian faith and tradition. However, as one editorial consultant stated: "let people gradually get used to the idea that a sane hermeneutics is both oriented in advance toward agreement/consent and is simultaneously exigent, discriminating, critical."

EDITORIAL CONSULTANTS

EX AUDITU

Volume 5 1989

CONTENTS

INTRODUCTION

"Salvation" emerged as the theme for this issue from the previous discussion of "The Church and Israel (Romans 9-11)," *Ex Auditu* 4 (1988). In Rom 11:26 Paul concluded his reflections about Israel's place in salvation history with the reassuring declaration that "all Israel will be *saved*" (11:26). Whereas most of the articles had focused in one way or another on "Israel," the meaning of being "saved" never surfaced and the question has led to the present volume on "salvation."

In certain Christian circles salvation language brings back earliest memories of the Christian message. Phrases like "Jesus saves," "being saved," and "accepting Jesus as personal Savior" correlated with the poignant question—"Are you/have you been saved?" In short, the gospel had to do with "salvation." "All Israel will be *saved*" meant "all Israel" would be "saved" from eternal judgment, that is, hell.

As valid as such salvation language may be personally and theologically its limits can be illustrated in two ways. First, a personal story illustrates the cultural limits of that language. Having been raised in the Bible belt where one frequently saw "Jesus saves" painted on rocks, road signs, and bumper stickers and having awakened on Sunday mornings during my childhood to Charles E. Fuller and the Old Fashioned Revival Hour's theme song, "Jesus Saves," I was stunned one day during my graduate studies by some graffiti on the wall of the New York subway. In bright red paint was inscribed—"Jesus saves." Below it in green ink and a different hand was painted—"S & H Green Stamps." The graffiti vividly expressed what I had already come to understand. "Jesus saves" says it all, but it can say much too little.

Second, the series of articles in this issue illustrate the biblical, theological, personal and social complexity of "salvation." They remind us not only of what "salvation" means but of how much "salvation" means. We are foced inevitably to look at "soteriology" and its multiple expressions in Scripture and the Church. We soon discover how inadequate salvation language is today. Yet the question remains—what does "salvation" mean?

Donald Gowan in "Salvation as Healing" traces the concept of healing from the Old to the New Testament as the middle term which led to the connection of salvation and forgiveness in the Synoptics and in the ministry of the early church. He suggests that "healing" may be the more appropriate expression to convey the biblical meaning of "salvation," especially as it has to do with the individual and societal need and experience of "salvation" ("healing") today.

Three articles follow that focus on Luke, John, and Paul respectively. Joel Green in "'The Message of Salvation' in Luke-Acts" examines the NT writer who uses salvation language the most and raises again the question about the role the cross played in Luke's "salvation history." Marianne Meye Thompson looks at "Eternal Life in the Gospel of John" as the "term which connotes the totality of salvation" in the Fourth Gospel. Ben Meyer's "Did Paul's View of the Resurrection of the Dead Undergo Development?" reprinted from *Theological Studies* 47 (1986) 363-87 and his collected essays, *Critical Realism and the New Testament*, Princeton Theological Monograph Series 17 (Allison Park, PA: Pickwick Publications, 1989) 99-128, looks at the believer's ultimate "hope" or "salvation" as narrowly understood in terms of life, death, and resurrection.

Paul L. Hammer in "God's Health for the World: Some Biblical Understandings of Salvation" looks at the salvation language embedded in several Old and New Testament writings to discover the breadth of meaning behind the biblical concept of "salvation," of what it means biblically to "be saved." His survey of "salvation" texts leads him, like Gowan, to the theme of "health" and "healing."

Jonathan Rainbow in "Double Grace: John Calvin's View of the Relationship of Justification and Sanctification" shifts our attention to the more classical expressions of soteriology by reviewing salvation in terms of Calvin's teaching on justification and sanctification. Alasdair I. C. Heron moves the theme into modern systematics by looking at "The Theme of Salvation in Karl Barth's Doctrine of Reconciliation" through selected citations from volume four of Barth's *Church Doamatics*.

As a contemporary theologian, John Weborg in "Be Not Far: A Reflection on the *Lifework* of Jesus Christ" looks again at the atonement in view of the *lifework* of Jesus Christ as the incarnate "expression of God's friendship and solidarity with sinners" which becomes the ground for a "fundamental trust" from and within which "saving faith can emerge."

David Bosch writing from a missiologist's perspective on "Salvation: A Missiological Perspective" surveys the understandings of salvation in missionary history, looks at the crisis of salvation in contemporary discussions and calls for a "comprehensive salvation" today.

Finally, in a sermonic essay, "Sin and Salvation: *Amadeus* in the Light of Romans," Robert Jewett applies his hermeneutical approach ("indigenized hermeneutic") of finding a "cultural artifact," such as popular films, novels and short stories, that "resonates at a deep level with a particular Biblical passage" and interpreting each so that the one throws light on the other.

The Editorial Board eagerly anticipates the resumption of the annual Symposium on Theological Interpretation of Scripture to be hosted by North Park Theological Seminary of Chicago, Illinois. This Symposium will provide a forum for discussion of the future themes of *Ex Auditu*. The inaugural Symposium is scheduled for Oct 12-14, 1990 on the theme, **Prophetic and/or Apocalyptic Eschatology**. Papers from this forum will appear in volume 6 of *Ex Auditu*.

March, 1990

Robert A. Guelich
The Editor

An Announcement

North Park Theological Seminary in Chicago, Illinois is pleased to announce that the first Symposium on Theological Interpretation of Scripture will take place October 12 -14, 1990. The Symposium will start at 1:30 p.m. on October 12 in Nyvall Hall and will extend through noon on October 14.

The theme of this year's symposium will be **Prophetic and/or Apocalyptic Eschatology**. The following persons have agreed to make presentations:

Professor Klaus Koch	*Old Testament*
Professor Leslie Allen	*Old Testament*
Professor John Collins	*Intertestamental Literature*
Professor George Beasley-Murray	*New Testament*
Professor David Scholer	*New Testament*
Professor Adela Yarbro Collins	*New Testament*
Sister Agnes Cunningham	*Church History*
Professor Timothy Weber	*Church History*
Professor Gabriel Fackre	*Theology*
Professor John Howard Yoder	*Ethics*

Persons interested in attending the sessions should write before September 1, 1990 to:

Dr. Klyne Snodgrass
North Park Theological Seminary
3225 W. Foster Avenue
Chicago, Illinois 60625

Meals may be taken at North Park, and assistance will be provided in finding nearby lodging.

SALVATION AS HEALING

DONALD E. GOWAN

The major themes of this paper may be introduced by referring to two passages in the Gospel According to Luke (7:36-50; 8:43-48). In the former, a woman "who was a sinner" washes and anoints Jesus' feet and he declares that her sins are forgiven. In the latter, a woman who had had a flow of blood for twelve years touches the hem of his garment and is healed. At the conclusion of both stories Jesus says the identical words, "Your faith has saved you; go in peace" (7:50; 8:48). Salvation = forgiveness; salvation = healing. This paper will trace the concept of healing from the Old Testament to the New, finding it to be the middle term which led to the connection of salvation and forgiveness in the Synoptics and in the ministry of the early church as well.

It was, in fact, a book on the early church which first aroused my interest in the association of healing with salvation. While working on the promises of healing in the Old Testament in connection with my book *Eschatology in the Old Testament* I found a reference to a fascinating chapter in Harnack's book, *The Expansion of Christianity in the First Three Centuries*, called "The Gospel of the Saviour and of Salvation."[1] In that chapter he showed how the early church understood Jesus' ministry and its own to be the healing of soul and body. Later I was surprised to find Harnack's views dismissed in passing by Werner Foerster, in his article on *sōzō* in the *Theological Dictionary of the New Testament*. This paper is set in deliberate contrast to these sentences from Foerster's conclusion:

> NT *sōtēria* does not refer to earthly relationships. Its content is not, as in the Greek understanding, well-being, health of body and soul. Nor is it the earthly liberation of the people of God from the heathen yoke, as in Judaism. It does not relate to any circumstances as such. It denotes neither healing in a religious sense [citing Harnack], nor life [citing Wagner, 1905], nor liberation from satanic or demonic power [citing Holzmann, 1911]. It has to do solely with man's relationship to God.[2]

It is clear from the evidence Foerster himself has set forth in his article that he has not only dismissed Harnack, but has also dismissed the evidence from the Synoptic Gospels and Acts. His definition of "New Testament *sōtēria*" is based on the Pauline use of the term. The Old Testament material on which I propose to concentrate will be seen to stand in direct continuity with the Synoptics and Acts, and I believe also with the teachings of the early church. Its relationship with Paul is very indirect, and so there will be no need to bring the Pauline literature into the discussion.

The evangelists make an explicit connection between the ministry of Jesus and the Old Testament's promises of eschatological healing, providing a natural starting point for this study. Jesus summarizes his work as follows:

> The blind receive their sight and the lame walk, lepers are cleansed and the deaf hear, and the dead are raised up, and the poor have good news preached to them (Matt 11:5; Luke 7:22).

The reference to the blind, the lame and the deaf is an evident allusion to Isa 35:5-6, where blind, lame, deaf and dumb are promised healing in the last days. Another of Matthew's summaries of Jesus' ministry contains a similar variation on Isa 35:5-6, listing the dumb, the maimed, the lame and the blind, and there is general agreement that, among other things, the healing stories in the Gospels are intended to be signs of the inbreaking of the eschaton.[3] Those stories have been interpreted at length, but not so much has been done with the original promises of the Old Testament, to which they refer, and it is with those descriptions of eschatological healing that this study begins.[4]

The most useful materials for the study of salvation as healing have been found to be the Old Testament's promises of healing "in that day," the Psalms of lament dealing with sickness, and the Synoptics. Each of them will be dealt with in turn, followed by a briefer selection of comments from scholars who have written on salvation and healing in the early church. Finally, some conclusions will be drawn concerning the potential value of language about healing for the ministry of the contemporary church.

We shall trace four themes:

a) the association in both Testaments of "save" with "heal, " noting that in the Old Testament "save" is normally used to refer literally to physical deliverance, while "heal" is used both literally and metaphorically;

b) the association of healing with forgiveness, in two ways: (1) considering sin to be a cause of sickness, so that forgiveness produces physical healing, and (2) using sickness and healing as metaphors for sin and forgiveness;

c) the association of "save" with "forgive" is a rare usage in the Old Testament but more common in the New Testament;

d) the importance of what we may call "alienation, " choosing a word which may cover the sense of isolation both from human and divine relationships, in what both Testaments say about salvation as healing.

I. PROMISES OF HEALING IN THE OLD TESTAMENT

It is well-known that the root *yshʿ* "save" is used in the Old Testament almost exclusively of rescue from physical danger of some kind, from enemies, from prison, from injustice, from sickness. [5] That it could be used of something like deliverance from one's sins is shown by Ezek 36: 29: " . . . and I will deliver you from all your uncleannesses, " but that is a rare case. Eventually we shall see that the use of *sōzein* in the Synoptics is in continuity with the meanings "rescue" and "heal, " carried by, *yshʿ* but that it is also possible to take that rare use of "save, " meaning forgiveness, and make it a key term for the understanding of Jesus ' ministry, as Matthew does when he interprets the very name

"Jesus" as derived from *ysh*ʿ with the explanation, "for he will *save* his people from their sins" (Matt 1: 21) . I believe there is a three-fold basis for that understanding of Jesus as "Savior": in the Old Testament's promises of eschatological healing, in the Psalms which speak of sickness, and in Jesus ' own healing ministry.

One might expect the promise of healing for the sick, or of perfect health for all in the last days, to be a major element of Old Testament eschatology, but in fact it appears in only a few passages.[6] They are significant largely because of the specific ailments to which they refer and to the setting in which healing is promised, but before looking at those details, it is necessary to look for the four themes mentioned in the introduction.

a) The most frequently quoted passage associating salvation with healing is not eschatological, but it is useful to recall it here: "Heal me, O Lord, and I shall be healed; save me and I shall be saved; for thou art my praise" (Jer 17:14) . The kind of salvation which appears most prominently in the Old Testament's pictures of the ideal future is the restoration of exiles to the Promised Land, but salvation of a specific kind is sometimes offered to those we may call the disabled, as a part of that promise of return and new life in the land. For example:

> The Lord has saved his people,
>   the remnant of Israel.
> Behold, I will bring them from the north country,
>   and gather them from the farthest parts of the earth,
> among them the blind and the lame,
>   the woman with child and her who is in travail together;
> a great company, they shall return here (Jer 31:7b-8).

The triumphal journey through the desert to Zion is announced in Isa 35:4b-5 as follows:

> "He will come and save you."
> Then the eyes of the blind shall be opened,
>   and the ears of the deaf unstopped;
> then shall the lame man leap like a hart,
>   and the tongue of the dumb sing for joy.

The term "save" is associated with promises of healing also in Isa 33:22-24 and Zeph 3:19.

b) The only eschatological passage which parallels sin and sickness is Isa 33:24: "And no inhabitant will say, 'I am sick'; the people who dwell there will be forgiven their iniquity." That physical infirmity is referred to is indicated by the reference to the lame in vs. 23; that iniquity is considered to have been the cause of sickness is not directly stated, but may be inferred from the parallelism. It is more common to use sickness and healing as metaphors for sin and forgiveness, as in Isa 57:17-18:

> Because of the iniquity of his covetousness I was angry,
>   I smote him, I hid my face and was angry;
>   but he went on backsliding in the way of his own heart.
> I have seen his ways, but I will heal him,
>   I will lead him and requite him with comfort.

Compare also Isa 57:15; 58:6-11; Jer 33:5-8. This apparently instinctive use of "sickness" as a metaphor referring to anything that has gone radically wrong in the life of an individual or in society as a whole can be found throughout the Bible, and of course we are familiar with it as commonplace in contemporary speech. More will be said about that in the conclusion.

c) It has already been noted that the association of "save" with "forgive" is rare in the OT. The one eschatological text which explicitly associates physical health with forgiveness has just been quoted (Isa 33:24).

d) The key to a proper understanding of the Old Testament's promises of healing in the last days can be found by considering the setting of Isa 35:5-6. In that day a highway will be made through the desert, which will bloom in order to provide an appropriate setting for the triumphant procession of exiles back to Zion (vss. 1, 6b-10). But they will have to walk, and such a journey would be physically impossible for the lame, and a great trial for the blind. The deaf could not even hear the good news of vs. 4: "Say to those who are of a fearful heart, 'Be strong, fear not!' " And the dumb could not participate in the singing of that joyful group, anticipated in vs. 10: "And the ransomed of the Lord shall return, and come to Zion with singing." Comparing this chapter with the other passages that have been listed helps us to understand why Israel's hope for a perfect future did not find it necessary to speak of freedom from illness of all kinds. Note that the ailments which are specifically mentioned are conditions we now call disabilities. Only four appear in the eschatological texts: blindness, lameness, deafness, and inability to speak.[7] As the ideal future is envisioned, the prophets think of people who would otherwise be left out of the full, joyful life of the restored community, and they do not believe God will allow that. They are not so concerned with headaches, toothaches, coughs, and ulcers. Given the state of medical knowledge in those days, probably most people did not feel good most of the time.[8] Our ideal of perfect health for everyone may be a peculiar outlook of the 20th century, and of the "First World."[9]

People with all sorts of ailments, many of them serious, have functioned and still do function as full members of their communities, and it is participation in the life of the community which the Old Testament authors consider to be of critical importance for the realization of one's full humanity, as we shall see more clearly in considering the Psalms. As the prophets thought about the future they could not ignore the problem of those whose condition excluded them from full participation in community life, and so as they dream of the perfection of this world, those people must be mentioned explicitly. Here we have encountered promises that the isolation of the sick, which regularly becomes alienation, as we shall see in the Psalms dealing with sickness, is a problem God intends to overcome, and we shall see that the Synoptics affirm the ministry of Jesus has done precisely that.

II. SICKNESS AND HEALING IN THE PSALMS

The complaints which occur most frequently in the psalms of lament concern enemies and illness, with the former by far the most prevalent. Most of the psalms which speak of sickness also mention threats from enemies. The problem of the identity of these enemies has been widely discussed, but much less has been written about illness, which appears in about eighteen psalms, including some genres other than lament.[10]

a) "Save" and "heal" are parallel to one another in a psalm of thanksgiving, Psa 107:19-20:

Then they cried to the Lord in their trouble,
and he delivered (*yosi-em*) them from their distress;
He sent forth his word, and healed them,
and delivered (*yemalleṭ*) them from destruction. (RSV)

Psalm 6 speaks in vivid terms of physical distress:

Be gracious to me, O Lord, for I am feeble,
heal me, O Lord, for my bones are trembling.
I am full of trepidation,
but you, O Lord, how long?
Turn, O Lord, and deliver me,
save me for the sake of your steadfast love. (vss. 2-4)

Salvation is also associated with deliverance from illness in Pss 22:20-21; 31:2,7,10; 69:1,4; 88:1-18; 116:8-13; and the psalm of Hezekiah in Isa 38:10-20.

b) The frequently stated conclusion that Israelites normally considered illness to be God's punishment for sin probably should be modified somewhat in the light of the bulk of the evidence from the Psalms. A few psalms do put it that way,[11] with considerable emphasis, and they have tended to influence the reading of the others, in which it is more common to express bewilderment at the alienation from God which the sufferer feels because of the sickness. Psalm 32 does associate sin with physical distress, although it does not say explicitly that forgiveness produced healing:

When I declared not my sin, my body wasted away
through my groaning all day long. . . .
I acknowledged my sin to thee,
and I did not hide my iniquity;
I said, "I will confess my transgressions to the Lord";
then thou didst forgive the guilt of my sin. (vss. 3,5)

Psalm 38 puts the matter more clearly than anywhere else, saying, "There is no health in my bones because of my sin" (vs. 3b; cf. vss. 4-5), and Psa 107:17 also says, " because of their iniquities suffered affliction." Psalm 41 is ambiguous, saying in vs. 4b, "Heal me, for I have sinned against thee!" then affirming in vs. 12, "But thou hast upheld me because of my integrity." The parallelism of "who forgives all your iniquity, who heals all your diseases" (Psa 103:3) does not necessarily indicate a cause and effect relationship.

It is more common for the psalmists to ask God why they are suffering than to confess that they deserve their sickness because they have sinned. The feelings of Psa 73:13-14, "All in vain have I kept my heart clean and washed my hands in innocence. For all the day long I have been stricken, and chastened every morning," are expressed in a variety of ways in Pss. 6, 22, 30, 31, 42, 69, 88, and 102. Each of them speaks of alienation, from God and/or humans, without being able to account for it as the result of the psalmist's own faults.[12] Samuel Balentine's study of one term expressing alienation, the hiding of God's face, found that in the psalms (in contrast to the prophets) words concerning sin are not associated with the term, and that often it is accompanied by protests of innocence.[13] Several of the references to the hiding of God's face occur in the psalms of sickness (Pss 13:1; 22:24; 30:7; 69:17; 88:14; 102:2), but there are various other ways of indicating the sense of alienation:

> O Lord, rebuke me not in thy anger,
> nor chasten me in thy wrath. (Psa 6:1)
> I say to God, my rock; "Why hast thou forgotten me?" (Psa 42:9)
> My eyes grow dim with waiting for my God. (Psa 69:3)
> O Lord, why dost thou cast me off? (Psa 88:14)

These examples remind us that frequently the laments see the problem as being on God's side, rather than the responsibility of the sufferer. Reasons for that will be explored in part d) below. Contrary to much that has been written about sin and sickness in the Old Testament, it seems fair to say that most of these laments recognize no doctrinaire explanation for illness as punishment for sin. Of course, the theory occurs elsewhere in the Old Testament, as in Elihu's classic formulation in Job 33:19-30, and we have seen it used in a few psalms, but a careful reading of the laments over sickness should warn us not to assume that Israelites all accepted a neat explanation that every illness is a result of sin.

These preliminary observations already begin to show us that in the laments a sense of alienation is more regularly associated with sickness than is the confession of sin. In part d) below the fact that sickness regularly produces intense feelings of isolation will be pursued as the possible origin of the eventual doctrinaire explanation of sickness as punishment. So far, we have seen that although the idea is present it scarcely appears as a doctrine in the psalms dealing with illness.

c. The root *ys'* does not appear in association with sin in the Psalms dealing with sickness, but the idea of being saved from sin does occur, using the root *nṣl* in Psa 39:8: "Deliver me from all my transgressions." There is a possible relationship between saving and forgiving in the psalm of Hezekiah (Isa 38:10-20). After praying for healing, in vs. 16, and affirming that God has "cast all my sins behind thy back," in vs. 17, Hezekiah concludes his psalm with "the Lord will save me" (vs. 20). But words for saving or delivering are used with sin so rarely in the Old Testament that Stamm does not even include them among his terms denoting forgiveness.[14]

d) The laments reflect one of the disturbing, universal effects of sickness, the sense of loneliness in one's suffering which can develop into feelings of extreme isolation, and something stronger than that, which we may call alienation, with all the negative connotations that carries. It affects the way the sick person feels about both God and other human beings. It may be helpful to introduce our consideration of the emotive language of the Psalms with the insights into the psychology of sickness offered by some modern authors.

Near the end of Norman Cousins' *The Anatomy of an Illness as Perceived by the Patient*,[15] he lists the barriers which arise between the seriously ill and those who seek to minister to them. We shall find many of them expressed in highly emotional language in the Psalms. Among them he includes the feeling of helplessness; "a wall of separation between us and the world of open movement, open sounds, open expectations"; "the conflict between the terror of loneliness and the desire to be left alone"; and "the utter void created by the longing—ineradicable, unremitting, pervasive—for warmth of human contact." In addition to these feelings of isolation, he includes another feature that will be crucial to our evaluation of the relationship between sin and sickness: "There was the lack of self-esteem, the subconscious feeling perhaps that our illness was a manifestation of our inadequacy."

Martin Marty's moving reflections on the psalms of lament take us directly to the appropriation of the language of scripture by one affected by a critical illness.[16] In his chapter called "The Season of Abandonment" his use of winter-imagery as a way of speaking about the journey through a serious spiritual crisis leads him to move from "The January Thaw: A Hint of Presence" to the "psalms of the second winter, psalms that speak boldly of abandonment by friends and by God."[17] When we read what the psalmists have to say about friends and family, we shall be reminded of Marty's description of the cynicism of one who has been ill too long:

> You aren't exactly a cheery person with whom people will want to keep company. You would brighten the scene by staying hidden. Take a pill to get out of your misery. Brighten up before you reappear. We have our own loads to carry. What makes you so special?[18]

Leo Tolstoy produced a vivid, fictional account of this sense of isolation and unworthiness in the critically ill, in his short story "The Death of Ivan Ilych."

The phenomenology of sickness, as reflected in these modern descriptions and in our own experiences, may enable us to use the psalms of lament in order to trace the movement from feeling to doctrine in a way similar to that which Paul Ricoeur used in his examination of the relationship between defilement and sin.[19] Rudolph Otto's insights into the ways we rationalize the nonrational aspects of religious experience have also contributed to this approach.[20] Sickness or disability creates an emotional barrier between those in pain or unable to do things and those who feel good and have no limitations. It is created inevitably by pain and disability themselves, but is frequently aggravated by unconcern or impatience on the part of the healthy and may take the form of visible barriers.[21] One of the major effects of this isolation is the production of extreme feelings of resentment and self-pity in the sufferer.

They feel abandoned by friends and relatives:

> My friends and companions stand aloof from my plague, and my kinsmen stand afar off. (Psa 38:11)
> I have become a stranger to my brethren, an alien to my mother's sons (Psa 69:8).
> I am like a lonely bird on the housetop,
> All the day my enemies taunt me,
> those who deride me use my name for a curse (Psa 102:7b-8).

Those who once were dependable have betrayed them:

> Even my bosom friend in whom I trusted, who ate of my bread, has lifted his heel against me (Psa 41:9).

The sense of isolation produced by pain is compared to death itself:

> I have passed out of mind like one who is dead;
> I have become like a broken vessel (Psa 31:12).
> I am a man who has no strength,
> like one forsaken among the dead,

like the slain that lie in the grave (Psa 88:4b-5a).

Even more insidious, however, is the tendency not to blame one's abandonment entirely on others, but to begin to think it is deserved. Pain and disability in themselves attack one's feelings of self-worth, but the effects of the attack are exacerbated by the negative opinions of others who blame you for your ailment, take advantage of your weakness, or just ignore you:

> But I am a worm, and no man;
> scorned by men, and despised by the people (Psa 22:6).
> I am the scorn of all my adversaries,
> a horror to my neighbors,
> an object of dread to my acquaintances;
> those who see me in the street flee from me (Psa 31:11).
> I looked for pity, but there was none;
> and for comforters, but I found none (Psa 69:20b).
> Thou hast caused lover and friend to shun me;
> my companions are in darkness (Psa 88:18).

So this feeling of aloneness, typical of severe illness, may be expressed not only by words of separation, but also by expressions of the feeling that one has been judged unworthy to continue normal human relationships.

This sense of isolation and alienation becomes so extreme that it is then projected upon one's relationship with God, who is accused of deserting the one who depends on him:

> My God, my God, why hast thou forsaken me?
> Why art thou so far from helping me, from the words of my groaning?
> O my God, I cry by day, but thou dost not answer;
> and by night, but find no rest (Psa 22:1-2).
> Do not forsake me, O Lord!
> O my God, be not far from me (Psa 38:21).
> I say to God, my rock; "Why hast thou forgotten me?" (Psa 42:9a)
> For thou art the God in whom I take refuge;
> why hast thou cast me off? (Psa 43:2).

Furthermore, since the psalmist thinks of Yahweh as the source of all things, including sickness, the problem is worse than distance, or failure to hear the cry for help. God seems to be treating the sufferer as a human enemy would:

> O Lord, rebuke me not in thy anger,
> nor chasten me in thy wrath (Psa 6:1; cf. 38:1).
> Thy wrath lies heavy upon me,
> and thou dost overwhelm me with all thy waves.
> Thou hast caused my companions to shun me;
> thou hast made me a thing of horror to them. . . .
> O Lord, why dost thou cast me off?
> Why dost thou hide thy face from me? . . .
> Thy wrath has swept over me;
> thy dread assaults destroy me (Psa 88:7-8, 14, 16).
> For I eat ashes like bread,
> and mingle tears with my drink,

> because of thy indignation and anger;
> for thou hast taken me up and thrown me away (Psa 102: 9-10).

Some explanation must be found for this apparent anger of God, and it lies to hand in the feelings of rejection and unworthiness which naturally accompany illness or disability. And so the pain is rationalized by converting the sense of alienation into sin: Since I am worthless, this pain is deserved. God's apparent anger is thus justified by rationalizing sickness or disability as punishment for sin. Both the instinctive feeling of uncleanness and its explanation as sinfulness appear in a communal confession in Isa 64:5b-6a:

> Behold thou wast angry, and we sinned;
> in our sins we have been a long time, and shall we be saved?
> We have all become like one who is unclean,
> and our righteous deeds are like a polluted garment.

Most of the language of the Psalms, however, remains at the fundamental level of the emotions, for we have seen that bewilderment, a sense of betrayal, and pleas for help addressed to the psalmist's God whose failure to respond adds to his pain are the dominant elements in the laments. These prayers of the sick thus contain the materials which enable us to see why and how the explanation of suffering as punishment for sin developed.[22]

We may summarize what has been learned from the prophetic promises and the psalms of lament as follows: pain (including illness and every type of disability) produces a sense of loneliness, which can often be very intense. If severe enough and long-lasting enough the loneliness results in alienation, from one's community and from God. The effects of alienation from human companions are self-pity and a decreased sense of self-worth. A desire for vindication may also appear. Alienation from God is typically expressed in terms of distance or silence—feeling that God does not care; or in terms of anger—feeling that God is an enemy. But then that sense of weakness, worthlessness, uncleanness may become the means to justify God, as they lead to a confession of sin.

Thus sickness becomes a metaphor for sin and healing a metaphor for forgiveness. In the eschatology of the Old Testament, forgiveness can be described as healing (e.g. Isa 57:17-19). When actual physical healing is promised, however, it is the problem of alienation from the community which concerns the prophets most, as they name explicitly what must have been the most prevalent and most distressing disabilities (from the frequency with which they are mentioned) preventing people from achieving their full humanlty because they could not participate fully in the life of their community. Because healing is one of the forms of salvation longed for and promised in the Old Testament, and because healing has also become a metaphor for forgiveness, it is not surprising that by the New Testament period the word "save" can be readily used in a spiritual sense, even though such uses were rare in an earlier period.

III. SALVATION AND HEALING IN THE GOSPELS AND ACTS

That the writers of the Synoptics intended to represent Jesus as healer of body and soul is evident from their choice of language as well as from the number of healing miracles they record. Jesus uses healing as a metaphor for forgiveness when he says, "Those who are well have no need of a physician, but those who are sick; I came not to call the righteous, but sinners" (Mark 2:17; Matt 9:12-13; Luke 5:31-32, adding "to repentance"). Matthew takes "with his stripes we are healed" in Isa 53:5 literally, and thus applies vs. 4, "Surely he has borne our griefs [or diseases] and carried our sorrows [or pain]" directly to the healing ministry of Jesus, rather than to forgiveness (Matt 8:17). When Luke tells of Jesus' application of Isa 61:1-2a to his ministry he quotes the LXX, which speaks of "recovering of sight to the blind," a phrase not found in the Hebrew text Jesus read (Luke 4:18-19). Matthew finds a rather remote relationship between Jesus' healings and Isa 42:1-4, in order to represent them as a fulfillment of one more prophecy. And there is consistency in the summaries of his ministry which are provided here and there; Jesus came preaching and healing, and when specific ailments are mentioned they recall the traditional lists of the Old Testament promises, as we already noticed when Matt 11:5 (Luke 7:22) was compared with Isa 35:5-6. It is Matthew who makes the most of Jesus as a healer, as two recent articles have pointed out.[23] Duling notes that summaries such as the following are distributed throughout the Gospel:

> And he went about all Galilee, teaching in their synagogues and preaching the gospel of the kingdom and healing every disease and every infirmity among the people.(Matt 4:23).
>
> And great crowds came to him, bringing with them the lame, the maimed, the blind, the dumb, and many others, and they put them at his feet, and he healed them, so that the throng wondered, when they saw the dumb speaking, the maimed whole, the lame walking, and the blind seeing; and they glorified the God of Israel. (Matt 15:30-31).

Heil's comment, "In no other type of Synoptic Gospel material do people receive the gifts of salvation in a way that visibly improves their personal lives," provides an appropriate introduction to our survey of the ways salvation and healing are intertwined.

a) One of the standard meanings of the Greek word *sōzein* is "heal," and the Synoptics are distinctive in the New Testament for the prominence they give to that meaning. Especially important for our purposes is the continuity between the Old Testament's regular use of "save" to mean deliverance from physical distress and the predominance of the same meaning for *sōzein* in the Synoptics.[24] It refers to saving of life a total of nineteen times (ten times if parallels are discounted), to healing the sick fifteen times (nine times), to forgiveness of sin three times (Matt 1:21; Luke 1:77; 7:50), to eschatological salvation 5 times (Matt 19:25 par; 24:13; Luke 13:23, and is used eight times by Luke in what may be called a "general purpose" way, of all the benefits of believing in Christ (e.g. Luke. 19:10: "For the Son of Man came to seek and to save the lost."). This latter use appears to be the backward influence of the Book of Acts, where Luke evidently uses "salvation" in that broad way because it had become the language of the early church.

In Acts the word is used of saving life four times, of healing twice, of forgiveness twice, and in that general purpose way thirteen times (e.g. " 'Men, what must I do to be saved?' And they said, 'Believe in the Lord Jesus, and you will be saved, you and your household' " (Acts 16:30-31). John uses it twice of saving life (11:12; 12:27) and six times in a broad sense, with a more obvious contrast to divine judgment than is common in the Synoptics.[25] If we compare the Synoptics with the apocryphal books it becomes evident that they continue to use *sōzein* in the way it was used in Judaism of the first century, for seldom in the Apocrypha does it mean anything other than physical salvation.[26] As the

Synoptics portray the ministry of Jesus, then, salvation was literally the healing of the body for many of those he encountered.

b) The use of healing as a metaphor for forgiveness has already been noted, in Jesus' saying about the physician, which parallels "well" with righteous and "sick" with sinners (Matt 9:12 par). The literal association of sin with sickness is more problematical. The classic case (indeed it is the only case) is the story of the paralytic whose friends let his pallet down through the roof of the house where Jesus was (Matt 9:2-8; Mark 2:5-12; Luke 5:18-26). The word "save" is not used in any version of the story, either for healing or forgiveness, but consideration of the story cannot be omitted here. Jesus' immediate response to the appearance of the paralytic is to assure him his sins are forgiven, but this does not produce automatic healing. When Jesus' ability to forgive is challenged, he then compares forgiveness and healing, as to their relative difficulty. His act of healing, as the story is told, is then intended as proof that he also has power to forgive (Mark 2:10-11). Note that Jesus does not speak of sin and sickness in a cause-and-effect way, for he only compares forgiveness and healing rather than equating them. This is in continuity with his refusal to explain the condition of the man born blind, in John 9, as the result of sin of any kind. No doubt most of the readers of the story of the paralytic have assumed that the familiar doctrine of sickness as punishment lies behind it, but it is in the background, not the foreground, and it is important to note that this is the only healing story in which forgiveness of sin appears.

c) Forgiveness is associated directly with salvation only a few times, so we may look at all of them. The occurrence of Matthew's explanation of the name "Jesus"—"for he will save his people from their sins"—on the first page of the New Testament may lead us to expect to find it everywhere, but that is not true of the Synoptics. It occurs in the song of Zechariah: ". . . to give knowledge of salvation to his people in the forgiveness of their sins" (Luke 1:77), and the idea is probably present in Jesus' assurance to Zacchaeus, "Today salvation has come to this house" (Luke 19:9). Luke also makes the explicit connection in Acts 5:31: "God exalted him at his right hand as Leader and Savior, to give repentance to Israel and forgiveness of sins." The most interesting passage for our purposes is the text quoted at the beginning of this paper, Luke 7:50, in which Jesus, having offered forgiveness to the "woman who was a sinner," dismisses her with "Your faith has saved you; go in peace," the identical words addressed to the woman whose hemorrhage had been healed (Luke 8:48). Luke, in fact, speaks of being saved by faith six times, but in four of them the salvation received is healing of the body (8:48,50; 17:19; 18:42; the other two are 7:50 and 8:12).[27] Thus we have found that although Matthew and Luke can speak of salvation in a very natural way as forgiveness of sins, that equation is remarkably rare, and the Synoptics' use of "salvation" is close to that of the Old Testament.

d) The psalms of lament reveal the severity of the problem of isolation for the sick in Israel, and with that as background it seemed legitimate to interpret the prophets' specific mention of the healing of the blind (four times), the lame (six times), the deaf (twice), and the dumb (once) as a promise that in the people of God of the future, no one will be left out because of physical disability. The Gospels clearly present the work of Jesus as the fulfillment of such a promise. The details of the healings they record and the language used both of healings and of acts of forgiveness and acceptance show that these are more than signs that the eschaton is at hand. Around Jesus the new community foreseen by the prophets has begun to become a reality.

When lists of illnesses appear in the Gospels, they echo the specific choices of the prophets, and we are especially reminded of Isa 35:5-6 (blind, deaf, lame, dumb).

Matt 11:15 (=Luke 7:22) speaks of blind, lame, lepers and deaf; Matt 15:30-31 of lame, maimed, blind and dumb. Shorter lists typically include two of the four.[28] The addition of lepers in Matt 11:15 seems significant because of the stories of the cleansing of lepers in Matt 8:1-4 (=Mark 1:40-45; Luke 5:12-15) and Luke 17:11-19. As people considered to be unclean they are classic examples of alienation, in the New Testament, and so they fit the traditional list of disabilities, once we recognize the prophets chose those people for attention because they are regularly left out of participation in the life of their community. Several of the other healing stories may now be seen to fit the pattern. The woman who had suffered from a hemorrhage for twelve years had been ritually unclean for that whole time (Matt 9:20-22 = Mark 5:25-34; Luke 8:43-48). The healings of demoniacs are obviously restorations of people who had been alienated from normal life, and the detailed account of the wretched existence of the Gadarene (Gerasene) demoniac (Mark 5:1-20) is an especially moving story of Jesus' work to restore the sick to full life in community again.

Jesus does the same for others whose behavior had led to exclusion, such as tax collectors and the sinful woman, by offering them forgiveness of their sins and a new way of life, and it was his reputation for including those who until that time had been excluded that led to his saying, "Those who are well have no need for a physician" (Mark 2:15-17).[29] Sin and sickness do come together in Jesus' work, then; not because one is necessarily the cause of the other, but because he came to save us from both.[30] There is more than one kind of healing, and each kind is called salvation: forgiveness of sins (Luke 7:50; 19:9), psychological healing (as we would call the cleansing of demoniacs; Luke 8:36), and the healing of physical illness. Each involves a different kind of alienation, but each also has something in common with the others. Sin involves alienation from God because of one's own choices; demon possession, as the New Testament writers understood it, separated one because of an attack by an outside force; while physical illness leads to feelings of alienation from God, whether deserved or not. What they have in common is the likelihood that the person in need of healing will be alienated from normal community life, sometimes as a result of their own choices, sometimes in spite of their most fervent wishes. The salvation Jesus brought to all who responded to him, as he healed them physically, psychologically and spiritually, was the abllity to live a rich and full life, as the Old Testment prophets had hoped.

IV. SALVATION AS HEALING IN THE EARLY CHURCH

The healings recorded in Acts show significant continuity with the biblical material previously discussed. Concern for the lame reappears, in the stories of two healings in Acts 3:1-10 and 14:8-10. Unclean spirits are mentioned in 5:16; 16:16-18 and 19:11-12. Paul's sight is restored to him in 9:17-19. The other ailments specifically mentioned are palsy (9:32-35), fever and dysentery (28:7-10). For the most part, then, the stories in Acts continue the emphasis we have seen elsewhere in restoring people to full participation in the life of their community. The word *sōzein* is used only twice of healing (Acts 4:9; 14:9), but both are significant in that the latter is another case where being "saved by faith" means physical healing, and the former leads from "saving" (healing) a lame man to Peter's generalization: "And there is salvation in no one else, for there is no other name under heaven given among men by which we must be saved" (4:12).[31] The early church understood its message and ministry, as the Body of Christ on earth, to be to preach the forgiveness of sins, to establish a community of acceptance, and to reach out to care for the alienated in soul and body. All of this they summed up with the words salvation and healing.

The preceding section, dealing with the Synoptics, was to a considerable extent a gathering of the evidence which led Harnack to write, in the chapter referred to earlier, "The first three Gospels depict him as the physician of soul and body, as the Saviour or healer of men. . . . Jesus does not distinguish rigidly between sicknesses of the body and of the soul; he takes them both as different expressions of *one* supreme ailment in humanity. . . . The circle by which he was surrounded was a circle of people who had been healed."[32] But the burden of his chapter is to show that the early church understood its ministry to be the continuation of this two-fold healing carried out by Jesus, and to show how this contrasted with the common attitudes toward the sick of that day:

> In the world to which the apostles preached their new message, religion had not been intended originally for the sick, but for the sound. The Deity sought the pure and sound to be his worshippers. The sick and sinful, it was held, are the prey of the powers of darkness; let them see to the recovery of health by some means or other, health for soul and body--for until then they are not pleasing to the gods.[33]

On the other hand, "Christianity never lost hold of its innate principle; it was, and it remined, a religion for the sick."[34] Harnack summarizes the work of the early church in this way (italicizing the sentence):

> *Deliberately and consciously it assumed the form of "the religion of salvation or healing," or "the medicine of soul and body," and at the same time it recognized that one of its cardinal duties was to care assiduously for the sick in body.*[35]

The remainder of the chapter provides an abundance of examples of how the Ante-Nicene church both used sickness and healing as metaphors for sin and forgiveness in their preaching and also took seriously its responsibility to care for those who were physically ill.

Occasional, miraculous cures were reported, but the church seems not to have taken its inability to produce physical healing of all the sick who came to them to be evidence of the sinfulness of the sufferer or of a lack of faith or of the gifts of the Spirit on their part. Caring for the sick, some of whom did not get better, was considered to be a legitimate continuation of Jesus' healing work. Evelyn Frost's thorough study of healing in the Ante-Nicene church reminds us how radically this outlook differed from the flesh-spirit dualism which was the common worldview of its time, citing the lengthy arguments of Irenaeus and Tertullian. They were mostly intended to support their belief in the resurrection of the body, but in doing so they emphasized the wholeness of human existence.[36]

This is important for those of us who are not well-acquainted with the writings of the early church, since we may tend to think the church shortly after the New Testament period "spiritualized" and "eschatologized" their understanding of salvation.[37] In the light of the studies by Harnack, Frost and Garlick,[38] it seems more accurate to say that those early Christians took physical healing (hence, care for the sick) seriously, but that they also understood well there are other kinds of healing, as revealed by their metaphorical uses. As Frost puts it, "Christianity presents not a way of escape from suffering but a power over it."

> The triumphant participation in the victory of Christ over disease and death meant that the Christian was equipped by "the power of His Resurrection" for "the fellowship of His sufferings ." . . . It is not a way of escape *from* suffering but rather a way of *healing* through suffering.[39]

As long as Christians live in this world, they will be afflicted by the evil in it, but there is healing power in Christ to enable us not only to deal with suffering, but even to use it.

> Pain that assaults the regenerate from an evil source is only incorporated into the regenerate life in its transformed character, in which it is changed from an agent of destruction into an instrument of healing and life.[40]

It is this promise of true healing of more than one kind, contained in the salvation offered through faith in Jesus Christ, which I would like to develop a bit further in terms of the ministry of the contemporary church.

V. REFLECTIONS ON SALVATION

When I first read Harnack's exposition of the early church's understanding of salvation as healing, I found it to be a very attractive idea. As a person who grew up in the church, with a sense of dedication to Christ going as far back in life as I can remember, the idea of being "saved" has never had much personal relevance. I know very well I need forgiveness daily. "Forgive" and "reconcile" are meaningful words for me, but years ago when I first made a cursory study of "save" in the New Testment in an effort to understand how I could preach "salvation" I found to my distress that it seemed to be a much less important word for New Testament writers than it has been for the church. In addition to the physical salvation I have been emphasizing, rescue or deliverance from present distress, it does of course take on a meaning not found in the Old Testament, salvation from judgment to come, after death. Although I do not deny the reality of hell, that has not been a subject of great interest to me. In contrast to some of my fellow Christians, I do not think there is very much we can say about what God does with people in the afterlife. That is God's business. What concerns me very much is that there are people in hell here and now, in this life, and we have a responsibility for them. It is the hell of physical pain, mental despair, and spiritual guilt, and the church can do something about those things. We and everyone we know need to be saved from them, at one time or another, and so "saved" is certainly not a useless term. But in North America, at least, "save" and "salvation" inevitably have the overtones of the revivalist, the stench of hell-fire, and the implication of the need for a dramatic conversion experience for everyone. Hell-fire does not seem to worry many people just now, and not everyone who needs "salvation" needs a dramatic conversion experience. We do need healing, and this is terminology everyone uses and understands . We speak of sickness with reference to bodies, minds, and societies. "Sick," "well," "health," and "healing" are terms which can be used both literally and metaphorically without needing to explain them to anyone. I believe that the Gospel record of Jesus ' ministry, as understood and continued by the early church, provides for us a more useful vocabulary than the salvation-words, in order to help church members better understand what we are called to do, and to help the church explain to the world more clearly what we have to offer.

Understanding salvation as healing may do more for us than provide a useful vocabulary, however. "Justified but not yet perfected"—we can speak of that Pauline dilemma (e . g. Phil 3 :12) in terms of illness (or disability) and healing . Sometimes becoming reconciled with God makes sudden changes in life, just as the healing process sometimes produces dramatic improvements in our physical condition, but more often both experiences are slow and gradual, sometimes painful, and with occasional set-backs. Each of us has a "disability" of some kind which faith in Christ has the power to heal, but the overcoming of those disabilities, physical, psychological and spiritual may often be compared with the stroke victim learning to move his fingers or take a few steps again. When Paul speaks of the Christian being freed from the power of sin, born again to a new life, but still struggling with temptation and frequently failing (Romans 6 and 7) he is talking about real healing which has made a radical change in life, making it possible to function in a healthy way, but like other healings it is not complete to the extent of giving us a body like Superman's or a soul like Christ's. As Christians we work to carry out God's intention to heal the illness of body and soul, among individuals, and to heal sick relationships and the ills of society. The Swiss pastor, Dorothee Hoch, used healing language to speak of the church's social mission:

> Some of the illnesses which oppress humanity and Christendom are the result of a solidarity in sin: sickness among whole classes of people owing to bad social relationships and inhuman working conditions, or owing to poverty and unhealthy living conditions. There God waits for our responsible action and compassionate love and bids us put our shoulder too to the burden and co-operate. It is certain that God means to relieve and remove much suffering by means of *our* intervention.[41]

We do some good, and are challenged always by new opportunities, but we never succeed completely in curing anything. Like many a physical or psychological disability, real healing does occur, but some pain remains.

That means we dare not neglect the other forms of healing God offers, for even when the sickness or the disability does not completely go away, there can be healing. Some writers have made a distinction between curing and healing, speaking of a cure as the complete disappearance of the ailment, and of healing as a spiritual triumph over an ailment which may to some extent still afflict us. Madeleine L'Engle has written at some length about the distinction. She tells of a young man who moved from anger to acceptance of his father's impending death, who explained it by saying, "I knew that Dad was dying, that death was very close, but I also knew that Dad was healed. And so it was all right."[42] She explains her own understanding of the distinction in terms of her chronic eye disease. Her painful experiences included prayers for a complete cure, offered by one who believed firmly in faith healing, and as life goes, she soon became much worse. Her account of the result of that prayer is as follows, however: "And I was healed. Not my eyes." She sums up what she learned from it in this way: "I think God wants us to be whole, too. But maybe sometimes the only way he can make us whole is to teach us things we can learn only by being not whole."[43]

Real healing is experienced by people with an incurable illness who find it possible to face it without despair precisely because they are Christians, by people who cope with daily pain as they depend on Christ for strength, by those who remain healthy people even though they live in the midst of irresolvable family problems, and by those whose faith enables them to endure oppression and injustice without becoming victims of destructive hatred. For our time, a classic example comes from Allan Boesak's commentary on the songs in the Book of Revelation:

> Black people in South Africa have made freedom songs part of the struggle; in fact, the struggle is inconceivable without them. . . . In jail, they sing--songs of defiance and faith and freedom. . . . Prison wardens, policemen, and heavily armed soldiers cannot understand how people can sing under such circumstances. The more joyful the singing, the more aggressive they become. . . . But we sing because we believe, we sing because we hope.[44]

Others are destroyed by these afflictions, but the church has a gift to offer them which might enable them to triumph, as Christians we know have been able to triumph in the midst of their sufferings. Do not misunderstand me; I do not advocate the gospel as a painkiller, taking the place of vigorous action on behalf of health, peace, and justice.[45] The latter is essential, but in reality we often fail to obtain the physical freedom from oppression or pain we are striving for. That does not have to mean we have totally failed, however, if we do not forget that God heals in various ways.

We must work at healing the body, but until the eschaton pain will still afflict us. We must work to establish justice, but until the eschaton, evil will still afflict the societies of this world. But the gift of healing is available to everyone now, and it is desparately needed.[46] I am not sure that as a church we have even found the ways to explain to ourselves the value of the gift we have to offer, and I am certain we have not yet discovered how to offer it to our generation effectively enough.

NOTES

1. A. Harnack, *The Expansion of Christianity in the First Three Centuries*, vol. I (New York: G. P. Putnam's Sons, 1904) 121-151.

2. Werner Foerster, "*sōzō, sōtēria, sōter, sōtērios*" *TDNT* 7 (1971) 1002. I shall also find reason to differ from H. J. Cadbury's conclusion, "The normal time to which salvation is assigned is future, both in Paul and in the other New Testament writers. It is an eschatological consummation." F. J. Foakes Jackson, & Kirsopp Lake, *The Beginnings of Christianity,*, vol. V, (NewYork: Macmillan, 1933) 383.

3. E.g. A. E. J. Rawlinson, "The Divine Healer," *ExpT* 56 (1944/45) 183-184; R. McL. Wilson, "Sōtēria,"SJT 6 (1953) 413.

4. This paper will assume some of what I have written on eschatological healing in my *Eschatology in the Old Testament* (Philadelphia: Fortress, 1986) 83-96.

5. J. F. A. Sawyer, *Semantics in Biblical Research. New Methods for Defining Hebrew Words for Salvation* , SBT 24 (Naperville, Ill.: Allenson, 1972) and Sawyer, J. F. A., "ys' " *TWAT* 3 (1982) 1043-1059.

6. Literal healing is promised in Isa 29:18; 33:23-24; 35:5-6; 42:7,16; Jer 31:8; Mic 4:6-7 and Zeph 3:19. Jer 33:6 is probably metaphorical and Isa 57:15-19 and 58:8 are certainly so .

7. Jer 31:8 includes the pregnant woman and the woman who is giving or has just given birth in parallel with the lame and the blind because they are temporarily disabled, when a journey to the Promised Land is under consideration.

8. For general studies of sickness and healing in the Old Testament see, among others, R. K. Harrison,"Disease," *IDB* 2, 1962) 847-854; "Healing" *IDB* 2, (1962) 541-548; G. F. Hasel, "Health and Healing in the Old Testament," *AUSS* 21 (1983) 191-202; D. J. Wiseman,"Medicine in the Old Testament World" in *Medicine and the Bible,* ed. B. Palmer (Exeter: Paternoster Press, 1986) 13-42; K. Seybold & U. B. Mueller, *Sickness and Healing* (Nashville: Abingdon, 1981).

9. Luck comments that, as in the Old Testament, health is not especially valued in the New Testament. U. Luck, *"hugies, hugiainō,"* *TDNT* 8 (1972) 312. For a sixteenth century point of view, note Montaigne's comments on sickness and health in his essay, "Of Experience." Before a rather amusing rationalization of his own major affliction, kidney-stones, he offers generalizations such as this: "I have allowed colds, gouty discharges, looseness, palpitations of the heart, migraines, and other ailments to grow old and die a natural death within me; I lost them when I had half trained myself to harbor them. They are conjured better by courtesy than by defiance. We must meekly suffer the laws of our condition. We are born to grow old, to grow weak, to be sick, in spite of all medicine." *The Complete Works of Montaigne: Essays, Travel Journal, Letters,* trans. D. M. Frame (Stanford: Stanford University Press, 1957) 835. For nineteenth century views, see S. Sontag, *Illness as Metaphor* (New York: Farrar, Straus & Girouz, 1978) 2836. She quotes Camille Saint-Saëns as follows: "Chopin was tubercular at a time when good health was not chic. It was fashionable to be pale and drained . . . ."

10. K. Seybold, *Das Gebet des Kranken im Alten Testament,* BWANT 99 (Stuttgart: Kohlhammer, 1973); E. Gerstenberger, *Der bittende Mensch: Bittritual und Klagelied des Einzelnen im Alten Testament* , WMANT 51 (Neukirchen: Neukirchener Verlag, 1980) 113-168; K. Seybold, & U. Mueller, *Sickness and Healing* (Nashville: Abingdon, 1981) 43-56.

11. For a brief discussion of healing with reference to the language of sin and forgiveness, see J. J. Stamm, *Erlösen und Vergeben im Alten Testament: eine begriffsgeschichtliche Untersuchung* (Bern: A. Francke, 1940) 78-84.

12. Even Psa 69:5: "O God, thou knowest my folly; the wrongs I have done are not hidden from thee," may well be part of the protest in vs. 4b: "What I did not steal must I now restore?"

13. S. E. Balentine, *The Hidden God: The Hiding of the Face of God in the Old Testament* (Oxford: Oxford University Press, 1983) 51-55, 77.

14. Stamm, *Erloësen und Vergeben,* 47-86.

15. N. Cousins, *The Anatomy of an Illness as Perceived by the Patient: Reflections on Healing and Regeneration* (New York: Bantam Books, 1981) 152-154.

16. M. E. Marty, *A Cry of Absence. Reflections for the Winter of the Heart* (San Francisco: Harper & Row, 1983).

17. Ibid. 125.

18. Ibid. 143; and see pp. 126-128. Compare W. E. Oates, & C. E. Oates, *People in Pain: Guidelines for Pastoral Care* (Philadelphia: Westminster, 1985) 121: "A vicious cycle of abandonment, creating more abandonment, intensifies the temptation to isolation, forsakenness, and self-pity. Subtly the integrity of the patient is eroded."

19. P. Ricoeur, *The Symbolism of Evil* (Boston: Beacon, 1967) 25-99.

20. R. Otto, *The Idea of the Holy* (Oxford: Oxford University Press, 1950).

21. Stewart Govig's proposed civil rights resolution for the disabled emphasizes no one shall be shut out or looked down upon. S. D. Govig, *Strong At the Broken Places. Persons with Disabilities and the Church* (Louisville: Westminster/John Knox, 1989) 105.

22. Köhler's summary thus probably goes too far in explaining all the loneliness of the ill as the result of the conviction that they are sinners: "Loneliness is the lot of every sick man. The thought that he is guilty; the idea that to belong to him, to be with him, is shameful and suggests guilt; the conviction that one is stricken by God because afflicted with suffering--all this must be borne in mind and its nature felt if we are to get a real picture of the health and sickness of the Hebrew." L. Köhler, *Hebrew Man* (Nashville: Abingdon, 1956) 51. That his words reflect part of the truth concerning treatment of the sick in every age, however, has become painfully clear in the age

of the AIDS epidemic.

23. D. C. Duling, "The Therapeutic Son of David: An Element in Matthew's Christological Apologetic," *NTS* 24 (1978) 392-410; J. P. Heil, "Significant Aspects of the Healing Miracles in Matthew" *CBQ* (41 (1979) 274-287.

24. For a comparison of the uses of the root by the three evangelists, see W. C. van Unnik, "L'usage de'*sōzein* 'sauver' et ses dérivés dans les évangiles synoptiques" in *La Formation des Evangiles; probléme synoptique et Formgeschichte* par J. Cambier et al (Bruges: Desclée de Brouwer, 1957) 178-194.

25. For healing in John, see J. Wilkinson, "A Study of Healing in the Gospel according to John" *SJT* 20 (1967) 442-461.

26. The one exception is 2 Esdras, which speaks frequently of eschatological salvation, but this book is different from the mainstream of Jewish literature in many ways.

27. B. H. Throckmorton, "*Sōzein, sōtēria* in Luke-Acts" *Studia Evangelica* 6 (1973) 517.

28. Matt 12:22: blind and dumb; Matt 21:14: blind and lame; Mark 7:37, 9:25: deaf and dumb; Luke 14:13,21: maimed, lame and blind; John 5:3: blind, lame and paralyzed.

29. "At the very least, Jesus declared the petitioner clean, that is, acceptable and welcome in the community. Jesus, as it were, extended the boundaries of society and included in the holy community many who were otherwise excluded (lepers, tax collectors, prostitutes, and the like)." J. J. Pilch, "Understanding Biblical Healing: Selecting the Appropriate Model" *BTB 18* (1988) 65.

30. Note that James 5:15 says, ". . . and the prayer of faith will save the sick man, . . . and if he has committed sins, he will be forgiven." Cause-and-effect is not explicitly stated here, either. J. Wilkinson, "Healing in the Epistle of James" *SJT* 24 (1971) 326-345. Healing is mentioned in only one other place in the epistles; 1 Cor 12:9.

31. W. C. van Unnik, "The Book of Acts, the Confirmation of the Gospel" Nov T 4 (1960) 51.

32. Harnack, *The Expansion of Christianity*, 121-122.

33. Ibid. 125.

34. Ibid. 132.

35. Ibid. 131-32.

36. E. Frost, *Christian Healing. A Consideration of the Place of Spiritual Healing in the Church of To-Day in the Light of the Doctrine and Practice of the Ante-Nicene Church* (London: A. R. Mowbray, 1940) 33-37. The first two chapters of Clement of Alexandria's "Christ the Educator" use the healing imagery extensively, but the following sentence shows it was not exclusively metaphor: "The good Educator of little ones, however, Wisdom Himself, the Word of the Father, who created man, concerns Himself with the whole creature, and as the Physician of the whole man heals both body and soul." *The Fathers of the Church*, vol. xxiii (New York: Fathers of the Church, Inc., 1954) 7-8.

37. With reference to the Ante-Nicene literature, Frost writes, ". . . the salvation of Christ was for the whole man; body, mind, and soul were joint-partakers in the redemption from the powers of evil." *Christian Healing,* 225.

38. P. L. Garlik, *Man's Search for Health. A Study in the Inter-Relationship of Religion and Medicine* (London: The Highway Press, 1952) 186-196.

39. *Christian Healing*, 202.

40. *Christian Healing*, 238.

41. D. Hoch, *Healing and Salvation. An Investigation of Healing Miracles in the Present Day* (London: SCM, 1958) 40.

42. M. L'Engel, *The Irrational Season* (New York: Farrar Straus Giroux, 1987) 127.

43. Ibid. 133; cf. Hoch, *Healing and Salvation,* 39-40.

44. A. A. Boesak, *Comfort and Protest. The Apocalypse from a South African Perspective* (Philadelphia: Westminster, 1987) 60-61.

45. Elsewhere Boesak writes, "This song has nothing to do with the shallow, triumphalistic "Jesus-is-the-answer" theology with which oppressed people are so often taught to comfort themselves." *Comfort and Protest*, 87.

46. "So Christians have not had a 'solution' to the problem of evil. Rather thay have had a community of care that has made it possible to absorb the destructive terror of evil that constantly threatens to destroy all human relations." S. Hauerwas, "God, Medicine, and the Problems of Evil," *The Reformed Journal* 38 (April, 1988) 19.

"The Message Of Salvation" In Luke—Acts

JOEL B. GREEN

I. INTRODUCTION

"Brothers, children of Abraham, and those among you who fear God, to us the message of this salvation has been sent" (Acts 13:26). With these words, Paul comes to the hinge in his "word of encouragement" in the synagogue at Pisidian Antioch, as Luke narrates it (13:13-41).[1] The phrase itself, *ho logos tēs sōtērias* ("the message of salvation"), is reminiscent of a Pauline way of speaking. Thus, we find the apostle using similar wording as apparent synonyms for "gospel" in his correspondence–e.g. *ho logos . . . tou stauro*u ("the message of the cross," 1 Cor 1:18), *ho logos tēs katallagēs* ("the message of reconciliation," 2 Cor 5:19); and *logos zōēs* ("word of life," Phil 2:16).[2] Nevertheless, with both the theme raised by this phrase and the content of this "message," we are well within the frame work of Luke's understanding of salvation and the death of Jesus.[3]

Salvation, in fact, lies at the heart of Luke's theology and purpose in writing, as numerous interpreters have shown.[4] This is suggested initially by the preponderance of the vocabulary of salvation in Luke-Acts. Thus, the relevant term that appears in the speech at Pisidian Antioch, *sōtēria* ("salvation"), appears ten times in Luke-Acts, but never in the other Synoptic Gospels.[5] *Sōtēr* ("savior") and *sōtērion* ("salvation") are also missing in Matthew and Mark, but appear in Luke's writings four and three times, respectively. In the NT, *diasōzō* ("to save," "to bring safely through") occurs only twice outside of Luke-Acts (Mark 14:36; 1 Pet 3:20), but is employed six times by the Third Evangelist. The verbal form, *sōzō* ("to save"), appears in Luke-Acts some thirty times.

More importantly, the narrative itself returns again and again to the salvation-theme. For example, Luke 1:5-2:52, the story of the birth and childhood of Jesus, raises this concern in a number of ways. The announcement of John's birth (1:5-25), with its emphasis on conception out of barrenness, is narrated in such a way as to underscore how God has begun to act directly on behalf of his people to bring salvation. This is suggested by the form of the story itself,[6] as well as by the prophetic role predicted of John ("he will turn many of the children of Israel to the Lord their God," 1:16) and the promise that John's birth would be the cause of joy for many (1:14).

The annunciation of the birth of Jesus to Mary is equally evocative of the gracious work of God, particularly as interpreted subsequently. Thus, although Luke constructs no formal etymological identification of Jesus as the one who would save the people from their sins (cf. Matt 1:21), this notion is not far from view in 2:11 (cf. 1:77). Moreover, the repeated words of grace to Mary in 1:28, 30 (*chaire. kecharitōmenē. . . . heures garcharin para tō theō*) prepare for the opening words of the Magnificat: "My soul magnifies the Lord, and my spirit rejoices in God my Savior, for he has looked graciously on the humble state of his handmaid" (1:46-47). The specific language of salvation hardly appears in the verses we have noted, but the gracious, salvific work of the Savior God clearly occupies center stage.

The salvation-theme is at the fore even more pointedly in the hymnody of the narrative of Jesus' birth and childhood. The Magnificat (1:46-55) celebrates the merciful and powerful activity of God[7] on behalf of Mary and, through Mary, on behalf of "his servant Israel." That this activity is salvific is manifest from the initial appellation of God as Savior in 1:47. Similarly, in the words of the Benedictus (1:68-79) we hear of God's gracious visitation and deliverance of his people, his provision for a mighty savior[8] through the house of Israel, so that Israel might be saved from its enemies and be granted forgiveness of sins. In both hymns, God's salvific enterprise is understood as a manifestation of his mercy,[9] in continuity with past promises. In his words of blessing, Simeon identifies the child Jesus as God's salvation, and expands his redemptive work to include not only Israel, but also the Gentiles. The angelic message, delivered to the shepherds out in the field, summarizes well the message of the story thus far: "To you is born this day in the city of David a Savior, who is Christ the Lord" (2:11; cf. Acts 2:36).

The continued appearance of the salvation-theme in these early chapters of Luke's Gospel is particularly important to our discussion because 1:5-2:52 lays the theological foundation for the lengthy narrative to follow. Hence, we are hardly surprised to discover in Acts 13 that, in this programmatic sermon for the Pauline mission in Acts,[10] the salvation-theme is raised in this explicit way.

What is more, at least two, significantly *Lukan* emphases raise their head in this sermon. First, just as in the opening chapters of the Gospel God's redemptive work in Jesus was tied to his earlier promises, so here, in Acts 13:16-41, the message of salvation is represented as continuous with God's past activity and promises. God's bringing a Savior to Israel, Jesus, is only one more in a long line of God's actions on behalf of Israel listed in the opening of the speech: God chose . . . God made . . . God led . . . God bore with . . . God destroyed . . . God gave . . . and so on. Moreover, the resurrection of Jesus is portrayed as the "good news," the fulfillment of "what God promised to the fathers." As Madox and others have seen, this emphasis is related to the purpose of Luke-Acts--namely, the necessity of demonstrating to a largely Gentile audience how " . . . their faith in Jesus is no aberration, but the authentic goal towards which God's ancient dealings with Israel were driving."[11]

The second emphasis marking the soteriology of this speech as Lukan is the absence of any straightforward atonement theology--that is, of any Pauline-type interpretation of the cross.[12] This lack is particularly surprising in light of the language of justification in 13:39, which suggests some fundamental association with the Pauline way of expressing the kerygma. In a typically Lukan way, however, the sermon proceeds to a preeminent focus on the raising of Jesus without positing the death of Jesus as the basis for the offer of salvation.

With this, we engage what has become the centerpoint of a longstanding discussion in Lukan studies: How does Luke understand the means of salvation?, together with the closely related question, What is the nexus between Jesus' death in Luke-Acts and Luke's soteriology? By and large, Lukan scholarship has been content to reiterate what this speech makes abundantly clear–namely, Jesus' death was central to God's purpose (13:27-29)–without exploring further in what way his death might have functioned in Lukan theology.[13] Having pointed briefly to the centrality of salvation to the Lukan enterprise, we are now in a position to take up this problem in more detail.

In this essay, we will argue that it is precisely at the interface of Luke's view of Jesus' death and his understanding of salvation that one sees best the profundity of Luke's soteriology and is able to elucidate holistically its content. We will see that major aspects of the Lukan message–including the means and content of salvation, the shape of discipleship and ethics, and eschatology–intersect at the juncture of Luke's theology of the death of Jesus and his development of the salvation-theme.

II. LUKAN SOTERIOLOGY AND THE DEATH OF JESUS

Without a doubt, the problem of relating the death of Jesus to salvation in Luke-Acts has been complicated by the tendency to read Luke through lens provided by Paul.[14] Indeed, discussions related to "Luke's theology of the cross," simply by their choice of this vocabulary, set the question from the outset within the compass of Pauline conceptualizations. Descriptions of the "NT kerygma" that take their point of departure from Paul have led to a number of theses in which atonement-theology is said to be assumed in or lurking in the shadows of the Lukan narrative.[15] However, there now exists a near consensus that Luke was not interested in a soteriological interpretation of the death of Jesus along the lines of what we find in Paul. This consensus is based primarily on the absence of formulations in Luke-Acts which affirm the interpretation of Jesus' death as an atoning sacrifice. Conzelmann speaks for many when he observes that there is no " . . . direct soteriological significance drawn from Jesus' suffering or death. There is no suggestion of a connection with the forgiveness of sins."[16]

In support of this thesis, students of Luke-Acts have drawn attention to three lines of corroborative evidence.[17] (a) Luke neglects to recount the ransom-saying ("For the Son of Man also came not to be served but to serve, and to give his life as a ransom for many," Mark 10:45). Even those who regard Luke 22:24-27 as having been derived not from Mark 10: 41-45 but from non-Markan material[18] must somehow account for the fact that Luke has elected not to use the ransom-saying elsewhere in his Gospel . (b) The sermons in Acts underscore the salvation-historical necessity of Jesus' death and develop its significance especially in terms of a "contrast formula" (e.g. "You crucified and killed Jesus, but God raised him up," Acts 2:23-24),[19] but they do not draw a direct line between the forgiveness of sins and the cross. (c) Material in Luke-Acts borrowed from Isa 52 :13-53 :12 (e. g. Luke 22:37; Acts 8:32-33) fails to mention the vicarious, atoning significance of the Servant's suffering.

On the other hand, two Lukan passages nevertheless point to Luke's awareness of the interpretation of the death of Jesus along the lines of an atoning sacrifice, and this calls into question exaggerated theories that Luke intended to obliterate any reference to such an interpretation. First, the eucharistic words of Jesus in Luke 22:19-20 effectively root human salvation in the death of Jesus:

> And he took bread, and when he had given thanks he broke it and gave it to them, saying, "This is my body, which is given for you. Do this in remembrance of me." And likewise the cup after supper, saying, "This cup which is poured out for you is the new covenant in my blood."

In an explicit way, this passage speaks of the "new covenant" prophesied in Jer 31:31-34, a text which directly relates the new covenant to the forgiveness of sins. Moreover, both in the bread and cup-words, Jesus identifies his death as "for you." Therefore, Luke presents here an unmistakable reference to a soteriological interpretation of the death of Jesus.

Immediately the question is raised, however, whether these words, and thus this interpretation, were present in the Lukan text. Luke 22:19b-20 are missing in a minority of textual witnesses and some interpreters have argued against their originality in the Third Gospel.[20] Although we are unable to pursue this question in detail here, it is important to mention that the chief reason for doubting the originality of vss 19b-20 is that its language is not characteristic of Luke.[21] As we have argued elsewhere,[22] this evidence is insufficient to lead us to decide against the originality of the eucharistic sayings in Luke, but it does point more positively to the mechanical way in which Luke has reproduced the eucharistic tradition here. In short, Luke has neither drawn attention to the redemptive themes of the Last Supper nor has he made this material more a part of his own thinking by integrating it into his style.

The second text wherein an interpretation of Jesus' death as an atoning sacrifice is found in Luke-Acts presents a similar situation. This passage comes in the midst of Paul's farewell discourse to the elders at Ephesus: "Watch yourselves and all the flock, in which the Holy Spirit has made you overseers, to shepherd the church of God, which he bought with his own blood." This reading of Acts 20:28 represents only one way in which the text might be understood. Due both to textual variants and stylistic ambiguity, this is a difficult admonition to translate: Is it the "church of God" or the "church of the Lord"? With whose blood was this church purchased? God's? The Lord's? God's son's? Paul's?[23] It is true that the notion of purchasing with blood is found elsewhere in the NT (e.g. Eph 1:7), but never with reference to "*God's* own blood"—and herein lies the scandal of this text. Apparently, Luke has again borrowed traditional language without embracing its theology as in anyway integral to his narrative.[24]

In summary, Luke was certainly aware of the interpretation of Jesus' death as the basis for human salvation, but he did not choose to develop this notion as a critical or significant element either of his understanding of the crucifixion of Jesus or of his soteriology.

More important for any discussion of Luke's understanding of the means of salvation is another line of evidence. This has to do with those texts in which the evangelist outlines more explicitly how salvation is made available to humanity.[25] Three texts come to mind--Acts 2:33; 5:30-31; and 10:43--though, as we shall see, these only bring into sharper relief what is otherwise evident throughout the Lukan narrative.

The first passage is perhaps the most oblique. It comes toward the close of Peter's Pentecost address, just before the peak of the sermon in 2:36. As such it functions as an explanation for the pneumatic phenomena experienced by the disciples earlier in the chapter and prepares for the confession of Jesus as "both Lord and Christ" in 2:36. It reads: "Being exalted, therefore, to the right hand of God, and having received the promise of the Holy Spirit from the Father, [Jesus] has poured out this which you now see and hear." In addition to laying out the significance of the outpouring of the Spirit on this day, this affirmation identifies Jesus as the one who subsequently administers the Holy Spirit. And the subsequent narrative makes clear that salvation is realized above all in the reception of the Spirit (cf. 2:38; 9:17; 10:43-44; 11:15-17). As Luke narrates it, Peter makes clear the basis of Jesus' position: it is as the one exalted to God's right hand that he has received the promised Spirit and is therefore able to administer the giving of the Spirit.[26]

The logic of Acts 5:30-31 is more straightforward. Here, Peter, speaking for the apostles before the Jewish leadership, asserts,

> The God of our fathers raised up Jesus, whom you killed by hanging him on a tree. God exalted him at his right hand as Prince and Savior, to give repentance to Israel and forgiveness of sins.

As a result of his exaltation, Jesus is now *archēgos* and *sōtēr*, Prince and Savior; as such he gives repentance to Israel and forgiveness of sins. Having previously noted the centrality of the gift of the Spirit to Luke's understanding of salvation, we may go on to observe similarly the importance of repentance (cf. Luke 19:9; Acts 2:38; 3:19; 9:35; 14:15; 15:19; 16:34; 17:30; 20:21; 26:18; 26:20) and the forgiveness of sins (cf. Luke 1:77; 7:47-50; Acts 2:38; 3:19; 10:43; 13:38-39; 26:18). Hence both with the mention of these themes and with the appellation *sōtēr* ("Savior"), Jesus is identified as the one who makes salvation available to humanity--this as a result of his exaltation.

Finally, in the context of Peter's sermon at the home of Cornelius we find these words: "To [Jesus] all the prophets bear witness that everyone who believes in him receives forgiveness of sins" (10:43). The obstacle to our understanding of this text arises from the reality that the prophets nowhere associate the offer of forgiveness with Jesus or with a messianic figure. Rather, it is the Lord himself who will offer pardon, according to the prophets. On the one hand, one might simply draw attention to the importance for Luke of thus rooting the work of Jesus in the OT, and especially the prophets.[27] On the other, it is worth noting that Luke's christological argument has already prepared us for Peter's affirmation before Cornelius and his household. In the Pentecost address we may follow a programmatic christological development, taking its point of departure from the citation of Joel 2:32 in Acts 2:21—"And it will be that whoever calls on the name of the Lord will be saved"—and reaching its climax in Jesus' reception of the title "Lord" at his exaltation (cf. 2:36). In other words, in Acts 10:43, "what is asserted of God in 'all the prophets' can now be asserted of the exalted Jesus."[28]

In conclusion, taken together these three texts indicate for us how Luke understood the basis of the offer of salvation. He declares that the availability of salvation for men and women is founded above all in Jesus' exaltation. How, then, is the death of Jesus related to this schema?[29]

Lukan scholars have often observed the multiple assertion of Jesus' innocence in Luke 23 and the many parallels between the Jesus of Luke's passion account and the Suffering Righteous One in the Psalms and Wisdom. On this basis, they have postulated for Luke a view of Jesus' passion as the suffering and death of God's Righteous Sufferer who goes to his death in spite of his innocence but is subsequently vindicated by God.[30] This view accounts for the theme of innocence in the passion story, embraces the contrast formulae in the speeches in Acts, and demonstrates in Jesus' life how God overturns injustice--all important motifs in Luke-Acts.

It is clear that this interpretation provides an insufficient matrix for the totality of Luke's understanding of Jesus' death, however, for it falls short of explaining the salvation-historical necessity—a critical Lukan theme.[31] An alternative model, one that accounts more fully for Luke's concerns, concentrates on the Suffering Servant of Isaiah, a more focused embodiment of the notion of the OT Righteous Sufferer.

That Luke is interested more pointedly in the Suffering Servant is manifest in the passion narrative itself and elsewhere in Luke-Acts. In the passion story (a) Jesus cites Isa 53:12 as a general allusion to his suffering and death (22:37), thus communicating that in his passion he fulfills the role of the Suffering Servant; (b) Jesus' struggle on the Mount of Olives (22: 39-46) is cast in terms reminiscent of the Isaianic Servant;[32] (c) Jesus is declared innocent (23:4, 14-15, 22) and acclaimed by the centurion as a "righteous man" (23:47), an allusion to Isa 53 :11 (cf. the conjunction of *dikaios* ["righteous"] and Jesus' suffering in Acts 3 :13-14, where Jesus' passion and exaltation are described in language derived from Isa 52:13-53:12); (d) Jesus refuses to speak in his own self-defense (23:9; Isa 53:7); and (e) in the mockery scene, Jesus is ironically called "the Chosen One," a designation for God's Servant (23:35; Isa 42 :1). Outside the passion story, numerous references to Jesus' role as the Servant appear, the most explicit in the citation of Isa 53: 7-8 in Acts 8: 32-33 and the prophetic reference to Jesus ' mission by Simeon in words borrowed from Isa 49: 6 (2: 32).

The significance for Luke of the identification of Jesus' passion as that of the Suffering Servant is three-fold. First, it explains how Luke can emphasize the salvation-historical necessity of the cross *and* spotlight Jesus' exaltation or vindication as the salvific event. The Isaianic portrayal of the Suffering Servant holds together these twin motifs, particularly in Isa 53:11, where, following his suffering, "my righteous servant will justify many." In other words, Luke's portrayal of Jesus as the Servant indicates the necessity of his death and the salvific import of his vindication, *without* depending on the interpretation of the Servant's suffering as a vicarious sacrifice.

By dispensing with thoughts of self-glorification and obediently accepting the role of the servant (cf. 12:37; 22:25-27), Jesus embodied the righteousness and lowliness of the Servant. The cross was the consequence, but God overturned this humiliation, vindicating his Servant, exalting him and, in this way, opening the way of repentance and forgiveness.

Second, Luke's emphasis on the Servant provides a framework for drawing out the universal implications of Jesus' mission. That Jesus would be "a light for revelation to the Gentiles" was predicted by Simeon (2:32; Isa 49:6), so it is noteworthy that at Jesus' death he was acclaimed as the Righteous One by a Gentile. The importance of Jesus' mission is not only for the Gentile, but also for the Jew (e.g. 23:34, 48) and the criminal (23:43). In Jesus' death one finds the culmination of a life lived for others, including (or especially!) outsider.[33]

Third, by portraying Jesus' career, and especially his death and exaltation, as that of the Suffering Servant, Luke demonstrates in the ultimate way his understanding of the way of salvation, a discussion to which we may now turn.

III. SALVATION AS REVERSAL IN LUKE

The career of Jesus is portrayed in Luke-Acts as the reversal of fortunes. Thought righteous before God and declared innocent by the political authorities, he is put to death. Though put to death as though he were a criminal, he is raised up by God. That is, as the Servant of Yahweh, Jesus goes to the cross in obedience to God, and is exalted by God. Thus vindicated, as a result of his exaltation, he fulfills the role of Savior. Luke's understanding of Jesus' own career, developed against this Isaianic reversal-theme, sets the stage for Luke's understanding of the way men and women experience salvation.

The importance of the theme of salvation-as-transposition is highlighted in those texts where Jesus' missionary agenda comes to the fore. Luke 4:16-30 functions in this way, as do a number of related passages, including 1:46-55; 5:27-32; 7:21-22; and 19: 10 .

The Magnificat (1:46-55) develops the salvation-theme in two stanzas, the first related to Mary's experience of "God my Savior" (vss. 46-50), the second broadening the field of view to embrace Israel (vss. 51-55). The parallelism of these two stanzas is noted above all in Mary's description of herself as *doulē autou* ("his handmaid") in vs. 48, and her designation of Israel as *pais autou* ("his servant") in vs. 54, both as recipients of the mercy of God. The role of Mary progresses in the song from the one on whom God has looked graciously, to the one who symbolizes all Israel and through whom the salvation of God comes. Contrary to any attempts to read this hymn as "a call to revolutionary action,"[34] we must take full account of the reality that, according to this song, the redemptive work is God's doing. And this revolutionary doing is best understood as a reversal of positions. Mary herself, an humble maidservant, is regarded by God and will be blessed henceforth. Moreover, she affirms,

> he has scattered the proud in the imagination of their hearts, he has put down the mighty from their thrones, and exalted those of low degree; he has filled the hungry with good things, and the rich he has sent away empty (vss. 51-53).

What are we to make of the fact that Mary repeatedly speaks of God's activity in the past tense? Her perspective seems to be that the coming of Jesus is the decisive act of God. Hence, even though the child has yet to be born and carry on his divine mission, the redemptive work of God has already been set in motion in the promise of his birth.

In an important sense, Luke's audience has been introduced to this way of understanding the gracious work of God even before Mary is introduced in the narrative . In 1: 6-7, the tragedy of Zechariah and Elizabeth's circumstance is presented to the reader in carefully balanced phrases.[35] They are righteous, but they are childless. God hears their prayers (1:13), however, and Elizabeth bears a son; hence, rather than Elizabeth's having reproach before others (1:25), her relatives and neighbors recognize how the Lord has shown her mercy (1: 57) .

This notion of transposition is also at center stage in the Lukan version of the beatitudes in 6:20-22. Here, the blessings that accompany the new epoch are matched, point-for-point, by pronouncements of woe: "Blessed are the poor, for yours is the kingdom of God . . . but woe to you that are rich, for you have received your reward," and so on. Clearly, in Luke's mind, a reversal of fortunes occurs in the kingdom of God.

The other passages singled out for development–4:16-30; 5:27-32; 7:21-22; and 19:10–are related to each other insofar as they are concerned more directly with Jesus' commission. The blind receiving their sight, the lame walking, lepers cleansed, the deaf hearing, the dead being raised up, captives being released, and the poor having good news proclaimed to them--all are embodiments of the eschatological message that characterizes Jesus' Spirit-anointed mission (4:18; 7:22). What is more, each represents a concrete manifestation of the reversal motif with which we are concerned, and each is related to what is happening then-and-there in the ministry of Jesus.

These expressions of God's mercy are characteristic of the mission of Jesus as portrayed by Luke. Indeed, O'Toole and Tannehill have recently drawn attention to Jesus' role as the savior of the disadvantaged–e.g. "sinners," tax collectors, the demon-possessed and sick, the poor, Samaritans, and women.[36] To the contemporary reader of the Third Gospel, this concern of the Lukan Jesus may seem self-evident, since we so often find Jesus among characters such as these, people considered by others as irreligious, outside the boundaries of God's grace. However, it is worth reminding ourselves that, even in this century, students of Luke have found ways of downplaying this central aspect of the Third Gospel, substituting for this concern for concrete manifestations of God's redemptive grace in the here-and-now an interpretation of salvation in Luke as oriented around transcendent, next-worldly, and spiritual categories.[37]

By way of addressing further this tendency, as well as introducing some reflections on the remaining passages related to Jesus' commission, we may note how often Lukan scholars have drawn attention to the special use of *sōzō* ("to save") in Luke. The verb is employed by Luke with reference both to the preservation and healing of physical life (i.e. "to heal"; cf. 8:36, 50; 17:19[?]) and to a more spiritual-oriented, transcendent salvation (e.g. 7:50; 8:12; 13:23; 17:19[?]; 19:10).[38] It is this latter, spiritual use of *sōzō* that stands out in Luke when compared with the usage of the other Synopticists.

In Mark one finds the spiritual nuance explicitly in 8:35; 10:26; and, perhaps, in 13:13, where deliverance from eschatological tribulation is in view. Elsewhere, the term has to do with miraculous healing (3:4; 5:23, 28, 34; 6:56; 10:52) or, in 15:30-31, with the deliverance of Jesus from distress on the cross. In those passages related to healing, only twice is this "saving" related to faith (5:34; 10:52). Matthew's usage of *sōzō* follows that of Mark. In addition to Mark, though, he employs the verb twice in the sense of "to deliver from danger" (8: 25; 14: 30) . The primary point of departure from Mark appears in Matt 1: 21, however, where it is shown that Jesus ' name is descriptive of his vocation: "he will save his people from their sins." It is against this backdrop that Luke's use of *sōzō* stands in sharp contrast, for he is much more apt to use the verb in its transcendent, spiritual sense. For example, in 7:36-50 *sōzō* is related explicitly to the forgiveness of sins and to the pronouncement of peace.

Of course, the importance of forgiveness of sins and other, more transcendent nuances of salvation in Luke-Acts should not be downplayed. Forgiveness of sins and the reception of the Spirit are integral to the experience of salvation in Luke-Acts, as we have observed. It is equally clear, however, that there is more to the story than this. In fact, Luke's use of *sōzō*, both with reference to healing and to spiritual salvation, must be understood against the even broader categories of salvation-as-tranposition Luke develops. On this, Luke's narrative descriptions of Jesus' mission in 5:27 and 19:1-10 are instructive.

Luke 5:27-32 and 19:1-10 are similar in a number of key ways. Both narrate the encounter of Jesus with a toll collector—Levi and Zacchaeus,[39] respectively. Both disclose the generally poor status of toll collectors in the eyes of the Pharisees and teachers of the Law (5:30) and the general public (19:7). Both name toll collectors as "sinners"—by means of vituperative apposition in 5:30 (cf. 7:34; 15:1; 18:11) and, in 19:7, by an added descriptive phrase. Both narrate the radical response of the toll collector to Jesus' offer of grace--Levi by leaving everything, following Jesus, and throwing a feast in Jesus' honor;[40] Zacchaeus by making fourfold restitution to those he had defrauded and by giving half of his goods to the poor. And both generalize from this encounter to clarify the contours of Jesus' mission: "I have not come to call the righteous but sinners to repentance" (5:32) and "For the Son of Man came to seek and to save the lost" (19:10).

What is of special consequence for our reading of these texts is the oft-documented social status of toll collectors in antiquity, both among Jews and Gentiles.[41] Their low status is underscored by their identification as "sinners," particularly when it is understood that, in a factional context, a "sinner" would be one whose behavior departs from the norms of an identified group whose boundaries are established with reference to characteristic conduct.[42] That is, "sinner" receives concrete explication especially in terms of group definition. And in a social setting like first-century Palestine, where "faithfulnes to God" was measured differently by different sects,[43] self-differentiation of this sort would have become an urgent enterprise indeed.

This process of determining group boundaries is clearly evident in our stories, and the first is narrated in such a way as to indicate that Jesus' opponents have one view of things, Luke and Jesus another. Thus, in the story of 5:27-32, Jesus' associates at the table are regarded as "toll collectors and sinners" by the Pharisees and teachers of the law, whereas the narrator had identified them only as "toll collectors and others." The word "sinners," then, is introduced by Jesus' opponents (cf. 7:34, 39; 15:2); subsequently, Jesus borrows the word and turns it on its head, as if to say, "You may call these people 'sinners,' but people like Levi are precisely those to whom I have come to extend the call to discipleship."

Similarly, in 19:1-10, the man for whom the crowd would not make room, who was forced to climb a tree in order to see Jesus, is precisely the man whom Jesus seeks out. The man referred to as a "sinner" by them all (*pas*) is actually a "son of Abraham," according to Jesus, albeit a "lost one." Taken together with other, similar phrases in the Third Gospel (cf. 1: 54-55; 3:7-9; 13:10-17; 16:22-31), the designation of this man's relationship to Abraham suggests that, though regarded by others as a person outside the boundaries of God's grace, he is nevertheless one who needs and is granted mercy from God.

In these ways, Luke provides further clarification of Jesus' mission *programme* as set forth in Luke 4:16-30. There, we are told, having been anointed by the Spirit, Jesus will evangelize the poor, proclaim release to the captives and recovery of sight to the blind, and set at liberty those who are oppressed. Now, we see that Jesus has come for "those who are sick," "to seek and to save the lost," to call "sinners," like these toll collectors, to discipleship.

What is the linkage between these mission statements? They point to the inclusion of people in God's reign who otherwise have no claim on God. They point to the profound socio-religious meaning of salvation in Luke's understanding. They underscore the inadvisability of any attempt to define narrowly the terms of Lukan soteriology. And they extend our understanding of salvation in Luke as it is focused on the reversal-of-positions theme.

IV. SALVATION . . . WHEN?

The theme of salvation-as-reversal can be traced elsewhere in Luke-Acts--such as in Jesus' teaching on economics and hospitality (e.g. 12:31-21; 14:1-24; 16:19-25) and on the nature of discipleship (e.g. 22:25-27). It is also integral to the fabric of Luke's characterization of the growth of the church, as Barnabas and Paul recognize: "It is through many trials that we must enter the kingdom of God" (14:22).

Data of this nature points to an inescapable conclusion regarding the "when" of salvation in the Lukan writings. Lukan soteriology is not focused on the eschaton, as though the blessings of salvation were somehow held in reserve until the *parousia*. For him, the transposition of places is taking place now, today! (4:21), and this raises the long-debated question of Luke's eschatology.

Since Conzelmann it has been customary to recognize in the Third Gospel a keen interest in salvation history over against a hope in the imminent *parousia*.[44] Subsequent scholarship has focused especially on the degree to which Luke has downplayed the hope of an imminent *parousia*, with the result that Conzelmann's thesis has been revised on both primary fronts. On the one hand, Lukan scholars generally have been more hopeful of finding a *parousia*-hope in Luke-Acts than was Conzelmann; on the other, they have been much less willing to associate Luke's enterprise with an attempt to explain the delay of the *parousia* by replacing it with a theory of the progress of the church in history.[45]

The most recent full-scale examination of the relevant material is the important thesis of John T. Carroll. His is a mediating view between those who insist that Luke has downplayed the earlier Christian stress on the end of the age and those who believe Luke maintains (though adds his own interpretation to) that emphasis. Others have argued this mediating view, however, and it is now generally held that, though Luke was most concerned with the present, he still gives some weight to a future-oriented eschatology.

Carroll's chief contributions lie elsewhere. First, in his view, "The baseline, as Luke sees it, is the unpredictability of the *parousia*."[46] The chronology of the end is subject to the prerogative of God and cannot be known by anyone else (cf. Luke 12:35-48). The coming of the end is certain, but as regards its timing Luke advises agnosticism. Second, Carroll sets forth a plausible situation for the Lukan eschatology:

> Both the contours of the entire narrative and details of Lukan redaction (e.g., Luke 19:11; 21:12) reflect Luke's concern to assimilate delay and duration into the eschatological program. Yet this was not a theoretical exercise. Rather, in adopting and adapting the traditions that had come to him, Luke addressed the prevailing ethos of Christian communities known to him. He witnessed a loss of urgency in mission activity (cf. Acts 1:6-11), complacency in execution of assigned responsibilities (Luke 12:35-48), and a "business as usual" orientation to life (17:26-30) that no longer reckoned with Jesus' return.[47]

Carroll goes on to argue, *contra* Conzelmann, that the delay of the *parousia* itself was not the motivating factor for Luke's approach. Rather, "delay-and-duration" had led to a loss of motivation for discipleship and mission--a loss Luke hoped to counter by highlighting the certainty and unpredictability of the *parousia* and the significance for the future of *present* discipleship and service.

As Carroll recognizes, his analysis of the Lukan eschatology suggests a significant measure of continuity between the perspective of the Third Evangelist and that of other authors of the NT writings. This analysis also dovetails well with the larger Lukan concern to ground Christian faith and praxis in the past and future of God's redemptive activity.

Additionally, we may point out how well this way of understanding the Lukan eschatology interconnects with the perspective on the Lukan soteriology we have outlined. We have argued that the focal point in Luke's presentation is Jesus' exaltation—i.e. Luke's interpretation of Jesus' resurrection and ascension to the right hand of God. The exaltation, then, becomes the basis for the offer of salvation. As the Pentecost story (Acts 2) also makes clear, however, the reception of the Spirit constitutes one of the primary blessings of salvation, but also compels the Christian community to involvement in God's salvific activity. Just as the parallel between Mary and Israel in the Magnificat suggests an invitation to partnership in the redemptive plan of God, so the parallelism between Luke 3:21-22; 4:18-19 (the anointing of Jesus) and Acts 2:1-47 (the anointing of the community) proposes the essential nexus between Spirit-anointing and redemptive engagement. In a context wherein Christians have begun to question the rootage of their faith in God's redemptive activity, Luke's interpretation of the exaltation of Christ serves to recall the connection of Jesus' career with the OT and OT promise, demonstrates how the blessings of salvation are made available in this period of delay-and-duration, indicates how the trials of the church relate to the way of salvation as set forth in Jesus' own career, and provides present impetus for vital engagement in the missionary endeavor.

Luke, then, understands salvation as a reversal of positions, and sees in Jesus' career the decisive beginning of this salvation. Indeed, this transposition motif finds its zenith in Jesus' passion and exaltation. The cross, then, is not the contradiction of Jesus' divine mission, but is the means by which he fulfills God's purpose, after which he is exalted to God's right hand. In thus fulfilling the role of the Servant of Yahweh, Jesus effects salvation for all humanity, establishes the true character of discipleship as reversal, and lays claim on all who would follow him in faithful discipleship.

NOTES

1. Inasmuch as the authorship of Luke-Acts is still debated and the argument of this essay does not depend on this identification, we will use "Luke" to denote the author of these two volumes without prejudice as to the question of authorship. For the most recent defense of the composition of Luke-Acts by the traditional Luke, sometime companion of Paul, see J. A. Fitzmyer, S.J., "The Authorship of Luke-Acts Reconsidered" in *Luke the Theologian: Aspects of His Teaching* (New York/Mahwah: Paulist, 1989) 1-26.

2. See also Eph 1:13: "the message of truth, the gospel of (your) salvation."

3. This is not to say that this address is a Lukan creation, as though there were no traditional basis for its substance. Thus, for example, the traditional credo of 1 Cor 15:3-7 corresponds at key points with vss. 27-39 of this sermon:

Acts 13:27-39	1 Cor 15:3-7
1a Jesus was condemned	
1b according to the Scriptures	
21 Jesus was unjustly executed	2a Christ died
	6 for our sins
2b according to the Scriptures	2b according to the Scriptures
3 Jesus was laid in a tomb	3 He was buried
4a Jesus was raised from the dead by God	4a He was raised on the third day
4b according to the Scriptures	4b according to the Scriptures
5 Jesus was seen by many	5 He appeared to Peter
6 Forgiveness of sins through him is now proclaimed. . .	

As is generally recognized, Philipp Vielhauer was right to posit a "Paulinism" in Acts, even if his portrait was largely exaggerated ("On the 'Paulinism' of Acts" in *Studies in Luke-Acts: Essays Presented in Honor of Paul Schubert,* ed. L. E. Keck and J. L. Martyn (Nashville: Abingdon, 1966) 33-50. On historical and tradition-critical questions, see now G. Lüdemann, *Early Christianity according to the Traditions in Acts: A Commentary* (Minneapolis: Fortress, 1989) 153-154; and C. J. Hemer, *The Book of Acts in the Setting of Hellenistic History,* ed. C. H. Gempf, WUNT 49 (Tübingen: J.C.B. Mohr , 1989) 415-443.

4. Recent studies of salvation in Luke-Acts include: F. Bovon, "Das Heil in den Schriften des Lukas" in *Lukas in neuer Sicht,* BTS 8 (Neukirchen-Vluyn: Neukirchener, 1985) 61-74; M. Dffmer, *Das Heil Gottes: Studien zur Theologie des lukanische Doppelwerkes, BBB 51* (Kffln-Bonn: Peter Hanstein, *1978);* Dom J. Dupont, *The Salvation of the Gentiles: Essays on the Acts of the Apostles* (New York: Paulist, 1979); J.A. Fitzmyer, S.J., *The Gospel according to Luke,* 2 vols., AB28-28a (Garden City, New York: Doubleday, 1981/85) I. 22-23, 219-231; N. Flanagan, O.S.M., "The What and the How of Salvation in Luke-Acts" in *Sin Salvation. and the Spirit,* ed. Daniel Durken, O.S.B. (Collegeville, Minnesota: Liturgical, 1979) 203-213; J. ; Richard Glöckner, *Die Verkündigung des Heils beim Evangelisten Lukas* (Mainz: Matthais-Grünewald 1975); J. B. Green, "The Death of Jesus, God's Servant," in *Reimaging the Death of the Lucan Jesus,* ed. D. Sylva, BBB (Bonn: Peter Hanstein, 1990) ; Robert Maddox, *The Purpose of Luke-Acts,* SNTW (Edinburgh: T. & T. Clark, 1982); I. H. Marshall, "Luke and His 'Gospel'" in *Das Evangelium und die Evangelien: Vorträge vom Tübinger Symposium 1982,* ed. P. Stuhlmacher, WUNT 28 (Tübingen: J. C. B. Mohr, 1983) 289-308; *idem, Luke: Historian and Theologian* (Grand Rapids, Michigan: Zondervan, 1971). R. F. O'Toole, S.J., *The Unity of Luke's Theology: An Analysis of Luke-Acts,* GNS 9 (Wilmington, Delaware: Michael Glazier, 1984);

5. *Sōtēria* does appear in a secondary ending to the Gospel of Mark as an addition to 16: 8 .

6. Recent form-critical work by E. W. Conrad ("The Annunciation of Birth and the Birth of the Messiah, " *CBQ* 47 [1985] 656-668) has revised R. E. Brown's earlier identification of a "biblical annunciation of birth" form (*The Birth of the Messiah: A Commentary on the Infancy Narratives in Matthew and Luke* [Garden City, New York: Doubleday, 1977] 156), with the result that Brown's fundamental argument—that the NT annunciations of birth are strongly evocative of the patriarchal narratives—has been strengthened. This contributes emphatically to the impression this passage leaves of God's redemptive plan coming to fruition.

7. R. C. Tannehill (*The Narrative Unity of Luke-Acts: A Literary Interpretation,* vol. 1: *The Gospel according to Luke* [Philadelphia: Fortress, 1986] 26-32) observes how the verbs of this hymn repeatedly occupy an anterior position in each clause, emphasizing this celebrated activity as God's undertaking.

8. Greek: *keras sōtērias* ("horn of salvation") . See M. L. Süring, *The Horn Motif: In the Hebrew Bible and Related Ancient Near Eastern Literature and Iconography* (Berrien Springs, Michigan: Andrews University, 1980).

9. For the Benedictus, this has been emphasized recently in an interesting way by M.J.J. Menken, "The Position of *splagchnizesthai* and *splagchna* in the Gospel of Luke," *NovT* 30 (2, 1988) 107-144.

10. See Walter Radl, *Paulus und Jesus im lukanischen Doppelwerk: Untersuchungen zu Parallelmotiven in Lukasevangelium und in der Apostelgeschichte,* EH 23:49 (Frankfurt-am-Main: Peter Lang, 1975) 82-100.

11. Maddox, *The Purpose of Luke-Acts,* 187. For related discussions, see O'Toole, *The Unity of Luke's Theology*.

12. The absence of atonement-theology in the speeches of Acts has long been noted--e.g. C.H. Dodd, *The Apostolic Preaching of the Cross* (London: Hodder and Stoughton, 1936) 25; H. J. Cadbury, *The Making of Luke-Acts,* 2d ed. (London: S.P.C.K., 1958) 280-281.

13. Thus, J.B. Tyson, *The Death of Jesus In Luke-Acts* (Columbia, South Carolina: University of South Carolina, 1986) 170: "The conviction of divine necessity constitutes Luke's main contribution to the theological discussion of Jesus' death. But he seems uninterested in piercing through to an understanding of the theological reason for the death or in analyzing what it was intended to accomplish."

14. See W. G. Kümmel, "Current Theological Accusations against Luke," *ANO* 16 (1975) 131-145; "Thus from its beginnings it has been characteristic of the redaction-critical investigation of Luke's theology that the description of this theology has been accompanied by a sharp criticism based based primarily on comparison with Paul" (132).

15. Cf., e.g., L. Morris, *The Cross in the New Testament* (Grand Rapids: Eerdmans, 1965) 63-143; G.E. Ladd, *A Theology of the New Testament* (Grand Rapids: Eerdmans,1974) 330.

16. Conzelmann, *The Theology of St. Luke,* 201.

17. See J. B. Green, "Death of Jesus," in *Dictionary of Jesus and the Gospels,* ed. J. B. Green, I. H. Marshall, and S. McKnight (Downers Grove, Illinois: InterVarsity, forthcoming).

18 .See Marshall, *Luke: Historian and Theologian,* 170.

19. See J. Roloff, "Anfänge der soteriologischen Deutung des Todes Jesu," *NTS* 19 (1972-73) 38-64.

20. See most recently, G.D. Kilpatrick, *The Eucharist in Bible and Liturgy*: The Moorhouse Lectures 1975 (Cambridge: Cambridge University, 1983) 28-42.

21. See Kilpatrick, *The Eucharist in Bible and Liturgy,* 31-32; J. Jeremias, *The Eucharistic Words of Jesus* (Philadelphia: Fortress, 1966) 154-155.

22. See J. B. Green, *The Death of Jesus: Tradition and Interpretation in the Passion Narrative,* WUNT 2:33 (Tübingen: J.C.B. Mohr ,1988) 35-41.

23. This last, rather implausible suggestion was argued by W. Schmeichel, "Does Luke Make a Soteriological Statement in Acts 20:28?" in *Society of Biblical Literature: 1982 Seminar Papers,* ed. K. H. Richards (Chico, California: Scholars, 1982) 501-514.

24. See E. Schweizer, *Luke: A Challenge to Present Theology* (London: S.P.C.K., 1982) 45.

25. See Green, "The Death of Jesus, God's Servant."

26 .See M.M.B. Turner, "The Spirit of Christ and Christology" in *Christ the Lord: Studies In Christology Presented to Donald Guthrie,* ed. H. H. Rowdon (Downers Grove, Illinois: InterVarsity, 1982) 179-181.

27. Cf., e.g., Luke 18:31; 24:27, 44; Acts 3:21, 24; D. L. Bock, *Proclamation from Prophecy and Pattern*: *Lucan Old Testament Christology,* JSNT 12 (Sheffield: JSOT, 1987); U. Wilckens, *Die Missionsreden der Apostelgeschichte:Form-und traditionsgeschichtliche Untersuchungen,* 3d ed., WMANT 5 (Neukirchener-Vluyn: Neukirchener, 1974) 148; J. A. Fitzmyer, "The Jewish People and the Mosaic Law in *Luke -Acts" in Luke the Theologian, 175-202.*

28. See Marshall, "The Resurrection in the Acts of the Apostles," 104.

29. Our conclusion receives indirect support from Fitzmyer, "'Today You Shall Be with Me in Paradise' (Luke 23:43)" in *Luke the Theologian,* 203-233. In an attempt to rehabilitate a soteriological meaning for the death of Jesus in Luke, Fitzmyer exegetes this saying from the Lukan passion story with impressive detail and creativity. On this basis he insists that Luke portrays God's

plan as coming to fruition through, not in spite of, the suffering and death of Jesus. Two factors are at work. First, in his narrative, Luke portrays Jesus exercising his regal and messianic power of salvation from the cross. Second, Luke emphasizes Jesus' entrance into glory as the sequel to his death and burial, and this "transfer to paradise" has soteriological effect. What is missing from Fitzmyer's analysis, and what we hope to provide below, is a more far-reaching interpretation of the nexus between the death of Jesus and his exaltation within the framework of Luke's soteriology.

30. Cf., e. g. , R. J. Karris, O. F. M., *Luke: Artist and Theoloaian. Luke's Passion Account as Literature,* TI (New York: Paulist, 1985); *idem,* "Luke 23:47 and the Lucan View of Jesus' Death," *JBL* 105 (1986) 65-74; A. Büchele, *Der Tod Jesu im Lukasevangelium: Eine redaktionsgeschichtliche Untersuchung* zu Lk 23, FTS 26 (Frankfurt-am-Main: Josef Knecht, 1978) .

31. See, e.g., Luke 9:22; 17:25; 22:15, 22; 24:26, 46; Acts 1:3; 3:18; 17:3; C. H . Cosgrove, "The Divine Dei in LukeActs," *NovT* 26 (2, 1984) 168-190; Büchele, *Der Tod Jesu im Lukasevangelium, passim;* Dömer, *Das Heil Gottes,* 70-93.

32. See J. B. Green, "Jesus on the Mount of Olives (Luke 22:39-46): Tradition and Theology," *JSNT* 2 6 (1986) 29-48 .

33. A further advantage of this proposal, then, is its capacity to encompass the whole of Jesus' career as portrayed by Luke as soteriologically meaningful, an emphasis suggested in a different way by Büchele, *Der Tod Jesu im Lukasevangelium,* 168-169 .

34. So R. McAfee Brown, *Unexpected News: Reading the Bible with Third World Eyes* (Philadelphia: Westminster, 1984) 81.

35. Note (a) the appearance of *ēsan* ("they were") at the beginning and end of these two sentences, (b) the double use of *amphoteroi* ("both"), and (c) the fact that the first sentence has 17 words, the second 18 .

36. O'Toole, *The Unity of Luke's Theology,* 109-148; Tannehill, *The Narrative Unity of Luke-Acts,* 101-139.

37. See, e.g., the ways in which the Magnificat has been viewed in this century in D. M. Scholer, "The Magnificat (Luke 1:46-55): Reflections on Its Hermeneutical History" in *Conflict and Context: Hermeneutics in the Americas,* ed. M. L. Branson and C. R. Padilla (Grand Rapids, Eerdmans, 1986) 210-219.

38. See W. Foester, "*Sōzō* and *Sōtēria* in the New Testament," in *TDNT,* (1971) 989-98.

39. It is now generally understood that "toll collector" serves better to represent the role of persons named in the Gospels than the earlier translation "publican," from the Latin *publicani*--cf. E. Badian, *Publicans and Sinners: Private Enterpise in the Service of the Roman Republic* (Ithaca: Cornell University, 1972); J. R. Donahue, S.J., "Tax Collectors and Sinners," *CBQ* 33 (1971) 39-61.

40. Fitzmeyer (*Luke,* I. 589) draws attention to the *inclusio* marked by 27 and 32: "Jesus *calls* Levi to follow him, because he has come to *call* not the righteous but sinners to reform." Hence, Levi's response to Jesus (vss. 28-29) gives concrete expression to the *metanoia* of vs 32. Cf. 3:12-13.

41. See, e.g., Donahue, "Tax Collectors and Sinners"; L. Schottroff and W. Stegemann, *Jesus and the Hope of the Poor* (Maryknoll, New York: Orbis, 1986) 7-13.

42. See J. D .G. Dunn, "Pharisees, Sinners, and Jesus" in *The Social World of Formative Christianity and Judaism: Essays in Tribute to Howard Clark Kee,* ed. J. Nuesner, et al. (Philadelphia: Fortress, 1988) 264-289 (275-276). Dunn documents how, *within* Judaism, "sinner" might be used to designate those who gained disapproval by a given faction (276-280).

43. See P. D. Hanson, *The People Called: The Growth of Community in the Bible* (San Francisco: Harper & Row, 1986).

44. Conzelmann, *The Theology of St. Luke.* See already R. Bultmann, *The Theology of the New Testament,* 2 vols. (New York: Charles Scribner's Sons, 1951) 2. 116-118.

45. See the helpful survey of this discussion in J. T. Carroll, *Response to the End of History: Eschatology and Situation in Luke-Acts,* SBLDS 92 (Atlanta, Georgia: Scholars, 1988) 1-30 .

46. Ibid, 165.

47. Ibid, 166.

ETERNAL LIFE IN THE GOSPEL OF JOHN

MARIANNE MEYE THOMPSON

I. INTRODUCTION: QUESTIONS AND PROBLEMS

Even the casual reader of the Gospel of John can scarcely fail to be impressed by the prominence given to the theme of "life" in it. Early on the theme is introduced with the statement that in the Logos there was "life" (1:4). Towards the end of the book, the Gospel's purpose is succinctly presented in a statement formulated in terms of "life:" "Now Jesus did many other signs in the presence of his disciples which are not written in this book. But these are written that you may believe that Jesus is the Christ, the Son of God, and that believing you may have life in his name" (20:30-31). And throughout the Gospel one regularly finds the theme of life, especially in prominent places. Many of the beloved "I am" sayings of the Fourth Gospel have as their predicate a term or terms related or equivalent to life. The Johannine Jesus declares "I am the bread of life;" "I am the resurrection and the life;" "I am the way, the truth and the life;" "I am the light of the world; whoever follows me will not walk in darkness, but will have the light of life." In other formulations Jesus promises life to those who follow him: "I have come that they may have life, and have it abundantly" (10:10). "The water that I will give will become a spring of water welling up to eternal life" (4:14). "So also the Son gives life to whom he will" (5:21). And, of course, there is perhaps the most-oft quoted verse of John and, indeed, of the entire New Testament: "For God so loved the world that he gave his only Son, that whoever believes in him should not perish but have eternal life" (3:16).

One could adduce many more examples of verses which refer to "life" or its synonym "eternal life."[1] But statistics alone do not adequately convey the centrality of the theme of "life" in John. For as the verses cited above suggest, the purpose of the Son's mission as well as the purpose of the Gospel can be summarized in terms of the giving of life. But if it is easy to document the importance of the theme of life, it is more difficult to account for its prominence and to delineate the precise content of the Johannine concept of "life."

Some scholars argue, for example, that John has appropriated the term "eternal life" because it allows him to make more personal and individualistic the corporate concept of "kingdom of God."[2] Along these lines one finds also the suggestion that life is a "mystical" or perhaps "spiritual" conception, a description of internal experience or of the ultimate destiny of one's soul.[3] Often the view that John significantly reinterpreted the concept of "life" has been linked with the theory that John's Gospel was directed towards a Hellenistic readership. "Life" embodied the hope for salvation of the Hellenistic (Gentile) reader, a reader filled with a dread of death and yearning for life which could surpass and overcome the all too present experience of death.[4] Coupled with this theory one also finds an emphasis on eternal life as a "timeless" reality, in contrast to the "Jewish" conception of life as "life of the age to come."[5] Still another scholar has concluded that John's emphasis on "realized eschatology" comes from John's effort to deal with the problem of the delay of the *parousia*.[6] And Rudolf Bultmann pressed realized eschatology to its extreme, asserting that John had radically reinterpreted the future hope as an existential reality to be known in the present reality of "life." In the present, and in the present alone, one would know and find " salvation."[7]

Precisely the emphasis on the present possession of life throws into sharp relief the question of its content. Almost by definition it seems impossible that one should have *eternal* life now. And although John does seem to speak of receiving eternal life in the future (3:16, 36; 5:25, 29; 6:27, etc.), these references are ambiguous, and none of them relegates eternal life entirely to a future state. Those who believe *have* life (5:24), and they have "passed from death to life" (5:24). What, then, can it be that believers enjoy even in the present world?

In order to probe the question of the meaning of life and, specifically, of "salvation as life" in the Gospel of John, we will divide our study into three parts, each intended to answer a subsidiary question. These questions are as follows: (a) What can we learn from John's use of the vocabulary of "life" and "eternal life?" That is, what understanding of *life* is manifested in the use of these terms in John and in possible background material? (b) How does one receive *life*? Although this question might seem, at first glance, to be secondary to the issue of "salvation as life," it provides the framework into which one must fit the answer to the third question: (c) what is it that one has when one has *life?* After an investigation of each of these three questions, we shall close with some reflections on salvation as life in the Gospel of John.

II. THE GOSPELS' VOCABULARY OF LIFE

1. *The Synoptic vocabulary of life*

It will be helpful at the outset to review briefly the Synoptic use of the terms "life" and "eternal life." A few summary statements will suffice. First, the terms "life" and "eternal life" are equivalent. For example, in response to the rich man's question "What good deed must I do, to have *eternal life?*" Jesus responds, "If you would enter *life,* keep the commandments" (Matt 19:16-17).

Second, both "eternal life" and the absolute "life" refer to future blessings to be received by those who heed the call of Jesus. More specifically, these are not merely future blessings, to be received at some point in this life, but eschatological blessings, for the life promised is the life of the age to come" (Mark 10:29-30; Matt 19:29; Luke 18:29-30; cf. Matt

7:14; Luke 13:23-24). These passages point towards the future, the age of salvation (Mark 20:26; Matt 19:25; Luke 18:26), the "age to come."

Third, already in the Synpotic Gospels, "eternal life" and "kingdom of God" are used interchangeably. This does not imply that "eternal life" and "kingdom of God" are simply identical. Both are used to speak of that which God's saving work will grant to Jesus' disciples (Mark 9:43, 45, 47; 10:17-30; Matt 19:23-29; Luke 18:24-30). Specifically, "eternal life" refers to the inheritance of the righteous in the age to come, as it does in Jewish writings prior to or contemporaneous with the NT.[8] While it is sometimes said that by its etymology *zōē aiōnios* literally means "life of the age," in practice it typically meant "life of the age to come," and that is the usage which we see in Dan 12:2, the only use of *zōē aiōnios* in the OT, where the LXX renders the Hebrew phrase *ha we'olam*. There "eternal life" means "everlasting life" for the righteous, as opposed to everlasting punishment, following a general resurrection of all the dead. "Eternal life" as life of the age to come is also reflected in other Jewish apocalyptic writings (e.g., *Ps Sol* 3:12, 13:11, 14:10; 1 *Enoch* 37:4, 58:3; cf. also 91:10, 103:4; see also 2 Macc 7:9, 14, 36; 4 *Macc* 15:3), as well as in rabbinic sources (*m. Aboth* 2:7, 4:16-17; *b. Bez.* 15b; *b. Shab.* 33b; *Sifra Lev.* 5.85d [on 18:5]; *Sifre Deut.* par. 47-8; *Mek. Exod* 13.3; *b. Berak.* 28b).

In short, *zōē aiōnios* did not simply mean life appropriate to "an age," but rather life appropriate to the "age to come." This life was understood to be everlasting in character, antithetical to life which was merely temporary and fleeting. "Eternal life" implied a quality of life, and not merely a quantity of life, for it was contingent upon and subsequent to the resurrection to life in the age to come. This is the conception of life found in the Synoptic Gospels. Further, in those Gospels, "life," "eternal life," and "kingdom of God" are used interchangeably to speak of what is promised to those who in this life respond to the call of Jesus. These promised blessings are viewed as predominantly future, although reception of them in the future depends on one's action in the present. Moreover, these three terms speak of what can also be called "salvation," or participating in the future state of blessedness. That age is to be characterized by the fullness of the knowledge of God and perfect human response to God, and all the spiritual blessings attending such a relationship, as well as by material and physical well-being.[9] To have eternal life means to live in the age brought by God or, in short, to live with God.

2. *The Johannine vocabulary of life*

When we come to the Gospel of John, we find that the situation is sometimes analogous to, and sometimes less clear than, the situation which obtains in the Synoptics. John uses the simple noun "life" (*zōē*) nineteen times; and the phrase "eternal life" (*zōē aiōnios*) eighteen times. In addition, the verb "to live" *(zaō)* appears seventeen times. Again, it is apparent from Johannine usage that "life" and "eternal life" are synonymous. Thus in 5:24, Jesus says, "Those who hear my word and believe him who sent me, have *eternal life*; they do not come into judgment, but have passed from death to *life*." Later we read, "You search the scriptures, because you think that in them you have *eternal life*; and it is they that bear witness to me; yet you refuse to come to me that you may have *life*" (5:39-40). In the following chapter, Jesus says "whoever believes has *eternal life*. I am the bread of *life*" (6:47-48). And in John 10, Jesus speaks of himself as the good shepherd who has come that his sheep may have life. He later states that he gives his sheep *eternal life* (10:10, 28). Finally, we may note that verses previously cited, John 3:16 and 20:31, speak of what Jesus brings as, respectively, *eternal life* and *life.* These parallel passages suggest that what is the case in the Synoptics holds true here as well: "eternal life" and "life" are synonymous.

More difficult to answer, however, are the questions whether "life" and "eternal life" are also interchangeable in the Johannine vocabulary with kingdom of God and whether we may understand "eternal life" as the "life of the age to come." To the first question we may answer, somewhat cautiously, in the affirmative. "Kingdom of God" appears only twice in John, and there it is not so clearly in parallelism with life, eternal life, or salvation, as it is in the Synoptics. And yet where "kingdom of God" does appear, we find that "eternal life" follows close in its train. In the discourse with Nicodemus, Jesus states that no one can see (or enter) the kingdom of God unless they are "born again" (3:3, 5). Subsequently we read that "the Son of man [must] be lifted up, that whoever believes in him may have eternal life" (3:15). Appropriate to the new birth is new life, eternal life. Not surprisingly, in 3:17, "eternal life" and salvation are also linked; the Son comes to give eternal life; the Son comes to save. In Johannine thought, no less than in the Synoptic Gospels, kingdom of God, eternal life, and salvation may be used interchangeably.[10]

We may then ask, second, whether the Johannine conception of "eternal life" is essentially the same as the Synoptic understanding. That is, should we understand "eternal life" in John as the "life of the age to come"? And if "eternal life" is the "life of the age to come," how can the Johannine Jesus say, "Truly, truly, I say to you, whoever hears my word and believes him who sent me, has *eternal life;* they do not come into judgment, but *have passed from death to life.*" The promise of the present possession of "eternal life" seems virtually to preclude the Jewish and Synoptic understanding of "eternal life" as "life of the age to come." And yet it is probably true that a majority of scholars today believe that precisely this understanding of "eternal life" forms the necessary background for understanding the Gospel of John.[11] Some, however, do dispute it. Schnackenburg, for example, in responding to Dodd, writes that Dodd's view that "eternal life" is connected with the Jewish idea of the life of the age to come "can hardly be right."[12] Schnackenburg takes this view because he sees the contrast in John between "life of this world" and "eternal life" not in terms of temporal succession, but in terms of a qualitative distinction between the earthly and heavenly realms from which come the two vastly different kinds of life.[13] Stated otherwise, the Synoptic dualism is temporal, but Johannine dualism is spatial.

Schnackenburg has correctly noted that for John "life" is "eternal" because it is brought from above, from God. And yet one may lodge two caveats here. First, even Jewish thought does not think of the "age to come" only in future or temporal terms. There is a spatial element to Jewish "dualism" as well as a temporal element.[14] Second, although Schnackenburg argues that nowhere in John is life relegated entirely to the future, so that it *must* be understood as life "of the age to come," it nevertheless remains true that the *resurrection* is understood to be future. The Johannine eschatology, while emphasizing what is present now for believers, does not lose its future aspect. We shall take this up below in section IV.

Briefly, we must turn to a discussion of another word that John uses, also translated in English as "life," and that is the word *psychē* (10:11, 15, 17, 24; 12:25 [2x]; 12:27, translated "soul;" 13:37, 38; 15:13). Its usage in these cases sheds light on the more pregnant term *zōē.* In every case, *psychē* denotes human life which can be given up. Jesus thus lays down his life (*psychē;* 10:11, 15, 17, 24); Jesus' audience is challenged to give up its life (*psychē*) to gain "eternal life" (*zōē aiōnios;* 12:25); Peter promises to lay down his life (*psychē*) for Jesus (13:37, 38); and in the well-known words of 15:13, Jesus asserts that "No one has greater love than this, that they lay down their life (*psychē*) for a friend."

John's use of *psychē* helps to define *zoe*. In contrast to *psychē*, which one can give up or lay down, *zōē* is life which cannot be taken away, life which is imperishable. *Zōē* cannot be lost, since it is true, heavenly, God-given life. But *psychē* can be lost, since it is bound to this world, which is temporal and passing way. Yet this should not be taken to imply that the *psychē* which human beings possess is any less the gift of God than the "eternal life" granted to believers. John's dualism is not absolute but, as it is often described, modified. All life comes from God. And yet while all human beings may have *psychē*, not all have *zōē*. This leads us directly to the second main question to be investigated, namely, how does one receive life which is properly designated eternal, *zōē*?

III. HOW DOES ONE RECEIVE ETERNAL LIFE?

In pursuit of an answer to the question of how or why "life" images "salvation" in the Gospel of John, it will be helpful to first answer the question, How does one receive eternal life? For how one receives eternal life tells us much about what that life is. If, for example, one holds that salvation is received through gaining information, then ignorance is the "plight" to which "knowledge" is the solution. If one is saved through physical healing, then the state from which one is to be rescued is disease, and salvation is health. In any case, the way in which salvation is effected and mediated helps to resolve the problem of what salvation is. We may test this as we seek to answer the question, How does one receive eternal life? The answer to this question is two-fold: (a) One receives eternal life as a gift *from* God, who is the source of all life; and (b) One receives eternal life *through* the mediation of the Son, Jesus Christ. Indeed, hidden within these simple statements is John's whole "theology" of eternal life. Therefore, each of these statements demands more detailed discussion and development.

1. *God as the source of eternal life*

First, we must note that John bases his view of eternal life upon the understanding that God is the *living* God. Two sets of statements in John make this clear. On the one hand, there are statements which explicitly link "life" with God. Thus in 5:26 it is said that "the Father has *life* in himself." In 6:57, Jesus speaks of the "*living* Father." And there are statements which imply the eternal existence of God. For example, 1:1 evokes the "beginning" of Gen 1:1. In the prayer of consecration of John 17, Jesus speaks of the glory that he had with God "in thy own presence . . . before the world was made" and, again, in 17:24, refers to the love God had for the Son "before the foundation of the world." God is the God who is alive eternally.

This conception of God can be found in the OT, in Jewish sources prior to and contemporaneous with John, and in the NT as well. John does not need to argue for this understanding of God; indeed, it is precisely what he assumes. A few examples must suffice to illustrate what could be documented much more extensively. From the OT come the expressions the "living God" (Deut 5:26; Jer 10:10), the "everlasting God" (Isa 40:28), or various combinations, such as "the living God and everlasting King" (Jer 10:10). God lives forever (Deut 32:40; cf. Isa 48:12; Ps 41:14, 106:48). God is the source of life (Ps 36:9; Jer 2:13; Ezek 37:1-4). The LXX translates the "I am who I am" of Exodus 3:14 as "I am the one who is" (*egō eimi ho ōn*). Philo echoes the LXX at this point, repeatedly referring to God either as *ho ōn* and, more frequently, *to on*, "that which is." Indeed, Philo's emphasis at this point has led one writer to comment that for Philo "God is just existence."[15] The conception of God as living is also thoroughly rabbinic.[16] The Apocalypse of John predicates eternal existence of God when it speaks of God as the one "who is and who was and who is to come" (1:4, 8; 4:8; 11:17). Taken together these references point to a conception of God as eternal and imperishable, in short, the "living God."

Second, the living God is the *creator and source of life*. As numerous writers have noted, eternal life is virtually synonymous with "divine life."[17] Life is eternal precisely because it comes from the God who is eternal, the God who lives. Thus the Father is the ultimate source of life, even for the Son: "As the Father has life in himself, so he has granted the Son also to have life in himself" (5:26). And, again, "For as the Father raises the dead and gives them life, so also the Son gives life to whom he will" (5:21). It is not enough to say that God gives only "eternal life." For if we go back to the prologue of the Gospel, we read that "All things were made through [the Word], and without him was not anything made" (1:3). And yet not all things that were created can also be said to have "eternal life." For "that which is born of the flesh is flesh, and that which is born of the Spirit is spirit" (3:6), and "it is the Spirit that gives life" (6:63; cf. Isa 31:3). In other words, God is the source not only of eternal life, but of all life, including natural or physical life.

What, then, is the relationship between physical and eternal life? Frequently the relationship between "natural" and "supernatural" life is taken to be such that the former symbolizes the latter; the giving of physical life provides a natural image or analogy to the granting of spiritual or eternal life.[18] On the other hand, the assertions of Corell are well-taken when he writes, "*Zōē* in the Fourth Gospel is not opposed to physical life: it is life in its perfection, including physical life. For there is only one 'life'—life given in creation. The [new birth] of which St John speaks is no metaphysical re-creation, but the realization and fulfilment of created life."[19] The prologue, deliberately echoing the creation account in Genesis, sets the story of the Gospel in a cosomological framework and simultaneously informs us about the meaning of life.[20] All life, in short, comes from God; but God alone has it eternally.

Third, then, it is implied that those who have eternal life *share in something that characterizes and comes from God alone*. They share in God's own life. Thus John writes "This is eternal life, that they know thee, the only true God, and Jesus Christ whom thou hast sent" (17:3). Some scholars deny that 17:3 should be construed as a *definition* of eternal life, and the point is well taken.[21] For eternal life is the more comprehensive term. And yet John does not write that knowing God is prerequisite to or leads to eternal life; rather, knowing God *is* eternal life. As Ernst Haenchen puts it, "True life is living in harmony with God."[22] Only those who know God, who live in fellowship with God and in harmony with the purposes of God, have eternal life, not because living in fellowship with God merits eternal life as a reward, but because fellowship with the eternal God is already to have a share in God's own life.

This understanding of eternal life as knowing God leads to the Johannine understanding of election. Chapter 6 especially links together God's gift of life with God's calling. "My father gives you the true bread from heaven. For the bread of God is that which comes down from heaven, and gives life to the world. . . . All that the Father gives me will come to me; and whoever comes to me I will not cast out. For I have come down from heaven, not to do my own will, but the will of him who sent me; and this is the will of him who sent me, that I should lose nothing of all that he has given me, but raise it up at the last day. For this is the will of my Father, that every one who sees the Son and believes in him should have eternal life; and I will raise him up at the last day . . . . No one can come to me unless the Father who sent me draws him; and I will raise him up at the last day" (6:32, 37-40, 44).

This passage underscores four main points: (a) Ultimately it is God who gives life; (b) through the Son who has been sent; (c) to whose who have been "drawn" by God; and (d) who believe in the Son. It is the first and third point that are of interest here, for they point to the fundamental question of the Gospel of John, namely, the question of God. John is ultimately concerned with *theo*logy in its proper sense, with the question of who God is and how God is known. Thus he is also concerned with the question, who are those who truly know God? The absoluteness of revelation through the Son (1:18), which surpasses all other revelation, including that through Moses and the Torah (1:17; 5:39), suggests that because God is revealed fully only in the Son, then only those who know the Son know God. And since, as the statement of 17:3 suggests, knowledge of God is eternal life, only those who know the Son share God's eternal life. In short, only those who know the Son can claim to be the elect of God. For now that the Son has come into the world, "living in harmony with God" means to live in harmony with the Son. If once God fed the people with manna in the wilderness and mediated the Torah through Moses, now God's purposes are to be seen in the giving of bread from heaven and the incarnate Word. "Salvation is from the Jews," but it is now mediated through Jesus Christ. Only those who are drawn to Christ are drawn by the Father.

In the predestinarian tone of the Fourth Gospel we hear the claims of the Johannine community . But we hear a theological statement as well as a sociological one. That eternal life is God's gift, given to those whom God has "drawn," suggests that life is not attained by personal achievement.[23] Rather, it is received as a gift from the hand of God. In this way, the ultimate gift of "eternal life" mirrors what is already true of the gift of sustenance or physical life. Life is received in continual dependence on God.[24]

Indeed, if eternal life is knowing God, fellowship with God, then it demands a continual, ongoing, mutual relationship. Life is not an object to be seized apart from the Giver, and precisely in the continuing knowledge of the Giver of life does one find and know God's own life, eternal life.

The dialogue with Nicodemus affords a good opportunity to examine John's conception of how eternal life is gained. Several items in this discourse merit comment. First, statements about Jesus' identity point to his soteriological role. Jesus is indeed a teacher come from God (3:2), who can instruct Nicodemus about the "new birth" made efficacious by the Spirit. But he is also the descending Son of man (3:15), who not only brings knowledge about heavenly things, but eternal life itself. He is the mediator between heaven and earth, the realm above and below. He brings Spirit to flesh, love to the world, God to earth.

Second, the dualism expressed here is not a cosmological schema but a soteriologically oriented construct.[25] The world "above" belongs to God, the Word, life, truth, Spirit, and to those who share in that world through faith, who have passed from death to life, who have been born anew by the Spirit. Earth cannot ascend to heaven; but heaven can come down. Flesh cannot become Spirit, but Spirit can vivify flesh. Those who have died cannot live, unless they are born anew, from above, and "live" by the vivifying power of that realm. And it is in the Incarnation that the two worlds are linked in such a way that those who have been bound in death to the world below can participate in life in the world above. The Johannine dualism, then, also sheds light on the meaning of eternal life, for it reminds us that the life which is sought and available is God's life, brought from a realm to which human beings cannot attain on their own, by the one who shares the life of God.

Third, one shares the life of God only by being born of the Spirit, for one is not born to such life naturally. Although the Johannine phrase *gonnao anōthen* can be translated either "born anew" or "born from above" it is clear that the emphasis falls on the fact that the the birth which makes one a child of God happens solely by the initiative and action of God's own Spirit (cf. 1:12-13): "new birth" is "birth from above." And the image of birth is in itself instructive As an image of salvation,"birth" suggests not monism or identity or mystical union with the Creator, but rather dependence upon the Creator for existence, sustenance, and life.[26] In keeping with the conception of " birth from above" is the Johannine designation of believers as "children of God." God nourishes those who depend upon him. God gives living water; provides the bread of life, and tends the vine so that the branches may bear much fruit. Indeed, in the image of the vine and branches the Johannine conception of life is graphically portrayed: God is ultimately responsible for the health of the vine; Jesus himself is the vine; believers are the branches, who live only as long as they cling to the vine. This image not only points to God as the source of life and Jesus as the mediator of life, it also shows that life means continued dependence on and relationship to the one who gives it.

In this brief look at some statements from chapters 3 and 6 we are already anticipating the mediatorial role which Christ exercises in bringing God's life to human beings. We are, therefore, led to a consideration of the Christological dimension of eternal life in John.

2. *Christ as the Mediator of Life*

(a) Christocentric or theocentric?

It has become commonplace now for scholars to note the "radical Christocentricity" of the Gospel of John, and this judgment applies equally to the Gospel's conception of "eternal life." For example, Franz Mussner comments that John's understanding of eternal life as a present reality is a consequence of Johannine Christology.[27] This judgment has been frequently echoed.[28] Because Christ has come to the world, and because he is "eschatological salvation," then salvation, construed as eternal life, is truly present in the world. But this formulation already suggests that it would be better to speak of "eternal life" not as a consequence of John's christology, but rather as flowing naturally from his soteriology.[29] For when John takes up the theme of eternal life, his main concerns are how one has it and who has it. And these are best termed soteriological issues. This is not simply a matter of terminology; there is an important point at stake here, namely, the defintion of eternal life. Although there are clearly formulations in John which say that Jesus is life, it is best to paraphrase these by saying that Jesus is the mediator of God's life to human beings.[30] Moreover, since knowing God constitutes salvation or eternal life, then faith in Jesus is penultimate in the scheme of Johannine soteriology. Life should be construed primarily *theo*logically, since life comes from God, and soteriologically, since Jesus comes to bring what God desires to give, and directs our gaze and faith to God.

That Jesus *is* life means that Jesus *brings* life.

It should be noted that this keeps John's concept of eternal life firmly in line with the Synoptic description of the kingdom. The kingdom, after all, is the kingdom of heaven, the kingdom of God. Jesus is the messianic plenipotentiary, the intermediary who brings or administers the kingdom; he even embodies the kingdom in the world (Luke 17:20-21). But the kingdom comes from God, and those who are called by Jesus are called to live in obedience to the God whose kingdom it is, to live under the reign of God. John's preference for the terminology of life does not abandon the Synoptic view that salvation is from and will be achieved by God. Thus when the incredulous disciples ask, "Who can be saved?" Jesus answers, "All things are possible with God" (Mark 10:26-27). And when an equally incredulous Nicodemus queries, "How can these things be?" Jesus answers that they can come to pass only by the power of the Spirit of God (3:4-5).

(b) "I am" sayings with predicate

The "I am" sayings of the Gospel support the twin assertions that in John life comes from God through Jesus Christ. In John 6, Jesus asserts "I am the bread of life," and "I am the living bread." As the Son of man, he can give "food which endures to eternal life" (6:27). But he gives such food "because on him has God the Father set his seal." It is the "work of God" to believe in Jesus. Jesus' Father gives "the true bread from heaven." The bread of God "comes down from heaven and gives life to the world. And, as has been pointed out above, those who come to Jesus are given to him by the Father (6:37), whose will it is that they should have eternal life and be raised at the last day. God feeds people with the bread of life.

Embedded in the great Tabernacles discourse of John 7-10 we find, twice, "I am the light of the world" as well as the saying about Jesus as the good shepherd who comes to give his sheep life. As the world's light, Jesus supersedes the light brought through Judaism (7:37-8:1). He heals the blind man. And he will lay down his life so that his sheep may know fullness of life. This he does of his own volition (10:17-18). The light Jesus brings enables people to know God (8:19; 9:39), because he is from the world above (8:23, 26-27, 38, 42; 9:30-31, 33) and does the works and will of God (9:3, 10:18). Indeed, the healing of the man born blind is not the work of Jesus, but the work of God (9:3). Through Jesus, God brings light to the world, and "light" in the Fourth Gospel is "the light of life," that is, the light which confers or leads to life.

The saying "I am the way, the truth, and the life" further demonstrates that Jesus' role in bringing life consists primarily in mediating fellowship with God. The second half of the statement–"no one comes to the Father but by me"–explains the first half, the "I am" saying. And the next verse continues by way of explanation, "If you had known me, you would have known my Father also." That is, Jesus is the way to the Father, because he mediates knowledge of the Father.[31] Therefore, he is also the mediator of truth and life. Both the exclusive nature of Jesus' claim and his function as the mediator of knowledge of God and so of life come to the fore.

The "I am" sayings with predicate are really soteriological in their focus. They do not so much answer the question "who are you?" as they do the question "what do you bring?" Jesus brings life because he lives even as God lives.[32]

(c) The absolute claim "I am"

That the Son participates in the existence of God is the point of the somewhat enigmatic absolute "I am" sayings of the Gospel. There is an echo here of the LXX translation of Exod 3:14, "I am the one who is" (*egō eimi ho ōn*). God is. And God therefore gives life. In John 8, when the theme of life surfaces again, we see that Jesus participates in the life of God and therefore in God's purposes of giving life to the world. Life is contrasted sharply with death (8:21, 24). Whereas it is Jesus' mission and intention to bring life (8:51-52), it is the intent of his opponents, those who are "from below," to bring death, especially to Jesus himself. Jesus, in fact, makes the bold promise that he can give eternal life (8:52). The Jews correctly understand that Jesus is making a claim about the kind of life that he lives. But they misunderstand the statement when they construe it in terms of *chronological* age. They hear him saying that he existed prior to Abraham. He must indeed be older than fifty! But Jesus is making a claim to have quite another kind of life in himself, and that is eternal life, divine life, the very life of God. Therefore, he can confer it upon them.

Thus the contrast between the Son and Abraham (8:58) is between the kinds of life that they have. "Before Abraham was [came into being, was born], I am [exist, am alive, continue to live]." Abraham's life has a beginning point, but that of the Son does not. His existence is like that of God. He is "greater than Abraham" and greater than the prophets, precisely because "they died" (8:52-53), but Jesus is. There may be a reference to the divine "I am" of the OT in the claim of 8:58, but it is allusive or indirect. Jesus does not say "I am the I am." It is not until he makes the claim "to have seen Abraham," that is, to share in an eternal kind of life, that the people react. Now he is claiming to have what God alone has. Thus the link between Jesus' statement and the divine, OT "I am" is through the middle term, life. Jesus claims to share in God's kind of existence, eternal existence, existence which does not "come into being," but which simply "is" (8:35; 1:1, 2). This life he has from the *living* God (5:26; 10:18).

(d) The life-giving work of Jesus

In connection with the theme of "life," any one or all of the signs in John could be scrutinized, for, according to John, the signs are to lead people to faith so that they may have life (20:31), and the signs themselves image the gift of life that God bestows. Because Jesus shares in the very life of God, he also shares the prerogatives of God to bestow life. Perhaps the most interesting and helpful material in understanding life is provided by the sign and discourse of John 5.

The discourse is introduced by two healings, that of the official's son (4:46-54) and that of the man at the pool of Bethesda (5:1-9). The boy is in imminent danger of death; the man is not. And yet both come to "life." Jesus' command to the boy's father, "Go; your son will live" is both prophecy and promise—and yet it is more. It is a life-giving word. The command to the man at the pool, "Rise, take up your pallet, and walk" is no less a life-giving word. For although not threatened by death, in his thirty-eight years of suffering he has enjoyed less than the fullness of life, which includes physical wholeness, as the OT makes plain and promised in the messianic age. Thus two stories where someone "hears the word of Jesus" and so lives (5:25), introduce the claim that Jesus grants life.

Indeed, the following discourse makes as much of Jesus' life-giving powers, as it does of the fact that the healing of the man at the pool took place on a sabbath. Together these two factors—the kind of work Jesus does and the day on which he does it—lay the basis for the following discourse (5:17-47). Jesus argues that he works even as God works: that is, he both does the kind of work reserved for God— he gives life—and he does it on the day reserved for God—the Sabbath day. This clearly evokes the creation of the world as recounted in Genesis, and probably alludes to the argument—found, for example, in Philo and rabbinic writings—that although God ceased creative work on the Sabbath, God did not cease from work that sustained the creation.[33] Even on the Sabbath God gives life to the world. Thus, says Jesus, "My Father is working and I am working still." It is the character and prerogative of God alone to give life, but Jesus exercises those powers as he bestows life.

The discourse also speaks of Jesus' power to judge. This is simply the negative corollary of his power to grant life (5:22, 27-29, 30), as the following statement makes clear: "he who hears my word and believes him who sent me, has eternal life; he does not come into judgment, but has passed from death to life." But the pairing of judgment and life is scarcely a Johannine innovation. Of particular relevance here is the Jewish speculation on the names of God, especially as that speculation is connected with the "two powers" or "two measures" of God.[34] These two powers are judgment and mercy, and each is understood to be expressed by one of the Hebrew words for God. The rabbis understood Elohim to denote the judgment of God, and YHWH to point to God's mercy. Philo, on the other hand, took *theos* (Elohim) to mean mercy and the tetragrammaton (read as Adonai, and translated in the LXX as *Kyrios*, Lord) to connote judgment. But the point remains that the totality of God's work was understood to be expressed by these two "measures" of his providence, that of judgment, and that of mercy or goodness. Thus when the Gospel of John asserts that Jesus brings both life and judgment, it may well be calling on the current Jewish view that God's work is merciful and just. There is the healing touch, the life-giving touch, as well as the work of God in judgment. Jesus indeed works as the Father works.

3. *Summary of Section III*

It may seem that up to this point we have been avoiding the topic of "salvation as eternal life" in the Gospel of John. And yet much of the answer to the question of "what is eternal life?" is implicit in this section. It will be useful, then, to summarize briefly. Central to John's understanding of God is that God is "the living God." This means that "life" uniquely belongs to and characterizes God, that God exists eternally, and that God is the creator and source of all life. "Eternal life," then, reflects this understanding of God and virtually means "the life of God," or "divine life." "Life" is something that characterizes and comes from God; the adjective "eternal" makes this plain. Thus to have eternal life means to live in relationship to and dependence on the one who gives such life. "Eternal life" can then nearly be equated with "knowing God," where "knowledge" is understood in terms of personal relationship.

Because "life" characterizes God and an other-worldly realm, it must be mediated to human beings. If at one time such life was mediated through knowledge of and faithfulness to the Torah, it is now supremely and finally mediated through knowledge of and faithfulness to the Son, who has been with and comes from God, and thus knows God, and has also been granted life by the Father. Indeed, the Son exercises the divine prerogatives to bestow life, because he himself has been given life. This "giving" is apparently without beginning or end, for the Son exists so that he always is. He can say, as does God, "I am." Although he lays down his *psychē*, he never gives up the divine and eternal *zōē* which he possesses. So too believers are called upon the lay down their *psychē*; but those who believe in Jesus live. But what, then, does it mean to "live?"

IV. THE CONTENT OF ETERNAL LIFE

We are now led to the question, What is the "content" of eternal life in John? What does one "have" when one *has* "eternal life"? Up to this point, we might conclude that one has knowledge of, fellowship with, and dependence upon God, mediated through the person of Jesus. Yet why does John call this "eternal life"? How can one partake of the deathless existence characteristic of God and the Word? Has John spiritualized the concept of "eternality" ? Is "eternal life" primarily a qualitative term, so that one experiences a better or superior sort of life in this world? And if "qualitative" or "spiritual" adequately characterizes "eternal life," then what has happened to the hope of the resurrection and the understanding that "eternal life" is also "life of the age to come?" Would John say that believers now partake of "resurrection life?" We must, then, turn to a discussion of the "content" of eternal life in John. It will obviously build and depend upon the previous parts of this essay, but we must shift the focus to ask directly, what does one have when one has "eternal life?" And, as has been noted, this question is inextricably tied up with the temporal question.

It would be easy to understand the relationship of "eternal life" to the present if we could say that eternal life is promised and assured to those who, in the present life, have faith in the one who mediates life. This is the understanding of one author, who writes, "Those passages which apparently assert the possession of eternal life here, e.g., John 5:24; 6:47; 17:3, are to be understood as referring to it in prospect, and not in reality. The believer has eternal life in prospect and promise, but not in realization."[35] And, "neither Jesus, nor the Bible anywhere says a believer has everlasting life right now, in this life."[36]

But this interpretation founders on passages such as John 5:24-26: "Those who hear my word and believe him who sent me *have eternal life*," which is interpreted by the following clause, "they have passed over from death to life." Moreover, the "chain" of life which flows from the Father, to the Son, to the believer (5:21, 24, 26-7) suggests that even as the Son now has life, so the one who believes in the Son already has that life. Finally, statements which imply that those who do not believe have already passed judgment on themselves have as a natural corellate the assertion that those who do believe have already come into life.

Obviously, what it means to possess eternal life in the present depends to a large extent on what eternal life is. It is not, first of all, to be construed as a reward, whether present or future, for one's action or choice, not a *quid pro quo*, life for belief. Eternal life is, rather, a continuation into the future of a reality granted and experienced here, of which faith is already a constituent element.[37] John's stress on the necessity of faithfulness, as expressed in the word "abide" (*menein*) reveals his concept of the ongoing and continuing nature of the relationship in which believers stand to God. The branch must "remain" in the vine if it is to have the vitality of life, for a branch cut off from the vine cannot live. Believers must "abide" if they wish to "know the truth" and live. They must remain in the one who is life, for apart from God, there is only death. Eternal life is not something that one has as a gift apart from God, the Giver.

On the other hand, eternal life is not merely the unlimited prolongation of the existence known here on earth. Otherwise, John might well have spoken of *psychē aiōnios*, the enduring of the individual into the age to come. But the imagery of "new birth," for example, suggests life of a different order. Similarly, statements which assert that the Spirit is now present, manna is once again given, people may know God, sorrow and travail have become joy, the glory of God is revealed, and the people of God are gathered together point to the presence of the age of messianic fulfillment, with its attendant judgment on the wicked and vindication of the righteous. Statements in John which say that the age of the messiah has come may have a polemical edge aimed at those who deny that Jesus is the Messiah. They make a "religious" statement about those who have life by participating in that age, and so have an inescapable social dimension as well. For the appearance of the Messiah means the in-gathering of the people of God, an important theme of the Gospel (10:16; 11:52; 12:24). The good shepherd must protect and gather the sheep into the pasture of life.

It is not particularly helpful, then, to speak of the Johannine concept of "eternal life" as individualized or to say that John has used the concept of "life" because it was more easily adapted to the individual's participation in the gift of God. There is an inescapable social dimension to the concept of life.[38] Indeed, no Gospel emphasizes so adamantly the importance of love for others in the fellowship of believers. Love is not merely the human response to each other or to God; love comes from the same source as life, and these are not two entirely differentiated entities. As T.W. Manson states it, "The divine life is a self-giving life. The vitality of God overflows into the world: it is creative life and what it creates is a fellowship of love."[39] Not surprisingly, in the Johannine tradition those who fail to love are those who take the life of others: the devil, Judas, Cain. Love is life giving; and life produces the fruit of love. God's gift is not merely given to individual believers, but to a community: the people of the Messiah.

But it is not so much the presence of the messianic age that creates problems in understanding John's soteriological schema, as it is the assertion that the subsequent judgment and vindication have arrived. Here we come up against the temporal question and, specifically, the questions of the relationship of eternal life to the resurrection. Although eschatological hopes and conceptions in Jewish literature are far from uniform, we can with some confidence say that where there are the twin hopes of resurrection and eternal life, the resurrection precedes judgment and the inheritance of eternal life. If, then, the judgment is said to have occurred, and believers have eternal life, can we also conclude that "eternal life" is "resurrection life"? Or, even more radically, does John transmute the hope for a future resurrection into a present and spiritual experience of the believer? Ernst Käsemann, for example, writes that the Johannine community gives evidence of "an enthusiastic piety which affirmed a sacramentally realized resurrection of the dead in the present."[40] Similarly, Bultmann assigned to the Ecclesiastical Redactor all passages that refer to a future resurrection, for in authentic Johannine thought, eschatology was "historicized," and the eschatological event was fully present in the proclamation of Jesus.[41] Taking a somewhat different tack, C.H. Dodd writes that "the 'resurrection' of which Jesus has spoken [in 11:26] is something which may take place before bodily death." Dodd further states that the raising of Lazarus "anticipates the final resurrection," while it is also a "symbol of the real resurrection by which a man passes from a merely physical existence, which is death, into the life which is life indeed."[42] And C.F.D. Moule suggests that John's view of salvation, "could very easily give rise to that individualistic heresy alluded to in 2 Tim 2:18--that the resurrection had already taken place."[43]

If it were correct to say that in Johannine eschatology the resurrection has already occurred in the experience of the believer, then this also implies a significantly different conception of resurrection than one finds either in other documents of the NT or of Judaism. For though at times resurrection is the reward given to the righteous individual who suffers and dies, perhaps as a martyr, one also finds—and with increasing regularity by the first century—the view that the resurrection implies the raising of the *people* of God, the future vindication of the righteous.[44] Resurrection is not an individual but a social or corporate reality, for salvation is a corporate concept, and resurrection and salvation are intimately connected. If John mutes or discards the future resurrection, a logical-corollary might well be a highly individualized understanding of salvation.[45] John might well have interpreted the future hope of a people as a presently attainable possession of the individual. But John's conception of "life" is not so highly individualized as has been argued, for in John life is not given to disparate individuals, but rather to a community of believers. After all, it is the Fourth Gospel that insists there must be "one flock, one shepherd."[46] God gives life to the righteous and faithful people of God.

We may also take up the interpretation that eternal life in John is a "spiritual" reality. Here much depends upon our definition or terms. But if "spiritual" is intended to mean that the Johannine view of salvation does not draw in its train material and physical reality, then I would argue that this view is inadequate. In John life is given through material elements, such as bread and water. Physical healings serve as images of God's gift of life. The changing of water to wine is a tangible manifestation of the presence of the messianic age. God works through, not apart from, the material realities of this world in bringing salvation. Nor are these material realities to be understood merely as "symbols" of another realm of reality or life. Indeed, where all life is understood to come from the living God, then that same God touches, heals, and restores all that is. God gave and God gives life.[47]

Also consonant with at least some strands in Jewish eschatology is the Johannine hope for the resurrection of the body, which suggests that "eternal life" in John ought not to be limited to the "spiritual" or "mystical" realm. The dead are raised, not "spiritually" or metaphorically, but bodily. Moreover, the present possession of eternal life does not imply the actualization of the resurrection or the internal realization of the final resurrection. These assertions may be illustrated by looking at two key passages in John 5:25-29, and 11:25-26. Although these passages are typically cited as evidence for the transmutation or reinterpretation of the resurrection hope in John, this interpretation is tenuous. Both passages testify to the expectation of a future resurrection which is not simply equated with eternal life or with a "spiritual" state of being or internal and personal experience.[48]

The key question to be answered is whether the terms for "death" and "life" in these passages refer to physical or spiritual states, with the main problem being posed by the statement that the one who believes in Jesus "shall never die" (11:26). Since it seems unlikely that this refers to physical immortality, it is generally taken as a reference to an enduring of the spirit or of "true life," even beyond the grave. For example, Bernard writes of these verses, "If a man believe in Him, although his body dies yet his true self shall live (v. 25). Or, as it may be put in other words, no believer in Jesus shall ever die, *so far as his spirit is concerned* (v. 26)."[49] Another way to phrase the question is to ask whether the raising of Lazarus and the promise that the dead "will live" (5:25) refer to the raising of the physically or spiritually dead. Temple writes that the raising of the (physically) dead by Jesus "was a sign of the quickening of multitudes spiritually dead."[50] But Corell's corrective is apt: the contrast is not "spiritual life contra physical death, but life *contra* death."[51]

Perhaps the best evidence for the interpretation of "life" and "death" as indicating physical as well as spiritual states is the fact that Lazarus actually comes forth from the tomb, a graphic fulfillment of the promise in 5:25—already partially fulfilled by the healings of 4:46-54 and 5:1-9—that "the hour is coming and now is when the dead will hear the voice of the Son of God, and those who hear will live."[52] Yet this promise is not completely fulfilled in the single raising of Lazarus, nor in a spiritualized interpretation of that event. For Lazarus is only one example of what is expected yet in the future, for John also states that "the hour is coming when all who are in the tombs will hear his voice and come forth, those who have done good, to the resurrection of life, and those who have done evil, to the resurrection of judgment" (5:29). If the raising of Lazarus signals the fulfillment of the promise in 5:25, it does not exhaust the content of that promise. For there is yet the promise of a general resurrection, as is spelled out in 5:29. It is clear that this is a resurrection in which all who are in the tombs, and not just the faithful in Christ, will be raised. Resurrection is not to be experienced by the faithful only. As Plummer comments, "Spiritual resurrection must always be a resurrection of life, a passing from spiritual death to spiritual life. A passing from spiritual death to judgment is not spiritual resurrection."[53] Life, however, certainly belongs to the believer alone; death and judgment describe the fate of those who do not believe. But this time of resurrection to judgment and life is not said to be present.

In 11:25-26 Jesus declares that he is "resurrection and life." He explains the meaning of "resurrection" when he says "he who believes in me, though he die, yet shall he live." That is, the believer will be raised to live forever. The statement that Jesus is "life" is explained by the statement "and whoever lives and believes in me shall never die."[54] Those who are presently alive *with eternal life* will not be cut off from the resurrection to life.[55] In short, those who have life now will be resurrected to life in the future, while those who are now dead will be resurrected to judgment and death.[55] The resurrection confirms the present status of the individual; it seals the relationship that one presently has to the Father and the Son.

Jesus' own life, death, and resurrection guide our interpretation here. Although Jesus dies, he lays down only his *psychē*, and never gives up his *zōē*, the eternal life that he possesses. For his life is imperishable, properly spoken of with the self-designation "I am." And in this regard his "life" (*zōē*) does not provide a complete analogy to the life (*zōē*) of the believer. For the life of the believer knows a beginning point and depends upon Jesus' own life: "Because I live, you will live also" (14:19). And yet there is a true analogy between Jesus and the believer. Just as in his resurrection Jesus takes up the *psychē* which he had laid down, so too believers will live again. In no way is Jesus' death a signal of abandonment by God, disruption of fellowship with God, or in any way a loss of the life (*zōē*) derived from God. And neither can death rob the believer of eternal life (*zōē*). Physical death is a threat to the *psychē* but not to "eternal life" (*zōē*). Even the present possession of eternal life does not eliminate the hope and need for the future resurrection, for it is the resurrection that overcomes physical death. Eternal life and resurrection are not simply synonymous. Nor does John reinterpret "resurrection" as the quality of a life (*zōē*) now available to the believer or the church. Rather, resurrection is that event which seals the believer in life eternally and removes the threat of death to one's *psychē*..

V. SUMMARY COMMENTS: SALVATION AS LIFE IN THE GOSPEL OF JOHN

Numerous summaries and explanations of "eternal life" in John can be found. Alf Corell, for example, concludes that "*zōē* or *zōē aiōnios* is the eschatological life which through faith in Christ is received and lived in the Church, and which afterwards through the resurrection reaches its fulfillment in the world to come."[57] Paolo Ricca writes that "'Eternal life' designates the life of the future, which has become present, and at the same time, is life *eis ton aiōna*, that is, life directed toward the future, expecting its final completion in the future. Eternal life in John is an eschatological reality, which is lived fully in the present and, at the same time, is fundamentally oriented towards the future."[58] Or, again, as David Aune has aptly stated it, eternal life is "more than ethical transformation, but less than ontological transformation."[59] Captured in these two descriptions of eternal life in John are several crucial elements which we have mentioned in one way or another. Now we may draw together the threads of earlier discussion.

First, eternal life is not relegated to the future, although the believer has hope for the future in the shape of the resurrection. Eternal life is present now insofar as through Christ an intimate relationship with and knowledge of God the Father is made available. In that relationship the believer acknowledges dependence upon God who is the source of all life. And in being faithful to that living God, the believer may be said to "have life." The believer does not have life "in himself," as does the Son. The Son's life is unmediated. But the believer has life in a continuing and dynamic relationship with God, through the mediation of the Son.

Thus those who have life have it only and insofar as they depend upon the source of all life. In fact, the reality known as "eternal life" is not so much something that one has alongside dependence upon God; it is almost equivalent to that dependence upon God. For from God, and only from God, who alone can give life, does life come to the believer in every form in which it comes. For this reason, commentators prefer to speak of the reality of eternal life in active and dynamic terms. Lindars, for example, writes that John prefers to say that believers "live," rather than to say that they "are saved."[60] Manson speaks of life as vitality, and Barrett as "essential energy."[61] These are merely modern paraphrases of the allegory of the vine and the branches in John 15, where it becomes clear that life is not some discrete thing, but the dependence of the branch upon the vine.

At times the vitality of life takes the shape of God's mercy and goodness manifested in the physical realm. That is, healing and provision are the work of the living God to restore to wholeness and health, to fullness of life, the creation to which the same God also granted life. Life, then, is not "otherworldly," as though it does not touch the realities of the present world.[62] The experience of physical life is analogous to the experience of eternal life, not as a symbol or picture, but as manifestation of the complete dependence that the creature has on the creator.

Neither is "eternal life" otherworldly in the sense that it is experienced only in the future. Although it is only by "new birth" that one enters into eternal life, this new birth is experienced in the present. Jesus prays not that believers be taken out of this world, but that they be preserved in this world. But how is this "new life" experienced in this world? It is experienced in and as the commitment to "live by the strength of the invisible and uncontrollable."[63] That is, eternal life is the appropriation, by faith, of unseen yet real divine realities, the relationship to, by faith, the unseen yet real and living God. Eternal life is living by the power of God, and the recognition that one lives alone by this power. Eternal life becomes a reality through the power of the Spirit of God.[64]

Thus "eternal life" is life lived from God's perspective, by God's own values. Eternal life is life as it is lived understanding the ultimate questions of life and in relationship to the source of all that is. Such a vision may not be perfect, but as one appropriates it, one has joy and peace. These are the paramaters of eternal life. One may choose to call these "spiritual realities," but only if, again, we understand that these touch the way one lives, thinks, and acts in the world. Joy and peace are not simply feelings, but concrete expressions of one's commitment to life. That is, joy and peace are not gifts that one is given alongside life.[65] Joy and peace are experienced as one enters into fellowship or harmony with God and understands that God's purposes are being effected in the world, and that in Christ one participates in those purposes. Despite present appearances to the contrary, one sees that the powers of darkness cannot overcome light (1:5) ultimately the divine will is at work in the world; that there is and will be life out of death. Neither joy nor peace overlooks the reality of circumstances of the world; but neither do these circumstances provide the ultimate shape and definition to the life of believers.

As distinctive to "life" as peace and joy is love. The divine perspective on life necessarily includes the social dimension, expressed in Johannine parlance by the simple "love." In the Gospel of John–although not necessarily in the Johannine community--the focus is on love for each other in the community, because this is the community of life. It is the elect community, those to whom God has granted the fullness of life, eternal life. In love for each other, the community puts into action now the final unity that will be experienced in the resurrection to life.[66] Thus those who experience life now can never will death, in any sort or form, for others. Those who have life must be committed to life for the world, whether through the proclamation of the one who is life, the alleviation of physical pain, or the healing of emotional distress. The promise of "salvation" in John 3:16 is paralleled by the call to love of one's fellow believer in 1 John 3:16-18. Reception of life demands a commitment to life.

Understanding those who have life as those "elect" or graced by God also means, in John, that this state of living in dependence upon the life of God continues into the future, when after physical death one is brought again to life. In the future there is yet a fuller vision of God, which consummates our present understanding, just as there is the transformation of the believer (1 John 3:2). Aune writes that, "the final goal of eschatological salvation, according to John 17:24, is 'to see the glory of Jesus' in a protological and eschatological unity with the Father."[67] These realities are truly experienced now, as believers "behold the glory of the only Son" (1:14), and so enjoy unity with God through Christ; but John does not say that believers are presently with Christ in the heavenly abiding places (14:2-3). The enjoyment of life with the Father, as the Son knows it (1:18), lies in the future.

In summary, "life" is a term which connotes the totality of salvation. No more encompassing term could be imagined. One can attempt to describe life and to suggest what one enjoys when one has life. For example, one can speak of deliverance from sin and judgment, radical transformation and enrichment of existence, fellowship with God, or the experience of the "unification of one's life."[68] But if one insists on understanding life as something one can get, something apart from the Giver of life, one does not fully understand life. Perhaps one ancient writer said it well when he wrote, "And is it not life eternal to take refuge with Him that is, and death to flee away from Him?"[69]

NOTES

1. On the equivalence of these terms, see below, "The Johannine Vocabulary of Life."

2. See C.F.D. Moule, "The Individualism of the Fourth Gospel," *NovT* 5 (1962) 171-90.

3. On the appropriateness of speaking of "mysticism" in John, see F. Mussner, *ZOE. Die Anschauung vom "Leben" im vierten Evangelium* (Munich: Karl Zink, 1952) 145; H. Odeberg, *The Fourth Gospel: Interpreted in its Relation to Contemporaneous Religious Currents in Palestine and the Hellenistic-Oriental World* (Amsterdam: B. R. Gruner, 1968) 268; C. J. Wright, *The Meaning and Message of the Fourth Gospel*, (London: Hodder & Stoughton, 1933) 148-96. C .K. Barrett, *The Gospel According to St. John,* 2nd ed [Philadelphia: Westminster, 1978] 85-87 argues that the term "mysticism" does not aptly describe Johannine thought; cf. B. Lindars, *The Gospel of John (Grand* Rapids, Eerdmans, 1972) 58. For descriptions of "life" in John as "spiritual", see R. W. Thomas, "The Meaning of the Terms 'Life' and 'Death' in the Fourth Gospel and in Paul," *SJT* 21 (1968) 201; L. Morris, *Jesus is the Christ: Studies in the Theology of John* (Grand Rapids: Eerdmans, 1989) 194, 196, 198. A. Corell, *Consummatum Est: Eschatology and Church in the Gospel of St John* (London: SPCK, 1958) 142, speaks of "eternal life" as "purely religious."

4. C.H. Dodd, *The Interpretation of the Fourth Gospel* (Cambridge: University Press, 1953) 144-50, 366; R. Bultmann, *Theology of the New Testament,* (New York: Scribners, 1951, 1955) 2:11; and "*zaō*," in *TDNT* 2 (1964) 871-72; R. Schnackenburg, *The Gospel According to St. John,* 3 vols. (New York: Seabury Press, 1980, 1982), 2. 359-360.

5. For "eternal life" as a "timeless" state or quality, see, in addition to the references in the previous note, J. N. Sanders and B. Mastin, *The Gospel According to St. John* (New York: Harper & Row, 1968) 359 n. 3; and R.H. Charles, *Eschatology: The Doctrine of a Future Life ln Israel, Judaism and Christianity* (New York: Schocken Books, 1963) 426-28.

6. R. E. Brown, *The Gospel According to John,* 2 vols. (New York: Doubleday, 1966, 1970) I, lxxxv. While the question of John's emphasis on "realized eschatology" is not identical with the question why he so stresses "life," they are obviously related, for in John's view what one has in the present is "life."

7. Bultmann, "*zaō*," *TDNT* 2 (1964) 871-72.

8. A thorough and well-documented survey of "life" and "eternal life" can be found in David Hill, *Greek Words and Hebrew Meanings* (Cambridge: University Press, 1967) 163-201.

9. See Barrett, *John,* 80.

10. See T.W. Manson, *On Paul and John* (London: SCM Press, 1963) 110-111; Hill, *Greek Words,* 192; Thomas, "Meaning of Life and Death," 203; D. G. Vanderlip, *Christianity According to John* (Philadelphia: Westminster, 1975) 41; J. C. Davis, "The Johannine Concept of Eternal Life as Present Possession," *Restoration Quarterly* 27 (1984) 166.

11. For example, Paolo Ricca, *Die Eschatologie des vierten Evangeliums* (Zürich/Frankfurt: Gotthelf-Verlag, 1966) 195; Brown, *John,* 2:505-508; Hill, *Greek Words,* 195; D. E. Aune, *The Cultic Set-*

ting of Realized Eschatology in Early Christianity (Leiden: Brill, 1972) 105; Lindars, *John*, 158; Morris, *Jesus is the Christ*, 204.

12. Schnackenburg, *St. John*, 2:521 n. 5; Dodd, *Interpretation*, 146.

13. Schnackenburg, *St. John*, 2:353.

14. See Odeberg, *The Fourth Gospel*, 293-94; Aune, *Cultic Setting* 58 n. 2, 106. Although Hill (*Greek Words*, 181-82) comments that in Jewish thought, "the Age to come is conceived of as eternally existent: it always *is* in the heavens and we awake to it at death," he later speaks of Jewish dualism as "temporal" (p. 196).

15. E. Uhrbach, *The Sages: Their Concepts and Beliefs* (Cambridge: Harvard University Press, 1987) 40. Some examples of Philo's emphasis on the existence of God can be found in *Det.* 160; *Mut.* 10-12, 17; *De Som.* I.230-231.

16. For example, in *b. Ber.* 28b Johanan ben Zakkai is quoted in describing God as "the Holy One, who lives and endures forever." See also the chapter on "God and the World," in G.F. Moore, *Judaism*, 2 vols. (New York: Schocken, 1927) I.357-385.

17. For example, Manson, *On Paul and John*, 111-113; Simon, "Eternal Life," 109; Odeberg, *Fourth Gospel*, 258; Aune, *Cultic Setting*, 106.

18. See P. Borgen, *Bread From Heaven* (Leiden: Brill, 1965) 172; Brown, *John*, I.506; Thomas, "Meaning of Life and Death," 201; Morris, *Jesus is the Christ*, 194, 196, 198.

19. Corell, *Consummatum Est*, 140.

20. See Barrett, *John*, 157: "The Prologue claims no more than the rest of the gospel, but sets first in a cosmological aspect what later will appear in a soteriological."

21. Schnackenburg, *St John*, 3.173; Corell, *Consummatum Est*, 140; contrast Barrett, *John*, 503; G. R. Beasley-Murray, *John* (Waco: Word, 1987) 296; L. Morris, *The Gospel According to John* (Grand Rapids: Eerdmans, 1971) 719.

22. E. Haenchen, *John*, 2 vols. (Philadelphia: Fortress, 1984) I.114.

23. Simon, "Eternal Life," 104; Morris, *Jesus is the Christ*, 195.

24. Hill (*Greek Words*, 168) writes, "We may reiterate what is perhaps the most significant aspect of the Hebrew understanding of 'life,' namely, its dependence on God. Wherever there is life, it is God's gift. . . . That life in all its aspects should be so dependent on God need not surprise us, for the God of the Old Testament is himself the Living God, active and creative. He is the 'Living One.' . . . Life here and now, life after death, are given and sustained by him."

25. Mussner, *ZOE*, 54-56; Hill, *Greek Words*, 196; Schnackenburg, *St. John*, 2.353.

26. Simon, "Eternal Life," 105; Aune, *Cultic Setting*, 107; Barrett, *Gospel of John*, 85-87; Lindars, *John*, 58.

27. Mussner, *ZOE*, 145-47.

28. Vanderlip, *John*, 43; Ricca, *Eschatologie*, 82, 90, 92, 98, 128; J. Blank, *Krisis: Untersuchungen zur johanneischen Christologie und Eschatologie* (Breisgau: Lambertus-Verlag, 1964) 15, 38-39, 125; Schnackenburg, *St. John*, 2:353, 355, 426-27; Ernst Käsemann, *The Testament of Jesus* (Philadelphia: Fortress, 1968) 16.

29. The Judgment that John's eschatology is essentially a function of his Christology is disputed, on different grounds, by Aune, *Cultic Setting*, 86 and D. Allison, *The End of the Ages Has Come* (Philadelphia: Fortress, 1985) 52-59.

30. See, for example, the comments of Beasley-Murray on John 14:6 in *John*, 252.

31. See Barrett, *John*, 458; Brown, *John*, II.628; Beasley-Murray, *John*, 252.

32. As Morris, *Jesus is the Christ*, 192, comments, "To say that someone is living is easily understandable; to say that he is life is not." For John, there is not such a great distinction. That the Son is "living" means that he has life, the is is "life" means that he enables believers to live.;

33. See the discussion and references in Dodd, *Interpretation*, 320-23; Barrett, *John*, 256.

34. On the "two powers" of God, see the discussions in Moore, *Judaism*,, I.386-400; A. Marmorstein, "Philo and the Names of God," *JQR* 22 (1931-32) 295-306; Dodd, *Interpretation*, 320-23; N.A. Dahl and A. F. Segal, "Philo and the Rabbis on the Names of God," *JSJ* IX (1978) and A. F. Segal, *Two Powers in Heaven: Early Rabbinic Reports about Christianity and Gnosticism* (Leiden: Brill, 1977); Uhrbach, *The Sages*, 448-61.

35. G. N. Woods, "Commentary on 1 John" in *Gospel Advocate Commentary* (Nashville: Gospel Advocate, 1974) 317; cf. L. van Hartingsveld, *Die Eschatologie des Johannesevangeliums* (Assen:

Van Gorcum, 1962) 60ff; 74-80.

36. G. N. Woods, "Commentary on John," 105.

37. Or, perhaps better, eternal life extends from the future back into the present. Obviously there is some difficulty in speaking of a beginning point for "eternal life," yet the believer does not share in the "timeless" aspect of eternity, as do God and the Word, for the decision of faith marks the "beginning" of "eternal life." In this sense, everlasting is the more accurate description of the temporal dimension of life for the believer, but it does not offer an adequate parallel to God's own life or capture the qualitative superiority of "eternal life."

38. W .H. Rigg, *The Fourth Gospel and its Message for Today* (London: Lutterworth, 1952) 86; Corell, *Consummatum Est,* 78, 146-50, 202; Aune, *Cultic Setting* , 105-121; Thomas, "Meaning of Life and Death," 205; D. Wenham, "Spirit and Life," *Themelios* 6 (1980) 8; David Rensberger, *Johannine Faith and Liberating Community* (Philadelphia: Westminster, 1988) 44.

39. Manson, *On Paul and John,* 113.

40. *Testament,* 15; cf. 20, 75.

41. *John,* 261; *Theology,* II.37-40; cf. Haenchen, *John.*I.:88-89, 253-54; J. Becker, *Das Evangelium nach Johannes,,* 2 vols. Gutersloh: Gerd Mohn; Wurzburg: Echter Verlag, 1981) 1.235-36, 2.358-60.

42. Dodd, *Interpretation,* 148, emphasis added; cf. Barrett, *John.* 396; J. H. Bernard, *A Critical and Exegetical Commentary on the Gospel According to St. John,,* 2 vols. (Edinburgh: T. & T. Clark, 1928) 2. 387-88.

43. Moule, "Individualism," 184; B. W. Bacon, T*he Gospel of the Hellenists,* ed. C. Kraeling (New York: Henry Holt & Co., 1933) 162-64, 337.

44. Sometimes the resurrection of the righteous (as in *Ps. Sol.* 3:16, 14:2ff) is part of a general resurrection (as in Dan 12:2, 1 *Enoch* 51:1; 2 *Bar* 30:1-5, 50:1; 4 *Ezra* 7:32; *m. Sanh.* 10:1; *m. Aboth* 4:22; *m. Ber.* 5:2; *m. Sot.* 9:15), when all people are raised to be judged according to their deeds. Texts which speak of the resurrection of the "righteous" and/or the "wicked," meaning not individuals but a plurality of persons suggest a "corporate" understanding of resurrection. See G. W. E. Nickelsburg, *Resurrection, Immortality, and Eternal Life In Intertestamental Judaism* (Cambridge: Harvard University Press; London: Oxford, 1972); E. Schürer, *The History of the Jewish People in the Age of Jesus Christ,* eds. G. Vermes, F. Millar, M. Black (Edinburgh: T. & T. Clark, 1979) 2.539-547, and the bibliography in n. 90; Moore, *Judaism,* II.279-322.

45. See Moore, *Judaism,* II:319, who writes that "the ultimate salvation of the individual [understood as eternal life] is inseparably connected with the salvation of the people."

46. *Test Jud* 25:2 promises that in the resurrection, "you shall be one people of the Lord, with one language." 2 *Bar* 30:3 speaks of the "souls of the righteous" appearing together, "in one assemblage, of one mind." For the gathering of the dispersed, see Tobit 13:5, 13; Sir 36:1-17; *Ps Sol* 11:3-8.

47. Barrett, *John,* 80, aptly summarizes, "The miracles in particular show figuratively what salvation is—the curing of the sick, the feeding of the hungry, the giving of sight to the blind, and the raising of the dead. Salvation, that is, means the healing of the ills of mankind, and the imparting of light and life." I would, however, delete the word "figuratively," for the signs are manifestations of the work of God to bring life in all its fullness.

48. Those scholars who suggest that in John the resurrection is already a present fact do not necessarily deny that John also holds to the hope of a general, future resurrection. See, e.g., W. Temple, *Readings in St. John's Gospel* (London: Macmillan, 1955) 182; Dodd, *Interpretation,* 364-66; Morris, *John,* 550; Bernard, *John,* 2:386-88; Vanderlip, *John,* 40.

49. Bernard, *John,* 2.388, emphasis added.

50. Temple, R*eadings in John,* 113; Brown, *John,* 1.215; Vanderlip, *John,* 35, 40; Haenchen, *John,* 1.252. Thomas, "Meaning of Life and Death," 208; Beasley-Murray, *John,* 76.

51. Corell, *Consummatum Est,* 148.

52. Aune, *Cultic Setting,* 59, 120-21.

53. A. Plummer, *The Gospel According to St. John* (reprint; Grand Rapids: Baker, 1981) 139-40.

54. Dodd, I*nterpretation,* 365; J. R. Michaels, *John,* (San Francisco: Harper & Row, 1984) 188; Beasley-Murray, *John,* 190. "Resurrection" and "life" are not equivalent, as some have held, e.g. Bultmann, *John,* 403; Schnackenburg, *St. John,* 2.331; Becker, *Evangelium,* 2:359-61.

55. Beasley-Murray, *John,* 191; Van Hartingsveld, *Eschatologie,* 50-56; Aune, *Cultic Setting,* 120-21.

56. It should be noted that John does not spell out in detail the nature of the judgment and death to be experienced by the unbeliever.

57. Corell, *Consummatum Est,* 149; cf. Aune, *Cultic Setting.* 109, 112, 134.

58. Ricca, *Eschatologie,* 120-21.

59. Aune, *Cultic Setting,* 109, 134; Simon, *Eternal Life,* 106.

60. Lindars, *John,* 160.

61. Manson, *On Paul and John,* 113; Barrett, *Gospel of John,* 158.

62. Contrast Schnackenburg, *St. John,* II.361.

63. Bultmann, *Theology, II.* 7

64. However, the experience of life is not simply equivalent to the experience of the Spirit, contra Wenham, "Spirit and Life," 6.

65. Mussner, *ZOE,* 186-87.

66. Aune, *Cultic Setting,* 109.

67. Aune, *Cultic Setting,* 90.

68. These helpful terms come from Vanderlip, J*ohn,* 37.

69. Philo, *Fug.,* 78.

DID PAUL'S VIEW OF THE RESURRECTION OF THE DEAD UNDERGO DEVELOPMENT?*

BEN F. MEYER

"Is it not a remarkable thing that you should have started the idea—and the word—Development, as the key to the history of church doctrine, and since then it has gradually become the dominant idea of all history, biology, physics, and in short has metamorphosed our view of every science, and of all knowledge?" So wrote Mark Pattison to John Henry Newman in 1878,[1] thirty-three years after the publication of Newman's *Essay on the Development of Christian Doctrine.*[2] Rarely had a single idea so rapidly and thoroughly transformed a whole culture's field of vision. This implies, to be sure, that Newman had had predecessors and allies of sorts as well as kindred and alien successors.

Among the predecessors was G. W. F. Hegel, whose triad of thesis, antithesis, and synthesis impinged on biblical history and exegesis especially through the work of Ferdinand Christian Baur.[3] By the end of the century "development" had established itself in biblical studies as an indispensable heuristic resource. Likewise, by century's end Richard Kabisch and Johannes Weiss had discovered "eschatology" as the very form of early Christian consciousness, aspiration, and reflection.[4] Soon Albert Schweitzer would so effectively thematize the issue of eschatology as to make it foundational for the exegesis of the New Testament, the history of religions (Judeo-Christian sector), and New Testament theology. Moreover, these two thought forms, "development" and "eschatology," inevitably intersected. Kabisch was the first to bring development to bear on eschatology grasped as a controlling principle, and Schweitzer offered the first real appreciation of this effort as well as the sharpest critique of its shortcomings.[5]

----

* Reprinted by permission of the author from his *Critical Realism & The New Testament*, (Allison Park: Pickwick Publications, 1989) 99-128.

It soon became clear that eschatology—pervasive in the texts, but for long centuries overlooked by their readers—and development—burked in the texts, but highly conscious among nineteenth-century scholars after Baur—were not only great but intoxicating discoveries. Just because the eschatological consciousness had been a vital experience in earliest Christianity, but lay outside the experience of modernity, and just because the consciousness of development had been a stunning advance since the mid-nineteenth century, but was by and large alien to the whole of late antiquity, the combination of the two generated the most uninhibited hypotheses and far-ranging, free-wheeling reconstructions of early Christian thought.

Here I propose, first, to recall the main lines of the discussion of development in one sphere of Pauline eschatology, namely, the theme of the coming resurrection of the dead; second, to question whether the Pauline texts (1 Thess 4; 1 Cor 15; 2 Cor 5; Phil 1) support the maximalists or the minimalists in the debate on the "development" of Paul's view. Maximalists argue that he moved from a relatively crude, conventional affirmation of resurrection to a more refined conception of survival, and often enough they have characterized this as a transition from Jewish to Greek categories. Minimalists doubt or deny a change of categories, but often enough have acknowledged the appearance of new, if minor, doctrinal elements in the later texts, or at least some variation in Paul's personal attitude toward the prospect of death and resurrection. Third, I propose to reflect on the context in which this debate has a significance beyond antiquarian, or even historical, curiosity. Therefore, Part 1 is history; Part 2 is exegesis; Part 3 is hermeneutics.

I. HISTORY

It was Baur who initiated this kind of investigation, and Otto Pfleiderer who, prior to the realization that eschatology was not only an aspect but the very horizon of early Christian consciousness, framed the first influential hypothesis of development in Paul's eschatological thought.[6] The pattern of Pfleiderer's view of Paul went well with the dominant weave of Liberal theology. Tutored like many Liberals first by Baur, then by Hermann Lüdemann's study of Pauline anthropology, Pfleiderer saw distinct "branches," Jewish and Hellenistic, in the Pauline "doctrinal system."[7] Paul, moreover, had shifted from the one to the other. If the first branch grew out of the expiatory death of Jesus and formed "the negative part of the Pauline Gospel in opposition to the Jews or the Jewish Christians," the second branch grew out of Christ's risen life in the radiant element of *pneuma*, far beyond "transitory and unclean *sarx*.[8] "Life" here was eschatological, but "the *transcendent eschatological idea* became of necessity an *immanent ethical* one," for the Christian's future share in "resurrection life" depended on his having died with Christ in baptism and so on his having already participated in Christ's "*pneuma* life." Baptism, accordingly, marked the moment of entry "into mystical communion with Christ and of the reception of his pneuma."[9]

The great development in Paul was, then, away from the sphere of the eschatological into that of the mystical. The messianic *zoe* was thus "stripped of its one-sided, supernatural, apocalyptic character" and became ethical and spiritual. This transition followed "one of the deepest laws of development in the history of religion": profound mysteries are concealed and protected in the calyx of apocalyptic imagery "until they are capable of flourishing alone . . . . "[10]

Let this sketch suffice to suggest the tenor and style of Pfleiderer's thinking about Paulinism. Though differing in detail from Baur and Lüdemann, Pfleiderer reflected ideas from both and specifically reflected the tendency to reduce a many-faceted faith to a fairly breezy history of ideas—a besetting defect of the Liberal movement.[11] The sketch may also serve to provide some measure of context for Pfleiderer's retrieval of Pauline eschatology.

"Development" in Pfleiderer's view did not exclude inconsistencies and unresolved antinomies. Rather, it hinged on them. All through "the Apostle's dogmatic teaching" there ran a duality reflecting the trajectory of Paul's own career: "from a Pharisee and a zealous upholder of the law," he had become "a chosen instrument of the gospel of the favour of God in Christ."[12] To the two phases divided by this turnabout belonged the two categories of Pauline thought: "remnants from Judaism" and "Christian gospel." Ranged under the rubric of Jewish remnants were the ideas of final judgment eternally distinguishing the saved and the lost on the basis of "just due"; the *parousia* as the decisive moment of the resurrection and redemption of the body; the messianic reign, beginning with the *parousia* and the resurrection of those in Christ and ending with the reduction to impotence of the last enemy, death (=the resurrection of all) and the handing over of the reign to the Father (1 Cor 15:24-26). Ranged under the specifically Christian gospel were salvation by the pure *charis* of God, the indwelling *pneuma,* shaping in the believer the image of Christ's death and resurrection, and for those in Christ the unhindered union with the Lord--clothed with a heavenly body—immediately upon death (2 Cor 5:1-10; Phil 1:23). Pfleiderer abstained from all effort to reconcile these two quite "incompatible" sets of ideas; for that, he thought, could be done only by recourse to "arbitrary criteria."[13]

Pfleiderer was undeterred by the flat impossibility of finding significant Greek analogies for (to say nothing of Greek attestation of) any part or aspect of the specifically Christian gospel, be it the pure gift of righteousness by faith, or the indwelling, energizing, patterning *pneuma* of God/Christ, or entry into immortality with a radiant *doxa*body prepared in heaven. In 1887, fourteen years after his two-volume work on Paulinism, he returned to the theme of Paul's Hellenized eschatology in *Primitive Christianity*.[14] Here Paul's development away from Jewish thinking into Alexandrian Platonizing was attested by 2 Cor 5:1-10, supplemented by Phil 1:21-22. and 3:8-9. Paul, in a word, drew on Hellenistic resources to spiritualize the Christian hope of salvation and, incidentally, to provide a neat exit out of the dilemma of the delayed *parousia.* As Albert Schweitzer remarked of this confident, comprehensive view,

> Pfleiderer believes also that he can show the course of the development by which the new conception was arrived at. In 1 Thessalonians, he thinks, the Apostle still rested unquestioningly in that notion of a corporeal resurrection which primitive Christianity shared with Judaism. But in the explanations of 1 Cor. XV the influence of the Greek ideas become observable, while in 2 Corinthians and Philippians it becomes dorninant.[15]

Pfleiderer's Paul—who moved back and forth between Judaic resurrection and Greek immortality, without being conscious of the divergence between the two sets of ideas, yet without ever mingling them—was unmasked as an exegetical illusion by the superior (if still quite fallible) synthesis of Richard Kabisch.[16] In opposition to Kabisch, Ernst Teichmann in 1896 produced a monograph in the form of twin essays on the Pauline conceptions of resurrection and judgment.[17]

According to Teichmann's reconstruction, Paul's thought on the resurrection of the dead registered a movement from Jewish apocalyptic spirituality to Hellenistic Wisdom spirituality. Like Pfleiderer, Teichmann argued that this evolution could be traced through three stages. In the first stage (1 Thess 4:13-17) Paul affirmed a resurrection of the dead in the sense of a resuscitation of the corpses of the faithful, an event to take place at the parousia. In a second, mediating stage (1 Cor 15:50-55) he affirmed the annihilation of everything earthly, including the earthly body, and the appropriation of a new, spiritual body—still, however, to take place at the parousia. In a third and final phase, represented by 2 Cor 5:1-11 and, still better, by Phil 1:21-25, resurrection has been abandoned, or abandoned in all but name, in favor of the bestowal of a new body at the moment of death.[18]

This scheme of development drew attention to the intermediate stage represented by 1 Cor 15:50-55. In this passage Paul introduced the notion of transformation. In 1 Thess 4 resurrection had no more implied "transformation" than had, for example, the story of Elijah swept up to heaven in a fiery chariot. But now transformation must make its appearance as a consequence of the Pauline antithesis of *sarx* and *pneuma*. Moreover, for Teichmann "transformation" really meant "total annihilation."[19] *Sarx* would be annihilated and man created anew. Hence Paul's maintenance of the idea of *resurrection* was incoherent with the real character of his thought. By the time of 2 Cor 5 it had been dropped; for here the new *soma,* which had existed in heaven since the creation, has "replaced" the earthly body.[20]

On the text of 2 Cor 5:1-10 Teichmann made five points: (a) the earthly body, destined for decay, is an obstacle to our union with the Lord; (b) but for every individual believer God has prepared a heavenly body to clothe him at the moment of his death; (c) "nakedness" images the *pneuma* stripped of its earthly body and separated from Christ; (d) this fate, however, will not befall the believer; (e) the subject of old and new life is the *pneuma,* which appears before the tribunal of Christ immediately after death. We accordingly have here a sharp change from the parousia-oriented thought of 1 Cor 15. Resurrection, as Teichmann observes, has not become "entirely unnecessary."[21] Still, he finds it "interesting" that, despite this stunning development, Paul hangs on to the traditional term (2 Cor 1:9; 4:14; Phil 3:11).[22]

The basic idea in Teichmann's account was derivative from Pfleiderer: the "Spirit" of God bestowed in baptism was the seed of personal survival. At one time the Apostle's eschatological thought had been well represented in the image of the glorious return of Christ to earth; but, without ever abandoning this now empty image, Paul arrived finally at an eschatology better represented as the believer's ascent into the heavenly world. True, Paul never managed to shake off the hope of being united to Christ without having to die. But that merely betokened the inescapability of biographical limits: Jewish-Greek syncretism was the Apostle's daily bread.[23]

The Pfleiderer-Teichmann line has had unlikely success in England. R. H. Charles, in his 1899 study of "future life" according to Israel, Judaism, and Christianity,[24] maintained that 1 Cor 15 argued incoherently (a) for corporeal continuity between the dead and the risen, and (b) for the postponement of the resurrection to the *parousia.* When writing 1 Cor 15, Paul "does not seem conscious" of the contradiction, but by the time he wrote 2 Cor 5 he had "become conscious of the inherent inconsistencies of his former view" and abandoned it in favor of the resurrection of the righteous following immediately on death.[25]

H. A. A. Kennedy in 1904[26] observed that Paul's eschatological conceptions, though by no means worked into a systematic account *de novissimis*, had

> a far greater mutual congruity than some recent investigators have been willing to recognize. But *in an age when the notion of development is regarded as the key to all problems*, it is perhaps natural that scholars should use it in explaining certain phenomena which look like antinomies in the Pauline Epistles. This view has been worked out to its furthest limit by Sabatier, Pfleiderer, Teichmann, and others.[27]

Kennedy resisted it. First, he offered an account of 1 Cor 15 that was remarkable for the treatment given to vss. 50-55. Here he formulated the question to which the text was an answer, as follows: now that his readers could form some conception of the experience of their deceased friends, what of themselves? How were the survivors, the living, to pass into the final kingdom of God?[28] The answer was, "we shall all be transformed" (51b). That is, "the dead shall rise incorruptible, and we [the living] shall be transformed" (52bc). Second, he turned to 2 Cor 4-5. In the first verses of chapter 5 Kennedy interpreted the issue as that of survival to the *parousia* (*stenazomen* in vss. 2 and 4 had a striking parallel in Rom 8:23). But his recoil from the opinion that between 1 Cor and 2 Cor Paul had changed his mind about resurrection did not allow him to acknowledge that Paul might have meant what he said about dying and being "at home with the Lord" (vss. 6-9). Kennedy concluded at most to a negative result: for Paul death could not bring the believer into separation from his Lord.[29] Paul's yearning (vss. 2-8) was, as before, "for the immortality of the *sōma pneumatikon*" at the parousia.[30] Kennedy accordingly referred the two states contrasted in 2 Cor 5:6-9—"being at home in the body and absent from the Lord" 'being absent from the body and at home with the Lord"—to life in the natural or fleshly body and life at the *parousia* in the spiritual body.

Now, there is no argument over the sense of the first limb in this contrast: but, whereas there appears to be no visible support for Kennedy's reading of the second limb ("being absent from the body and at home with the Lord" = parousia), the parallel of Phil 1:23 positively militates against it. Respecting the latter text, Kennedy cited Paul Wernle's interpretation without making it any more cogent: "[Paul's] yearning overleaps all between death and resurrection, and hurries to its goal for reunion with Jesus."[31]

Albert Schweitzer's survey, *Paul and His Interpreters* (1911, ET 1912) traced the views of Paul especially from F. C. Baur to Schweitzer's own time. On the issue of development he noted that Auguste Sabatier had been the first to differentiate phases in Paul's development;[32] that Pfleiderer, inspired perhaps by Lüdemann's study of Paul's use of *sarx*, had fixed on Pauline eschatology as the privileged sphere of development;[33] that what Teichmann added to Pfleiderer was merely an overconfident extremism.

> Not one of [Teichmann's] "results" can be proved from the Apostle's letters. . . . He asserts, for instance, that in Thessalonians those who arise from the dead enter the kingdom of God in their earthly bodies. But from the Jewish Apocalyptic and from the teaching of Jesus it clearly appears that the resurrection included within itself a transformation of this creaturely corporeity into a glorified corporeity.[34]

Several factors have combined to keep Schweitzer's straightforward, devastating critique from delivering the *coup de grâce* to the Pfleiderer-Teichmann line. First, Schweitzer was unable to match his critique with a plausible positive retrieval of Pauline eschatology.[35] Second, the modern hankering to convert variations into "developments" meshed with the modern recoil from apocalyptic eschatology. As scholars yielded to both impulses, Paul became ever more dynamic and rational.

In C. H. Dodd's account of "the mind of Paul" the dynamism and rationality were attested by a many-sided evolution of attitudes.[36] The mature Paul—the Paul that matured between First and Second Corinthians—"has become reconciled to experience."[37] He has found a new value in human institutions, particularly the state and its magistrates, and, correlatively, a new distance from apocalypticism and its parousias. In Dodd's view, apocalypticism was "a form of compensation in fantasy for the sense of futility and defeat,"[38] its hallmark "a radical devaluation of the present world-order in all its aspects."[39] The newly mature Paul has broken with this. Whereas he had earlier thought of the saved as a tiny remnant,[40] he now foresaw the winning over of "all Israel" and, indeed, the redemption of the whole human race[41] and the whole material creation.[42] What brought about the "decisive change"[43] by which Paul suddenly "outgrew" his "harsh dualism"?[44] Apart from naming it a "second conversion," in which "the traces of fanaticism and intolerance disappear,"[45] Dodd did not say. This left room for others to come up with an answer.

To Wilfred L. Knox the answer lay not in a second conversion but in Paul's missionary strategy of accommodation to Hellenistic culture.[46] Knox observed that "the conception of a new age which had already begun and was shortly to be completed by the appearance of the Lord was fairly prominent in Christian preaching."[47] Paul kept to this in 1 Cor 15, but he did so in a spirit of accommodation to the Hellenistic readership. For example, the resurrection of the dead was no longer to a material but to a spiritual body.[48] This, however, was not enough to meet the difficulties of the Corinthians, rooted in their acceptance of popular Hellenistic philosophy. So, in 2 Cor 5 Paul took missionary accommodation to Greek categories further, to the "complete revision" of his eschatology.[49] He made the body the garment that the soul "was anxious to cast aside, the burden from which it longed to be delivered."[50] Present possession of the Spirit (2 Cor 5:5) could be equated with "the divine afflatus of Hellenistic belief."[51] Paul adopted the conception that the soul did not simply lay aside the body, but put on a new and glorious one. In imagery drawn from Babylon but at home in the mysteries and indeed everywhere in Hellenistic syncretism, Paul converted eschatology into "an accepted Hellenistic view of the life to come" (2 Cor 5:1-5).[52] Though he had substituted the immortality of the soul for the resurrection of the body and the gradual spiritualization of the soul for the great assize at the end of time, he strangely failed to abandon all talk of judgment (2 Cor 5:10), despite its having "ceased to possess any real significance. . . ."[53]

W. D. Davies has offered a detailed analysis of Knox's treatment of 2 Cor 5, but, though he accepted the view urged since Pfleiderer that Pauline eschatology underwent notable development between I Cor 15 and 2 Cor 5, he refused to accept Knox's answer to the question of what the change consisted in and what brought it about.[54]

Davies focused on three factors. First, the change consisted in rescheduling the acquisition of a heavenly body from the parousia to the death of the individual believer. Second, the occasion of this doctrinal development was partly psychological ("he himself had been at the gates of death"[55]) and partly pastoral ("the problem of Christians who died was becoming a pressing one"[56]). Third, the condition of the possibility of the change lay in the early Christian and Pauline consciousness of realized eschatology: the "conception of the Age to Come as having already dawned."[57] In 1 Cor 15 Paul's mind had been "centered on the *olam haba'* as the End of all history." In 2 Cor 5:1-2, however, "it is not resurrection as characteristic of 'the End' that concerns him;" his mind turns, rather, to what lies immediately beyond death.[58] In short, 1 Cor 15 corresponded to the Judaic notion of the age to come as reserved for the eschatological resurrection of the dead following the messianic age; 2 Cor 5 corresponded to the Judaic notion of the age to come as eternally existent: "it always IS in the heavens and we awake to it at death."[59]

In 1955 Joachim Jeremias espoused and developed an undeveloped indication in Adolf Schlatter's exegesis of 1 Cor 15:50.[60] Neither the living (*sarx kai haima*) nor the dead (*hē phthora*) could inherit the reign of God (that is, the existence proper to salvation in the age to come) as they were; rather, the condition of entry into the age to come, whether for the living or for the dead, was a divinely wrought transformation to take place at the parousia: "we shall not all sleep, but we shall all be changed."[61]

Jeremias not only championed this exegesis against the interpretation that took 1 Cor 15:50 to signify the flat incompatibility of the earthly or bodily with final salvation; he also explicitly related his reading of the text to Teichmann's reconstruction of Paul's thought on the resurrection of the dead. If in this reconstruction 1 Cor 15:50-55. was the link in an alleged transition from Jewish apocalyptic notions to Greek sapiential notions, Jeremias could argue that with the loss of this link the whole construct collapsed.

Jeremias's interpretation has been not only influential but decisive in its main point. Joachim Gnilka reported some years ago that the Teichmann reconstruction, setting immortality in opposition to resurrection, "is nowadays rightly without supporters."[62] Nevertheless, Gerd Lüdemann has recently reasserted the views of Teichmann at three points. First, at the time Paul founded the Christian community of Thessalonica, he conceived of salvation at the parousia without reference to the resurrection of dead Christians. Second, when Paul did integrate the resurrection of the dead with the salvation of the living at the *parousia* (1 Thess 4), he conceived of resurrection as a mere revivification of corpses. Third, Pauline dualism (spirit versus flesh) grounded Paul's view that the sphere of "flesh and blood" will be "destroyed" at the *parousia*.[63] From this it would seem that for some few, at least, the question of Paul's view of the resurrection of the dead is back to square one, i.e., to where it was roughly a hundred years ago.

Meantime, the opening lines of 2 Cor 5:1-10 continue to be a *crux interpretum*. Whereas Jacques Dupont found clues to the hope of the *parousia* in these first lines, Paul Hoffmann offered a detailed counterpart to Rudolf Bultmann's exegesis; that is, he deciphered the text as mirror writing, on the supposition that it reflected, by opposition, the eschatology of gnostic opponents.[64] Friedrich Lang has surveyed the variety of recent scholarship on 2 Cor 5:1 - 10.[65]

If Gnilka's assurance that the Teichmann line "is nowadays. . . without supporters" is no longer quite exact, still that particular line is a dead letter for the vast majority today. The influence of kerygma theology, however, is not quite so *passé* . Though it is notoriously difficult to say what will finally prove to have been going forward in our own time, it is nonetheless tempting to hazard a comment on the rich harvest of works dealing with 1 Cor 15 since 1970, namely, that special importance attaches to the analysis of parallels to 1 Cor 15 in ancient Jewish texts on the resurrection of the dead. The quest of such parallel material was of distinctly secondary interest to Barth, Bultmann, Scniewind, and their generation. Yet no small part of the scholarly literature designed to consolidate or resolve issues framed by these thinkers and exegetes has now been rendered all but obsolete by just such analytic work. An example of the latter is the series of articles, reflecting a Strasbourg dissertation, that Rodolphe Morissette published in 1972.[66]

Current opinion on the relevant texts resists consensus. Still, it seems to me possible that a contribution to greater order might well lie in locating and addressing the strategic exegetical issues that generate diverse opinion on "development" in Paul's eschatology.

II. EXEGESIS

For present purposes there is no need to offer (indeed, within the limits of a single essay there would be no excuse for offering) a fully detailed exegesis of the Pauline texts. I shall allow the main forms of the hypothesis of development to define the crucial points and shall limit my interpretative efforts to them. The hypothesis may be set out in three main propositions.

1) In 1 Thess 4 Paul affirmed salvation, at the *parousia,* of not only the living but the dead. Here he conceived of salvation in primitive Judaic terms: the dead return to the conditions of this life; then the living "will be swept up together with them on clouds into the air to meet the Lord" (Pfleiderer, Teichmann, Jeremias, G. Lüdemann. et al.). Crucial question: Does Paul understand the dead to return by resurrection to the conditions of the present life?

2) In 1 Cor 15 Paul affirmed salvation at the *parousia* of both the living and the dead, but by now he had arrived at the insight that

> Flesh and blood cannot inherit the kingdom of God, nor does corruption inherit incorruption (v. 50)

This means that Paul's affirmation of "resurrection"—which supposed some continuity between, on the one hand, "flesh and blood/the perishable" and, on the other, "the kingdom of God/imperishability"—was incoherent with his deepest soteriological thought (Pfleiderer, Teichmann, Charles, Dodd, W. L. Knox, et al.). Crucial questions: (a) Does 1 Cor 15:50 rule out corporeal participation in final salvation? (b) What does the *mystērion* (secret) of 1 Cor 15:51 refer to?

3) In 2 Cor 5:2-4 Paul reduced this incoherence by affirming that a foreordained heavenly body would be bestowed on the believer immediately upon death. This was an adoption of Greek categories (Pfleiderer, Teichmann, Knox, et al.) or a deployment of Judaic categories (W. D. Davies). Finally, in Phil 1:21-23 he supported this revision, establishing a certain primacy of the Greek theme of immortality (Pfleiderer, Teichmann, Knox, et al.). Crucial questions: (a) Does 2 Cor 5:2-4 refer to the *parousia* or to the acquisition of a resurrection body immediately upon death? (b) Is 2 Cor 5:6-9 concerned with the *parousia,* or with an intermediate state after death? (c) What light, if any, does Phil 1:23 throw on the matter?

Jeremias's 1955 essay all but put an end to the idea that "flesh and blood" (interpreted as the corporeal principle itself) had no part in final salvation. After 1955 that particular reading of the text of 1 Cor 15:50 was largely abandoned, few today being ready to follow Teichmann in suppressing the *prima-facie* sense of "change" ("we shall all be changed") in favor of making it mean annihilation and new creation.[67] With the loss of 1 Cor 15:50, the full-blown hypothesis of "development"—a complete trajectory with visible point of departure (1 Thess 4), apogee (1 Cor 15), and arrival at a new eschatology (2 Cor 5)—did indeed collapse.

Still, lesser developments could be maintained. Jeremias himself maintained a forward move from 1 Thess 4 to the mature Paul of the later correspondence. In 1Thess 4, according to Jeremias, something was missing: the idea of transformation. In this one particular he agreed with Teichmann and, in common with Teichmann, argued from. . . silence.[68]

But the notion that transformation from earthly to heavenly corporeity was in no way supposed by the resurrection theme in 1 Thess 4 is burdened with improbable consequences. First, this would not accord with the evidence of late Old Testament texts and Jewish noncanonical literature. Dan 12:2-3. is a keynote passage actualizing the destiny of the Servant in Isa 52-53 as the resurrection of the righteous (vs. 3) and assimilating the resurrected righteous to the angels (cf. the equation of "stars" and angels in Dan 8:10). See also Isa 26:19; *IQH* 11:10-14; *Pss. Sol.* 3:16; 2 *Bar*. 49-51, 61-63. Transformation belonged to resurrection even when, as in 2 *Bar*. 50:1-3, transparent apologetic considerations motivated a brief temporal dissociation of the two. Second, this view would not cohere with the indissoluble connection between transformation and resurrection in the tradition of Jesus' words (Mark 12:24-25.; parr. Matt 22:29-30; Luke 20:34-36) as well as in the Resurrection narratives (e.g., Luke 24:31, 36-53; John 20:19-23; Mark 16:12). Third, it is difficult to believe that Paul or any other early Christian could conceive of the resurrection of the dead in total abstraction from the resurrection of Jesus, which in the light of all available evidence was itself invariably conceived in terms of utter uniqueness respecting the past and prototypal status respecting the future (cf. pre-Pauline formulas correlating Jesus' resurrection with the exaltation of the Isaian Servant, such as 1 Cor 15:3-5; Rom 4:25; 8:34; Pauline and para-Pauline formulations such as 1 Cor 15:20, 45; Rom 8:29-30; Acts 26:23). All the material on Jesus' resurrection, early and late, quite unambiguously supposed a transformed corporeity from which, for example, the prospect of death was definitively banished. In short, nothing positively favors the view that in 1 Thess 4 resurrection signified merely the reconstitution of the earthly body, whereas several considerations tell decisively against it.

We return, then, to 1 Cor 15, the keystone in the hypothesis of development. The first part of the text is organized as follows: vv. 1-11; kerygmatic foundation; vv. 12-34 respond to the assertion *anastasis nekrōn ouk estin* (there is no raising of dead people). The question of how the rest of the text is organized has been diversely answered. Johannes Weiss proposed that vss. 35-57 were ranged under the rubric of the question *pōs* (how?).[69] Jeremias modified this by attributing a chiastic design to the text.[70] He first differentiated two questions in v. 35. *Pōs egeirontai hoi nekroi*? (How are the dead raised?) inquired after the event of resurrection; *poiǭ de sōmati erchontai*? (with what kind of body do they come [from the tomb]?) inquired after the new corporeity of the risen. In Jeremias's reading, the questions were answered in inverse order. Vss. 36-49 offered an answer to "with what kind of body?" and vss. 50-57 answered the "how?"

This beguiling view might well impose itself, if in vss. 50-57 we were to find some verifying particular, however, slight, showing that the text had been consciously conceived in relation to the *pōs?* (how?) of vs. 35. But no such verifying particular occurs in the text. Moreover, the *pōs* of v. 35 is explicitly concerned with "the dead," whereas the passage opening in vs. 50 is concerned with the living and the dead; indeed, it highlights the living ("we shall not all fall asleep, but we shall all be changed"). Again, the phrase in vs. 50, *touto de phēmi, adelphoi* (this I tell you, brothers), seems to open a new, if related, topic (cf. 1 Cor 7:29). It would seem likely, then, that in vs. 35 the words *poiǭ de sōmati*? (with what kind of body?) do not pose a question distinct from *pos*, but simply specify the intended thrust of *pōs*. (This, in fact, is how the great majority of interpreters take it.) With vs. 49, Paul's answer to *pōs* and to *poiǭ de sōmati* is concluded. But this generates a new question: How are vss. 50-57 related to what precedes them?

In quest of an answer, we might ask what the *mystērion* (secret) of vs. 51 refers to. The text furnishes an immediate answer: we shall not all fall asleep, but we shall all be changed. Fair enough; but what is it in these words that up to this point is still secret, i.e., that has not hitherto been dealt with by Paul? I shall proceed by a process of elimination.

First, it was hardly a secret among Paul's Christian contemporaries (for it was no secret in the eschatological instructions whether of Paul or of other early Christian teachers[71]) that not all would die. Though some had already died and others, including Paul himself, might still die, nevertheless the Christian faithful (and Paul hoped to be among them) would live to see the *parousia*. The secret, accordingly, was not future preservation of Christians from death, nor was it a differentiation of two classes at the *parousia*, the living and the dead.[72]

Was the secret, then, the fact of the transformation of those risen from the dead? Hardly. Earlier, Paul had already said:

> The sowing takes place in decay, the raising in immunity to decay;
> the sowing in humiliation, the raising in glory;
> the sowing in weakness, the raising in power;
> a natural body is sown, a spiritual body is raised.
>
> 1 Cor 15:42b-44a

Was the secret, then, that (unlike 2 *Bar*. 50:1-3) the transformation of the newly risen would take place simultaneously with their resurrection namely, at the parousia? Not likely. For Paul resurrection was always transformative resurrection (vss. 42-49), and it had already been ascribed to that moment, in vs. 23 (*en tę̄ parousia autou*, at his coming).

The secret, then, must be this: *although those still living at the parousia would not die, they too—like those raised from the dead—would at that same moment be transformed.*

The sense of the passage as a whole is clarified in the light of this interpretative option. The living would indeed not pass through death, but, like the dead and at the same moment as the dead, they would be "changed." Christ's victory over the last enemy, death, would be effected by the transformation of all. Neither flesh and blood nor corruption could enter into life without being changed.

Here we should emphasize that Archibald Robertson and Alfred Plummer,[73] Adolf Schlatter,[74] and Joachim Jeremias[75] were completely right in observing that corruption in the second line of the distich of vs. 50 is not synonymous with flesh and blood; for, contrary to the RSV and the NEB, *hē phthora* does not mean "the perishable";[76] it means "corruption" (NAB) or "decay" (Goodspeed). In context this must be an *abstractum pro concreto* referring to "the dead." The distich, then, states a predicament: neither the living nor the dead can enter the reign of God as they are. But with the triumphant announcement "we shall all be changed," the "secret" following the distich addresses and disposes of this predicament. The living as well as the dead will be transformed. Verses 53-54 accordingly celebrate the entry into the reign of God respectively of the dead (*to phtharton*, this being of decay) and the living (*to thnēton*, this mortal being).

The whole passage (1 Cor 15:50-57) was occasioned (as H. A. A. Kennedy had said as long ago as 1904[77]) by an implicit response and final question of the addressee: "We can now form some conception of the resurrection of our dead friends, but what of ourselves? How are those to enter into life who will live to see the parousia?" Just as Paul had insisted (in 1 Cor 15:35-49) that the dead would not return from the grave in earthly bodies, so he now taught (1 Cor 15:50-57) that those living at the parousia would not remain in their earthly bodies either. "We shall all be changed." Thus the duality of the living and the dead at the *parousia* commands the triumphant conclusion of 1 Cor 15, just as it had commanded the text of 1 Thess 4. Indeed, this duality is also a key to 2 Cor 5.

Of this passage W. D. Davies has asserted that "there is nothing in the text to suggest Paul's hope of surviving to the *parousia*."[78] Nevertheless, there are in the text two classes of specific indices to just that hope.

The first is a class of linguistic indices which connect 2 Cor 5:2-5 with two passages on final salvation at the parousia, namely, Rom 8:18-27 and 1 Cor 15:50-55. (a) The *stenazein* ("sighing" or "groaning") motif of 2 Cor 5:2-4 is paralleled by the sighing or groaning of Rom 8:22-23, which bears on "the redemption of our bodies" at the *parousia*; (b) the *pneuma-arrabōn* (Spirit-pledge) motif of 2 Cor 5:5 is paralleled by the *pneuma-arrabōn* passage of Rom 8:23 (cf. Rom 8:26-27). In the passage in Romans the presence of the Spirit as foretaste or first installment looks ahead to the final bodily redemption and the consummation of sonship at the *parousia*; 2 Cor 5:5 is structurally similar. (c) The combined motifs of *thnēton, endysasthai, and katapothēnai* in 2 Cor 5:4 are paralleled by the parousia passage of 1 Cor 15:53-54:

> this being of decay [the dead] must put on (*endysasthai*) immunity to decay and this mortal being (*thnēton*: the living) must put on (*endysasthai*) immortality and when this being of decay puts on immunity to decay and this mortal being puts on immortality, then the word of Scripture will come true: "Death has been swallowed up (*katepothē*) in victory. . . ."

Is there indeed nothing in the text to suggest Paul's hope of surviving to the *parousia*? In 2 Cor 5:4abc Paul expresses recoil from being stripped (of his earthly body) and desire of being able to "put on (his heavenly body) over" (*ependysasthai*) his earthly body. This "putting on over" evokes the secret of 1 Cor 15:51, we shall not all die but we shall all—the living as well as the dead—be changed at the *parousia*. The transformation of the living, that is, will not involve disembodiment. In 2 Cor 5:4d, moreover, Paul follows this with phrases inescapably reminiscent of 1 Cor 15:53-54, "so that this mortal being [*to thnēton*: the expression is applied, in 1 Cor 15:53-54, to the class of those still living at the parousia] may be swallowed up (*katepothē*) by life."

The second class of indices to hope of survival to the *parousia* in 2 Cor 5:2-5 is not linguistic so much as conceptual. The key ideas are antithetical: being "clothed" (=embodied) versus being "naked" (disembodied), these two states corresponding respectively to the living and to the dead; at the *parousia* those still living will "put on" a heavenly embodiment "over" their earthly embodiment. This was substantially established by J. N. Sevenster in a 1953 essay which, though sometimes unidiomatic and infelicitous, was a remarkable exegetical achievement.[79] Sevenster not only established the probable sense of *gymnos* (naked=disembodied); he went further, to trace the way in which the text, supposing three states (this life, the disembodied state of the dead, and the consummation-event of resurrection/transformation at the *parousia*), gave expression to two comparisons. In 2 Cor 5:1-4 the prospect of the third state is far more desirable than the prospect of the second; in 2 Cor 5:6-9 the second state, insofar as it means "being with the Lord," is simply superior to the first. The second state, when set against the third, is far from desirable (vv. 2-4); but, when compared with the first, it is objectively and subjectively preferable (vv. 6-9).

I would add two observations to those of Sevenster. First, the object of the *stenazein* (and *baroumenos*) motif is twofold; recoil from nakedness and longing for the *parousia;* but the second of these objects must not be overlooked, for it may be the more fundamental of the two (cf. Rom 8:22-23). Second, the three states are successive, but not in fixed universal fashion, for those living at the *parousia* will miss the second. From Paul's personal standpoint the best possibility of all would accordingly be immediate parousia (2 Cor 5:1-4), bringing the state that outstrips all others.

On the face of it, the text of Phil 1:23 simply confirms that Paul entertained the conception of an intermediate state between the present life and the parousia, entered into by death and aptly characterized as being "with the Lord." Those who deny that Paul harbored any such conception generally find themselves constrained to discover the parousia motif here. But in this text, at least, there really is not so much as a hint that the parousia is intended.[80]

Let me summarize our results by repeating and responding to the "crucial questions." Apropos of 1 Thess 4, did Paul understand resurrection as the return of the dead to the conditions of the present life? No; nothing in the text or context supports this reading, whereas numerous considerations tell against and exclude it.

Apropos of 1 Cor 15:50-57, does vs. 50 rule out the notion of corporeal participation in final salvation? No, the issue is not "body versus spirit" but "body in the present age—be it the flesh and blood of the living or the decayed body of the dead—versus body transfigured and immortal in the reign of God." Second, what does the *mystērion* (secret) of vss. 51-52 refer to? It refers to the destiny of the living at the *parousia*. They, too, like those risen from the dead, will be transformed at the *parousia*.

Apropos of 2 Cor 5, do vv. 2-4 refer to the parousia or to the acquisition of a resurrection-body immediately upon death? Linguistic and conceptual indices point to the parousia. Are w. 6-9 concemed with the parousia or with an intermediate state after death? They bear on an intermediate state, just as Phil 1:23 does.

Final result: there is a total lack of persuasive evidence that Paul's teaching on the resurrection of the dead underwent significant development either between 1 Thess 4 and 1 Cor 15, or between 1 Cor 15 and 2 Cor 5. Allusion to "the intermediate state" occurs at least in 2 Cor 5 and Phil 1, apparently without entailing any change in Paul's conception of the resurrection of the dead and transformation of the living at the *parousia.*

III. HERMENEUTICS

> Anyone who treats the charged expressions encountered in cultural history exclusively from the 'historical standpoint' is in that very measure incapable of genuine interpretation.
>
> Josef Pieper[81]

I have offered above a swift survey of the generations-long debate between maximalists and minimalists on whether Paul's view of the resurrection of the dead underwent significant development. I have concluded that the case of the minimalists is much stronger than that of their adversaries from Pfleiderer to the present day. But what is the significance of the debate itself and of the admittedly swiftly-sketched resolution thereof that I have just presented?

The debate has hermeneutical significance, and can perhaps be made to yield a hermeneutical lesson.

Hermeneutics bears on the understanding of texts. A basic feature of such understanding is the triangular structure of reader, text, and referent.[82] The reader understands the text by understanding what it is about, and he understands what the text is about by understanding the text. If in form this circle is vicious, in fact it is broken upon by acts of insight which, alternating between text and referent, spiral toward an ever clearer and firmer understanding of both.

Hans-Georg Gadamer recalled Luther's statement of the issue: "whoever does not understand the things cannot draw the sense from the words: (*qui non intelligit res non potest ex verbis sensum elicere*).[83] There are more positive formulations of essentially the same principle: (a) "preunderstanding" of the text is given in independent access to its referent (*die Sache:* not "the subject matter," but the referent in its integral relevant reality), and (b) an appreciative understanding of the text supposes a "life-relationship" to the referent and hence to the text.[84] It follows that there is nothing so futile as positivistic objectivism, with its "principle of the empty head,"[85] according to which the less the interpreter has in his head, the more likely he is to avoid "reading into the text" his own opinions and prejudices. To understand a lecture on color, it is no advantage to be free of prejudices by having been born blind. On the contrary, the blind man finds discussion of color obscure precisely because he lacks independent access to the referent, i.e., to color.

It may be worth our while, then, to pause over the referent or *die Sache*. And in the present instance this is—what? The resurrection of the dead, an event conceived as belonging to a climactic future, when the risen and glorified Christ will destroy the last enemy, death.

What can be our access to an as yet nonexistent event? It is not empirical in the sense that our access to the everyday events of our lives is. Nor is it well exemplified by access to history, though history, too, intends events nonexistent in our own present. The access to history is through a reconstructive activity of intelligence working on data variously mediated to us, but we cannot construct the future as we reconstruct the past. The past, however, is not irrelevant here, for in the texts on the resurrection of the dead the past event of the resurrection of Jesus grounds the eschatological future:

> Now the truth is that God has raised Christ from
> the dead,
> the first-fruits of those who have fallen asleep;
>
> for, just as through a man there came death,
> so the more surely through a man there shall come
> the resurrection of the dead;
>
> . . . just as we have borne the image of the man of dust,
> so the more surely shall we bear the image of the
> heavenly man as well (1 Cor 15:20-21, 49)

What is the carrier of meaning here, if not the correlatives, promise and hope? In the light of the election-historical mission of Jesus, the promise is fused with his victory over death; he is accordingly the ground of hope. So the texts are expressions of hope, suffused with hope, an intelligent hope that insists on coherent claims to truth (1 Cor 15:12-34).

Now, that ancients observed that interpretation belongs to the arts that do not impart wisdom, for the object of interpretation is not what is true but only what is said.[86] Formally, no doubt, this is true, but it is an ambiguous truth and can turn into a trap. For if the interpreter who wrestles with the truth of the text may easily find himself wringing from it just what he himself takes to be true, the interpreter who stands aside from the struggle over truth may just as easily, and perhaps more fatefully, trivialize the text, missing the drama of its depths.

This is the point of the above epigraph taken from Josef Pieper. The deadliest evasion of all, Pieper seems to be saying, is the assumption of a closed, impermeable "observer viewpoint," from which one may spend one's whole interpretative effort busily tracing "influences" and "derivations," "developments" in the writer and his record of subsequent impact (*Wirkungsgeschichte*).[87]

Here, it seems to me, lies the hermeneutical lesson of the last hundred years of disconcertingly shallow interpretation of Paul on the resurrection of the dead. In dealing with the Pauline texts, Teichmann, Dodd, and Knox (for example) practiced trajectory criticism. Each posited a distinctive sort of trajectory, but behind all three hypotheses lay a common repugnance toward apocalypticism as intrinsically perverse and illusory. None of the three pushed through this self-imposed barrier to *die Sache*. The upshot in each case was casual dismissal of the scenario which Paul presented as the central message of Christian hope.

The error common to the line that started with Pfleiderer did not lie simply in the assumption of an "observer viewpoint" and of an exclusively historical conception of the interpreter's task, nor did it lie simply in a too facile appeal to the category of "development." The main seeds of error were sown in estrangement from particularities of the text and, above all, from the referent itself *(die Sache)*. This controlling estrangement—the chronic vice of one great wing of biblical scholarship since Spinoza—converted the observer viewpoint into an alienated viewpoint and the historical task into the construction of chimerical trajectories, from supernatural Judaic fantasies to a reasonable Hellenistic wisdom (Teichmann), from harsh and fanatic dualism to maturity of experience (Dodd), from fumbling efforts to fairly effective efforts of accommodation to the Gentile mind (Knox). As *die Sache* disappeared from view, "development" dominated interpretation. Moving in a diametrically opposite direction, let me conclude with some positive considerations bearing on recovery of *die Sache*.

Peter Stuhlmacher has made the point that, as a pre-Christian theme, the resurrection of the dead was far more firmly rooted in the life of postexilic and postbiblical Israel than has generally been acknowledged.[88] With the Christian gospel, however, a new and unique hope was born in the world. It lay at the heart of the Christian movement, indissolubly bound to the risen Jesus, a fundamental facet of the Christ-event.

"Every historical event," wrote Heinrich Schlier in one of his later essays, "presses toward its text and has its text. Otherwise, it is not an 'event' in the full sense of the word. The complete text of the event we are considering—the resurrection of Jesus—is the New

Testament."[89] If the text corresponding to the resurrection of Jesus is the New Testament, this text has peak passages, where hope founded on the risen Christ finds powerful and eloquent expression. Among them is chapter 15 of Paul's first Letter to the Corinthians. Though the past few generations have shown intense interest in the retrieval of Christian eschatology, this particular text has repeatedly proved to be among the most vexatious and opaque, for subjective reasons such as I have just evoked.[90] On the other hand, since the Second World War the West has witnessed the flowering of a rich if extremely diverse literature—psychological, phenomenological, philosophic, and theological—on human hope: its role in the establishment of personality, in effecting the transition from absorption with "having" to communion with "being," its reference to personal fulfillment, its irreducibility to the this-worldly, its finally transcendent reference.[91] This literature is a resource for finding access to *die Sache*, the referent of the great hope-passages of the New Testament, preeminently including those on the resurrection of the dead.

Among the striking ascertainments to emerge from contemporary explorations of hope is the linguistic distinction between "to hope to" or "to hope that" and "to hope" simply.[92] Paul, for example, tells the Corinthians: "I hope to spend some time with you, if the Lord permits" (1 Cor 16:7). Here is hope that belongs to the vast category of human hopes (*espoirs*); it is not hope simply and absolutely (*espérance*), as in the words "if we have hoped in Christ for this life only, we are the most pitiable people of all" (1 Cor 15:19).

In one of his penetrating treatments of hope, Pieper alluded to the phenomenological studies of Herbert Plügge, a clinical physician who observed among his patients that these two classes of hope—everyday hope and fundamental hope—stood in paradoxical relationship to one another. Fundamental hope—not directed toward anything that one could "have," but bent on "being" and "selfness," on "salvation of the person"—emerged at the very moment that everyday hopes collapsed. "Out of the loss of common, everyday hope true hope arises."[93]

In Pieper's view, the test case was the situation of the martyr, for whom the last wisp of human hope was gone. "We can hardly speak of hope, if none exists for the martyr."[94] Indeed, this is precisely the level at which Paul pitched his passionate expositions and expressions of hope. He dealt with fundamental hope, having to do with being, with salvation of the person. What Paul added to the mysterious human phenomenon of such hope was reference to the gospel, that is, to the news of God's act on behalf of every human being in the death and resurrection of Jesus, made Christ and Lord. This gave a unique grounding to "fundamental hope" and, by adding certain dimensions to it through reference to Jesus' own resurrection, it gave this hope the profound and permanent form that it has in the Pauline letters.

I asked above why recognition of *die Sache* (which we may now characterize, shorthand-fashion, as fundamental hope transvalued by the gospel) was so fitful and dim in the tradition that began with Otto Pfleiderer's gratuitous guesswork. I first answered that hardly anything undermines interpretation more grievously than strict limitation to the stance of the outside observer. In the instance that we have been considering, this invited a too facile recourse to the heuristic category "development." I added that a deeper, more potent factor had been alienation *vis-à-vis* aspects of the text and its referent. Finally, I should remark that the fundamental hope of 1 Thess 4, 1 Cor 15, and 2 Cor 5 is among those "things of God" that according to Paul no one understands except by the Spirit of God (1 Cor 2:11; cf. Mark 4:11; parr. Matt 13:11; Luke 8:10; Matt 16:17; 11:25-27; par Luke 10:21f.; John 6:44; 15:5, etc.). This is more than a home truth repeatedly verified by experience. It is sheer hermeneutical realism, founded on a requisite proportion between the knower and the known.[95]

NOTES

1. See O. Chadwick, *From Bossuet to Newman: The Idea of Doctrinal Development* (Cambridge: Cambridge University Press, 1957) x.

2. J. H. Newman, *An Essay on the Development of Christian Doctrine* (Garden City: Doubleday, 1960). The Essay first appeared in 1845; a revised edition appeared in 1878.

3. This is not to say that Baur was above all and nothing but a Hegelian, nor that the Hegelianism of Baur was pure Hegel. It is to say that the pattern of Hegelian evolutionism had an impact on studies of early Christianity and that this was more through Baur than through any other single 19th-century biblical scholar (e.g., D. F. Strauss, Bruno Bauer, et al.).

4. R. Kabisch, *Die Eschatologie des Paulus in ihren Zusammenhängen mit dem Gesamtbegriff des Paulinismus* (Göttingen: Vandenhoeck & Ruprecht, 1893); J. Weiss, *Jesus' Proclamation of the Kingdom of God* (Philadelphia: Fortress, 1971) [German original, 1892; revised and expanded version, 1900].

5. A. Schweitzer, *Paul and His Interpreters: A Critical History* (London: Black, 1912 [German original, 1911]) 58-63.

6. O. Pfleiderer, *Paulinism: A Contribution to the History of Primitive Christian Theology,* 2 vols. (London: Williams and Norgate, 1877 [German original, 1873]).

7. H. Lüdemann, *Die Anthropologie des Apostels Paulus und ihre Stellung innerhalb seiner Heilslehre* (Kiel: Universitatsbuchhandlung, 1872); Pfleiderer, *Paulinism* I. 8.

8. Ibid I. 18.

9. Ibid I. 19.

10. Ibid I. 20.

11. See F. Schnabel, *Deutsche Geschichte im neunzehnten Jahrhundert. 4: Die religiöse Kräfte* (Freiburg: Herder, 1936, [3]1955.

12. Pfleiderer, *Paulinism* I. 276.

13. Ibid. I. 259; see also 260-71.

14. O. Pfleiderer, *Das Urchristentum, seine Schriften und Lehren in geschichtlichem Zusammenhang* (Berlin: Reimer, 1887).

15. Schweitzer, *Paul and His Interpreters,* 71.

16. See n. 4 above. For a summary see Schweitzer, *Paul and His Interpreters,* 58-63.

17. *Auferstehung und Gericht und ihre Bezlehungen zur jüdischen Apokalyptik* (Freiburg-Leipzig: Mohr, 1896).

18. Ibid. 33-62.

19. Ibid. ("Die völlige Vernichtung") 53.

20. Ibid. 62.

21. Ibid. 65-67.

22. Ibid. 67.

23. Ibid. 74.

24. R. H. Charles, *A Crltical History of the Doctrine of a Future Life in Israel, in Judaism, and in Christianity* (London: Black, 1899).

25. Ibid. 394-95.

26. H. A. A. Kennedy, *St Paul's Conceptions of the Last Things* (London: Hodder and Stoughton, 1904).

27. Ibid. 24; my emphasis.
28. Ibid. 261.
29. Ibid. 269.
30. Ibid. 270.
31. Ibid. 272.
32. A. Sabatier, *L'Apôtre Paul, esquisse d'une histoire de sa pensée* (Paris: Fischbacher, 1870).
33. See Pfleiderer, *Paulinism* I. 259, 265-66; Schweitzer, *Paul and His Interpreters* 69-72.
34. Schweitzer, *Paul and His Interpreters* 76.
35. For his attribution to Paul of an elaborately detailed eschatology, see Albert Schweitzer, *The Mysticism of Paul the Apostle* (New York: Holt, 1931) esp. 65-68. The main lines of this solution appear as a heuristic scheme in *Paul and His Interpreters*, 240-45.
36. C. H. Dodd, 'The Mind of Paul: I" (1933) and 'The Mind of Paul: II" (1934) in C. H. Dodd, *New Testament Studies* (Manchester: Manchester University Press, 1953, repr. 1967) 67-82, 83-128.
37. C. H. Dodd, 'The Mind of Paul: II," 108.
38. Ibid. 126.
39. Ibid. 113.
40. Ibid. 121.
41. Ibid. 123-24
42. Ibid. 124.
43. Ibid. 125.
44. Ibid. 126.
45. C. H. Dodd, "The Mind of Paul: I," 81.
46. W. L. Knox, *St Paul and the Church of the Gentiles* (Cambridge: Cambridge University Press, 1939) 1-26. Hereafter, *Paul and Gentiles*.
47. *Paul and Gentiles*, 126. Knox's phrase "fairly prominent" understates the matter. The concrete form of realized eschatology in early Christianity was the kerygma of Christ's resurrection, to which the supposition of "imminent parousia" long remained firmly attached. C. H. Dodd, in chapters 2 and 3 of his *Parables of the Kingdom* (London: Nisbet, 1935), presented a brilliant piece of detective work in explanation of the origins of this scheme. A deftly corrected version of Dodd's hypothesis appeared in a review essay by Joachim Jeremias, "Eine neue Schau der Zukunftsaussagen Jesu," *Theologlsche Blatter* 20 (1941) 216-22. This recovery of Jesus' own eschatology and its transformation in early Christianity had been presaged by Wilhelm Weiffenbach, *Der Wiederkunftsgedanke Jesu nach den Synoptikern kritisch untersucht und dargestellt* (Leipzig: Breitkopf und Härtel, 1873). For a summary of the whole, see B. F. Meyer, *The Aims of Jesus* (London: SCM, 1979) 202-9.
48. *Paul and Gentiles* 127.
49. Ibid. 128.
50. Ibid. 137.
51. Ibid. 140.
52. Ibid. 136.
53. Ibid. 141.
54. W. D. Davies, *Paul and Rabbinic Judaism: Some Rabbinic Elements in Pauline Theology* (Philadelphia: Fortress, 1948, [4]1980) 311-20.
55. Ibid. 311.
56. Ibid.
57. Ibid. 314.
58. Ibid. 317.
59. Ibid. 316.
60. J. Jeremias, " 'Flesh and Blood Cannot Inherit the Kingdom of God' (I Cor. XV. 50)" in *Abba: Studien zur neutestamentlichen Theologie und Zeitgeschichte* (Göttingen: Vandenhoeck & Ruprecht, 1966) 298-307.
61. Ibid. 298-302.
62. J. Gnilka, "Contemporary Exegetical Understanding of the Resurrection of the Body" in *Immortality and Resurrection*, ed. P. Benoit and R. Murphy (New York: Herder and Herder, 1970)

129-41; see 131 on Teichmann's thesis that hope of immortality undermined belief in resurrection.

63. On the first agreement with Teichmann, see G. Lüdemann, *Paul Apostle to the Gentiles: Studies in Chronology* (Philadelphia: Fortress, 1984) 212; on all three agreements, see G. Lüdemann, "The Hope of the Early Paul: From the Foundation-Preaching at Thessalonika to I Cor 15:51-57," *Perspectives in Religious Studies* 7 (1980) 195-201; cf. 195-96 on the first point, 197 on the second, 200 on the third. To be sharply distinguished from Lüdemann's work is the proposal of Joseph Plevnik, "The Taking Up of the Faithful and the Resurrection of the Dead in I Thessalonians 4:13-18," *CBQ* 46 (1984) 274-83. Plevnik argues that the transformative moment is present in 1Thess 4, but located in the "taking up" of the still living and of the resurrected dead "to meet the Lord." If Plevnik is correct, it follows that there is a development between 1 Thess 4 and 1 Cor 15: transformation is located in the very resurrection of the dead and in the simultaneous and parallel change of the living. This seems to me possible, but somewhat less likely than the view that I propose: Paul always conceived resurrection as transformative, but in I Cor 15 he added the "secret" that the living, too, would be transformed.

64. J. Dupont, *SYN CHRISTOI: L'Union avec le Christ selon saint Paul* (Louvain: Nauwelaerts; Paris: Desclée, 1952) 135-53; Rudolf Bultmann, *The Second Letter to the Corinthians*, ed. E. Dinkler (Minneapolis: Augsburg, 1985); Paul Hoffmann, *Die Toten in Christus* (Münster: Aschendorff, 1966, 31978).

65. F. Lang, *2 Korinther 5, 1-10 in der neueren Forschung* (Tübingen: Mohr, 1973).

66. R. Morissette, "L' Expression SOMA en I Cor 15 et dans la littérature paulinienne, " *Revue des sciences philosophiques et théologiques* 56 (1972) 223-39; "La condition de ressuscité, I Corinthiens 15:35-49: Structure littéraire de la péricope," *Biblica* 53 (1972) 208-28; "L'Antithèse entre le 'psychique' et le 'pneumatique' en I Corinthiens, XV, 44 a 46," *Revue des sciences religieuses* 46 (1972) 97-143; "Un midrash sur la mort (I Cor., XV, 54c à 75)," *Revue biblique* 79 (1972) 161-88. Perhaps the most striking exploitation of ancient Jewish parallels is found in the article published in *Biblica*. One result is the improbability that Paul's opponents in Corinth argued for a resurrection as having already taken place.

67. Lüdemann, as we have noted (see n. 63 above), is among the exceptions.

68. Jeremias, "Flesh and Blood," 307. This *faux pas* was occasioned, it seems clear to me, by Jeremias's defective specification of the referent of "secret" in I Cor 15:51-52. Having drawn a sharp conceptual distinction between "resurrection" and "transformation," Jeremias referred the "secret" to the timing of the latter. But, as we shall see, there is no evidence that Paul himself ever diferentiated resurrection and the transformation that was part and parcel of resurrection. If in 1 Cor 15:35-49 he had already thematized resurrection precisely as transformative, Paul must have referred the "secret" of v. 51, not (as Jeremias maintained) to the idea that the change of the living and the dead is to take place immediately at the parousia (rather than after the judgment, as in *2 Bar* 51), but simply to the transformation of the living at the Parousia (as the counterpart of the transformative resurrection of the dead). Günther Bornkamm, "*mysterion, myeo*," *Theological Dictionary of the New Testament* 4, 802-28, at 823: the secret in question is "what Paul tells the Corinthians about the change which will overtake Christians still alive at the parousia." This I take to be exact.

69. J. Weiss, *Der erste Korintherbrief* (Göttingen: Vandenhoeck & Ruprecht, 1910) 345, 353, 380.

70. "Flesh and Blood" 304-05.

71. Regularly assumed in Matthew, Mark, and Luke is an apocalyptic thesis according to which the Son of man will come to gather his own before they are exterminated in the eschatological ordeal. Two examples out of many: "But when they persecute you in one town, flee to the next; for truly I say to you, you will not have gone through all the towns of Israel before the Son of man comes" (Matt 10:23); "there are some standing here who will not taste death before the Son of man comes" (Mark 9:1 parr. Matt 16:28; Luke 9:27).

72. It should be remembered that in writing to the Thessalonians Paul's point was not that those still living would not die (that was taken as settled), but that the dead would not fail to join them in salvation at the parousia.

73. A. Robertson and A. Plummer, *A Critical and Exegetical Commentary on the First Epistle of St. Paul to the Corinthians* (Edinburgh: Clark, 21914) 375-76.

74. A. Schlatter, *Paulus der Bote Jesu: Eine Deutung seiner Briefe an die Korinther* (Stuttgart: Calwer, 1934) 441-42.

75. "Flesh and Blood," 299-301.

76. In Paul the sense of *phthora* as decay/corruption is usually quite clear; where a sense approximating "perishability" is required, it is expressed by combining *phthora* with some other term; see, e.g., Rom 8:21, "bondage to decay" (*he douleia tes phhoras*).

77. *Last Things* 259.

78. *Paul and Rabbinic Judaism*, 311.

79. J. N. Sevenster, "Some Remarks on the GYMNOS in II Cor V 3" in *Studia Paulina in honorem Johannis de Zwaan septuagenarii*, ed. J. N. Sevenster and W. C. van Unnik (Haarlem: Bohn, 1953) 202-14.

80. See the treatment of Dupont, *SYN CHRISTOI*, 171-84.

81. J. Pieper, *Was heisst Interpretation?* Rheinisch-Westfälische Akademie der Wissenschaften, Vortrage G 234 (Opladen: West deutscher Verlag, 1979) 21.

82. See E. Coreth, *Grundfragen der Hermeneutik: Ein philosphischer Beitrag* (Freiburg: Herder, 1969) 64-65; 116-17; 123-27.

83. See Hans-Georg Gadamer, *Truth and Method* (New York: Seabury, 1975) 151.

84. In biblical scholarship the widespread use of the term "preunderstanding" is attributable to the influence of Rudolf Bultmann, "The Problem of Hermeneutics" in *Essays Philosophical and Theological* (London: SCM, 1958) 234-61, 239. On the sense of *die Sache*, cf. Coreth, *Grundfragen* (page references as above, n. 82); on "life-relation" see Bultmann, "The Problem of Hermeneutics," 241-43, 252-53, 255-56.

85. See the analysis of Bernard Lonergan, *Method in Theology* (London: Darton, Longmann & Todd, 1972) 157.

86. *Epinomis* 975c (Platonic dialogue of doubtful authenticity).

87. Pieper, *Was heisst Interpetation*? 21f. Pieper refers to C. S. Lewis's brilliant evocation of the theme in *The Screwtape Letters*. See *The Screwtape Letters* and *Screwtape Proposes a Toast* (London: Bles, [24]1966) 121: "The Historical Point of View, put briefly, means that when a learned man is presented with any statement in an ancient author, the one question he never asks is whether it is true."

88. P. Stuhlmacher, "Das Bekenntnis zur Auferstehung Jesu von den Toten und die biblische Theologie," *Zeitschrift für Theologie und Kirche* 70 (1973) 365-403; see 383-89.

89. H. Schlier, *Über die Auferstehung Jesu Christi* (Einsiedeln: Johannesverlag, 1968, [4]1975) 6.

90. For evidence of the acute discomfort that this chapter caused Rudolf Bultmann, see the citations in J. M. Robinson, "Hermeneutic since Barth" in *The New Hermeneutic*, ed. J. M. Robinson and J. B. Cobb Jr. (New York: Harper and Row, 1964) 1-77, esp. 31-33.

91. A few representative works in which these themes have come to expression: J. Pieper, *On Hope* (San Francisco: Ignatius, 1986); G. Marcel, *Homo Viator: Introduction to a Metaphysics of Hope* (Chicago: Regnery, 1951); E. Bloch, *Das Prinzip Hoffnung* (Frankfurt am Main: Suhrkamp, 1959, rev. 1970); H. Plügge, *Wohlbefinden und Missbefinden: Beiträge zu einer medizinischen Anthropologie* (Tübingen: Niemeyer, 1962); R. O. Johann, "The Meaning of Hope," *The Theologian* 8 (1952) 21-30; P. T. de Chardin, *The Future of Man* (London: Collins [Fontana], 1959); J. Moltmann, *Theology of Hope: On the Ground and the Implications of a Christian Eschatology* (London: SCM, 1967).

92. See, e.g., J. Pieper, *Hope and History* (New York: Herder and Herder, 1969) 21-25.

93. See the account in Pieper, *Hope and History* 24-26; the last citation is from 26.

94. Ibid. 32.

95. Proportion in this context signifies, first, a broad isomorphism of structures of knowing and structures of being: see B. Lonergan, *Insight: A Study of Human Understanding* (New York: Longmans, 1958) 115, 499-502; second, a narrower correlation of knowing and being, which evokes the related themes of horizons, conversions, connaturality: see Lonergan, *Method*, 235-93. As the break with cognitional myth (or, in other words, intellectual conversion) is requisite to an adequate account of cognition, so "moral knowledge is the proper possession only of morally good men" (*Method*, 240) and real grasp of "the things of God" supposes religious conversion. As Pieper put it in *Interpretation?* 29: "So wenig ein amusischer Mensch ein Gedicht zu verstehen und zu interpreti-

eren vermag, so wenig kann es einen unglaubigen Theologen geben–wofern man. . . unter Theologie den Versuch versteht, Offenbarung gültig zu interpretieren."

God's Health For The World:

Some Biblical Understandings of Salvation

PAUL L. HAMMER

"Are you saved?" This is a question that we have been asked in the past and that continues to be asked today. It is language that we associate in part with revival meetings and going forward "to be saved" from hell for heaven, i.e. from eternal separation from God for eternal life with God. Sometimes we connect this with what we call a "fire and brimstone" kind of preaching that places the emphasis on the individual person's eternal destiny and seeks to elicit an immediate response which can "save" that person. But is such an understanding fully faithful to biblical understandings?

There can be no question that salvation language is an integral part of the biblical vocabulary. What we want to do to gain a fuller understanding of its multiple meanings is to explore the richness of that language as used by a number of the biblical writers. Such historical study is not an end in itself but a means for letting the full range of biblical witnesses to *salvation* inspire and encourage us "for the living of these days."

It is not possible for us to look at every occurrence of salvation language in the Bible. Almost all of the Old and New Testament writings use such language at least once. However, some writings use it much more extensively than others. Among Old Testament writings, the Psalms and Isaiah stand out in their use of all three forms of "salvation" language (e.g. *salvation, save, savior*), though 1-2 Samuel, Jeremiah, and Ezekiel use the verb *save* with some frequency.

In the New Testament only five writers use all three forms of salvation language: the Apostle Paul and the writers of Ephesians, Luke-Acts, the Gospel of John, and the Pastoral Epistles (1-2 Timothy, Titus). Matthew and Mark do use the verb *save* several times, and Hebrews and 1 Peter use both *save* and *salvation* more than once, as does 2 Peter *savior* and the Revelation of John *salvation.*

To limit our investigation of the various biblical uses of salvation language, we shall pursue those writers who have used all three forms of it. This means the Psalms and Isaiah in the Old Testament, and Paul's Letters, Ephesians, Luke-Acts, the Gospel of John, and the Pastoral Epistles in the New. In terms of the five New Testament writers, they may span the last five decades of the first century or so. Thus, our study of them may yield a view of the dynamic theologizing process among some New Testament writers in their understanding of salvation language.

After an overview of the Psalms and Isaiah (documents to which New Testament writers had access), our primary concern will focus on the five New Testament writers. Of course, wherever any of our New Testament writers demonstrate a dependency on any Old Testament writings, we shall indicate this as part of the historical, literary, and theological context in which they stand. This will show that, just as we are concerned to interpret our scriptures for our time, New Testament writers were concerned to interpret their scriptures for their time.

We use two technical terms, exegesis and hermeneutics, in the study of scripture (terms used in their Greek form by some New Testament writers). Exegesis is the historical task of "leading out" the understanding of a text in its own context in the past. Hermeneutics is the contemporary task of "interpreting" the meaning of a text for our context in the present. What we shall do here involves some of both, just as it did for New Testament writers. In fact, one New Testament writer uses forms of both terms in one chapter, Luke 24: "he *diērmeneusen* ("interpreted") to them in all the scriptures the things concerning himself (vs. 27); "Then they *exēgounto* ("told" or "led out") what had happened on the road, and how he was known to them in the breaking of the bread" (vs. 35).

Another verse in that same chapter points to a major reason for "opening" the scriptures (as voiced by the two Emmaus Road disciples): "Did not our hearts burn within us while he talked to us on the road, while he opened to us the scriptures" (vs. 32). A cognitive understanding of scripture that does not lead to affective heartburn stops short of the full intention in doing biblical study. To use categories of brain research, biblical study needs to engage both hemispheres of the brain in order to engage us as a whole. As a colleague of mine has said, "It takes a cool head and a warm heart." We hope that our study of *salvation* will nourish both mind and heart as we, like Jesus on the Emmaus Road, interpret the scriptures.

I. THE PSALMS

To use a concordance to locate salvation language, and then to read the psalms in which such language occurs, is to be almost overwhelmed with how central "the God of our salvation" is to the song and prayer book of Israel. Salvation language occurs some ninety times in at least forty-eight of the psalms, and the multiple ways in which it is used is rich indeed.

Savior. This term is used only twice, but its use reflects very major emphases about salvation in many of the psalms. One is a cry of prayer:

> Wondrously show thy steadfast love,
> O *savior* of those who seek refuge from their adversaries
>   at thy right hand (Psa 17:7).

The other proclaims what God has done in the exodus and indicts the sin of idolatry:

> They exchanged the glory of God for the image of an ox that eats

grass.
They forgot God, their *Savior,* who had done great things in Egypt
(Psa 106: 20-21; note "save" also in vss. 8, 10).

But such a proclamation occurs in the context of prayer at both the beginning and end of the psalm, and near the end we find:

Save us, O Lord our God, and gather us from among the nations,
that we may give thanks to thy holy name and glory in thy praise
(Psa 106: 47).

Though we shall not here seek to explore the historical contexts out of which each of these two psalms may have come (that would enrich our study further), already on the basis of its use in two psalms we can see that salvation language involves: a) God as savior *from* personal adversaries (as manifesting God's steadfast love); b) God as savior *from* political/economic exploitation and slavery in international life *for* confessing idolatry and giving thanks and praise to God.

Save, Salvation. The Psalms use the verb "save" and the noun "salvation" each some forty times. Here we shall look at them together (grouping similar usages) and seek to discover further the rich employment of salvation language in the Psalms.

1. *The God of salvation.* The Psalms frequently use such phrases as "God of my salvation" (e.g. Pss 18:46; 25:5; 27:9; 38:22; 51:14) or "God of our salvation" (e.g. Pss 65:5; 68:19-20; 79:9; 85:4). The use of both "my" and "our" underscores both individual and corporate relationships to the God of salvation.

Further, other images often are linked to salvation language:

The Lord is my rock, and my fortress, and my deliverer,
my God, my rock, in whom I take refuge,
my shield, and the horn of my *salvation*, my stronghold
(Psa 18:2; note also 18:35; 27:1; 62:2; 89:26; 95:1; 118: 14) .

Another important linkage connects God's "steadfast love" to salvation language:

Let thy steadfast love come to me, O Lord,
thy salvation accordng to thy promlse
(Psa 109: 41; note also 6: 4; 57: 3; 85 :7; 109: 26).

What the above linkages show is that one cannot isolate salvation terms from other major terms needed to describe the God of salvation; and the above references include only immediate ones, i.e. in the same verse. If we were to include the entire psalm, the linkages would be expanded still further.

We turn now to the contexts in which the Psalms depict the saving God at work. Who are the subjects of God's saving action?

2. *God saves those threatened by external factors:*

a) *Those with enemies.* We noted this earlier under *Savior* in texts that speak of deliverance from adversaries and from political/economlc bondage. A cry for salvation from enemies, foes, evildoers, the ruthless, occurs frequently in the Psalms:

> Deliver me from my enemies, O my God,
> protect me from those who rise against me,
> deliver me from those who work evil,
> and *save* me from bloodthirsty men (Psa 59:1-2;
> see also e.g. Pss 6, 13, 18, 27, 31, 37, 54, 68, 74).

b) *The poor, needy, weak, oppressed.* This is another major emphasis in the Psalms:

> For he delivers the needy when he calls,
> the poor and him who has no helper.
> He has pity on the weak and the needy,
> and *saves* the life of the needy.
> From oppression and violence he redeems their life;
> and precious is their blood in his sight
> (Psa 72:12-14; note also e.g. Pss 34, 40, 70, 76, 86, 109, 132).

c) *Those threatened by death.*

> Turn, O Lord, *save* my life;
> deliver me for the sake of thy steadfast love.
> For in death there is no remembrance of thee;
> in Sheol who can give thee praise?
> (Psa 6:4-5; note also e.g. Pss 18, 68, 116).

3. *God saves those with an internal sense of sin/anguish.*

> Help us, O God of our *salvation*, for the glory of thy name;
> deliver us, and forgive our sins, for thy name's sake
> (Psa 79:9; note also e.g. Pss 38, 51, 69).

4. *God saves the upright and those who love God.*

> O continue thy steadfast love to those who know thee
> and thy *salvation* to the upright of heart
> (Psa 36:10; see also 7:10; 37:39).

> May all who seek thee rejoice and be glad in thee!
> May those who love thy *salvation* say evermore,
> "God is great!" (Psa 70:4; see also 40:10, 16).

5. *God's salvation can challenge military solutions.*

A king *is not saved* by his great army;
a warrior *is not saved* by his great strength
The war horse is a vain hope for victory,
and by its great might it *cannot save* (Psa 33: 16-17).

For not in my bow do I trust, nor can my sword *save* me,
But thou *hast saved* us from our foes,
and hast put to confusion those who hate us (Psa 44: 6-7).

6. *God's salvation is a universal hope.*

By dread deeds thou dost answer us with deliverance,
O God of our *salvation,*
who art the hope of all the ends of the earth
and of the farthest seas (Psa 65:5).

Sing to the Lord, bless his name;
tell of his *salvation* from day to day.
Declare his glory among the nations,
his marvelous works among all the peoples (Psa 96:2).

Summary of salvation understandings in the Psalms.

The above references in no way exhaust the ways salvation language is used in the Psalms, and there is no substitute for reading the entire psalm. However, the above references make it abundantly clear that the overwhelming use of such language has to do with God's saving deeds *in this world* in terms of both individual and corporate well being. It has to do with external realities, both personal and political/economic, that threaten human wholeness and health, as well as with internal struggle over personal sin that mars the relationship with God.

Salvation in the Psalms is not a matter of human achievement; it is God who, in the midst of the many experiences of human life, seeks to save, to make whole all relationships, within and among persons, among nations, and with nature. Such a saving God calls for response in joyous gratitude and in saved and saving living.

II. ISAIAH

The three forms of salvation language we are pursuing (e.g. *savior, save, salvation*) occur in all three parts of what scholars perceive to be the three major parts of Isaiah (Isa 1-39; 40-55; 59-66), *savior* occuring a total of eight times, *save* and *salvation* each some twenty times. Though we shall not seek here to develop the historical contexts, it is well to note that the first part comes primarily from the 8th century B.C.E., the second from a period related to the Babylonian exile in the 6th century, and the third from the post-exilic 5th and 4th centuries. Though the Psalms do include political elements in a wide-ranging use of salvation language, Isaiah is primarily, though not exclusively, political.

Here again we shall deal first with *savior* language and then with *save* and *salvation* together.

Savior. There is a quite astounding use of this term in Isaiah 19. This chapter is an oracle against Egypt about an altar built in Egypt.

> It will be a sign and witness to the Lord of hosts in the land of Egypt; when they cry to the Lord because of oppressors he will send them a savior, and will defend and deliver them . . . and the Lord will smite Egypt, smiting and healing, and they will return to the Lord, and he will heed their supplications and heal them . . . . In that day Israel will be the third with Egypt and Assyria, a blessing in the midst of the earth, whom the Lord of hosts has blessed, saying, "Blessed be Egypt my people, and Assyria the work of my hands, and Israel my heritage" (Isa 19:20-25).

Here Israel's *Savior* (from the time of the exodus) now is ensioned also as the *Savior of* Israel's ancient political enemies. Here is a vision with universal scope that moves beyond national chauvinism and any domestication of God. A vision for us too?

The term *savior* occurs five times in the Servant Songs of Second Isaiah (40-55). Given the experience of political exile, God is Israel's *savior* to bring them home.

> For I am the Lord your God, the Holy One of Israel, your *Savior* . . . . I, I am the Lord, and besides me there is no *savior* (Isa 43:3, 11; note also 45:15, 21; 49: 26).

God saves Israel *from* political exile, as well as from transgression and sin (43:25), but *for* being God's witness and chosen servant (43:10). Other Servant Songs spell out that witness and service in terms of bringing forth justice and being a light to the nations (e.g. 42:1, 3, 6). Israel's *Savior* is no parochial God but a God who wants justice for all nations, as well as the renewal of nature (note e.g. 43:19; 42:10).

We would note a final reference to *savior* in Third Isaiah (56-60). Though the Lord has to deal with a rebellious people, the memory of Moses and the Exodus elicit the following:

> Surely they are my people, sons who will not deal falsely;
> and he became their *Savior.*
> In all their affliction he was afflicted,
> and the angel of the Lord *saved* them;
> in his love and in his pity he redeemed them;
> he lifted them up; and carried them all the days of old
> (Isa 63: 8-9; note also 60:16).

God's salvation from political/economic Egyptian slavery in the exodus event throbs throughout much of the Old Testament as the basis for a continuing affirmation of God as *Savior* in subsequent historical periods, including those of the various "Isaiahs." The annual celebration of Passover witnesses to such a *Savior,* and spirituals sing, "Go down Moses . . . Let my people go." It is a witness still relevant to many peoples in our world today.

Save, Salvation. Though salvation language in Isaiah is predominantly political, there are other texts to note. Yet even some of the below have politlcal overtones or contexts.

1. *The God of personal salvation.*

Behold, God is my *salvation;*
I will trust, and will not be afraid;
for the Lord God is my strength and my song,
and has become my *salvation.*
With joy you will draw water from the wells of *salvation*
(Isa 12:2-3).

Oh, restore me to health and make me live . . . !
for thou hast cast all my sins behind thy back.
For Sheol cannot thank thee, death cannot praise thee . . .
The living, the living, he thanks thee, as I do this day. . . .
The Lord will *save* me,
and we will sing to stringed instruments
all the days of our life, at the house of the Lord (Isa 38:16-20).

2. *Salvation as swallowing up death.*

He will swallow up death for ever, and the Lord God will wipe away tears from all faces . . . . It will be said on that day, "Lo, this is our God; we have waited for him, that he might *save* us . . . , let us be glad and rejoice in his *salvation* (Isa 25:8-9).

3. *Salvation in returning and rest.*

For thus said the Lord God, the Holy One of Israel
"In returning and rest you shall be *saved;*
in quietness and confidence shall be your strength."
And you would not, but you said,
"No! We will speed upon horses" (Isa 30:15-16).

4. *Salvation as linked to justice and righteouosness.*

The Lord is exalted . . ,
he will fill Zion with justice and righteousness;
and he will be . . . the abundance of *salvation,*
wisdom, and knowledge (Isa 33 : 5-6; cf. 45:8).
Thus says the Lord:
Keep justice and do righteousness,
for soon my *salvation* will come,
and my deliverance be revealed (Isa 56:1; cf. 59:11).

5. *Idols cannot save.*

They have no knowledge who carry about their wooden idols,
and keep on praying to a god that *cannot save* . . . .
And there is no other god besides me,
a righteous God and a *Savior* (Isa 45:20-21; cf. 46:6).

6. *Salvation is for all nations and for ever.*

"I will give you as a light to the nations,
that my *salvation* may reach the end of the earth" (Isa 49:6).

How beautiful upon the mountains are the feet of him . . .
who publishes *salvation* . . . .
The Lord has bared his holy arm before the eyes
of all nations; and all the ends of the earth
shall see the *salvation* of our God (Isa 52:7-10).

My *salvation* will be forever,
and my deliverance will never be ended . . .
my deliverance will be forever,
and my *salvation* to all generations (Isa 51: 6-8).

7. *Some images of salvation.*

We have a strong city; he sets up *salvation* as walls and
barracks (Isa 26:1).
He put on righteousness as a breastplate,
and a helmet of *salvation* upon his head (Isa 59:17).

I will greatly rejoice in the Lord . . .
for he has clothed me with garments of *salvation* (Isa 61:10).

For Zion's sake I will not keep silent . . .
until her vindication goes forth as brightness,
and her *salvation* as a burning torch (Isa 62:1).

Violence shall no more be heard in your land,
devastation or destruction within your borders;
You shall call your walls *Salvation*,
and your gates Praise (Isa 60:18).

Shower, O heavens, from above,
and let the skies rain down righteousness;
let the earth open, that *salvation* may sprout forth,
and let it cause righteousness to spring up also;
I the Lord have created it (Isa 45:8).

Summary of salvation understandings in Isaiah.

Given the strongly political contexts of Isaiah material in relation to the Assyrian deportation, the Babylonian exile, and the post-exilic period of reconstruction, it is no wonder that salvation language in Isaiah, rooted historically in the exodus, has to do heavily with the political salvation of a people. But that salvation is linked strongly to social righteousness and justice; i.e. without them there can be no political wholeness and health.

Further, though Isaiah material is much concerned with the salvation of Israel *from* political bondage, it also involves salvation *for* being a light of justice to the nations. God's concern for the health of all peoples and nations, also for Israel's ancient enemies, calls Israel to that prophetic task.

There also is a concern for personal salvation, i.e. for a renewed personal relationship with God that can deal with the sins of idolatry and rebellion. The nourishment of that relationship involves "returning and rest . . . quietness and confidence;" and it also can deal with sorrow and death through God's saving power to "swallow up death forever."

As in the Psalms, the understanding of salvation is primarily *this worldly* and has to do with the political health of both Israel and all other nations, as well as with the personal health of individuals in their relatedness to God, to others, and to God's whole creation. Among other images, Isaiah wants salvation to sprout forth from the earth to bring God's health to all.

III. PAUL

As we turn to the New Testament, we shall look first at the oldest of the New Testament writings, those written by the Apostle Paul himself. This means those seven Letters that most scholars agree Paul wrote largely between 50 and 60 C. E. or so (Romans, 1-2 Corinthians, Galatians, Philippians, 1 Thessalonians, Philemon). Others written in Paul's name (using a widespread practice of pseudonymous writing then) may have been written by others to let the authoritative Paul speak again in the decades after his death.

Paul uses salvation language some thirty times in five of these seven Letters (only Galatians and Philemon do not). Here we shall not deal with Paul's use Letter by Letter (though such a contextual approach would enrich our study further). Rather, we shall seek to group the various ways he uses such language throughout his Letters.

1. *Salvation as God's Good News in Jesus Christ.* Paul's use of salvation language centers in what God has done in the gospel, and for Paul that focuses in the proclamation of the death and resurrection of Jesus Christ. God's outreaching love in Jesus effects a new relationship with God and a new life for those who receive that reconciling gift. Several texts make this clear.

> For I am not ashamed of the gospel; it is the power of God for *salvation* to everyone who has faith (Rom 1:16).

> But God shows his love for us in that while we were yet sinners Christ died

> for us. Since, therefore, we are now justified by his blood (i.e. by God's outpoured love), much more *shall we be saved* by him from the wrath of God. For if while we were enemies we were reconciled to God by the death of his Son, much more, now that we are reconciled, *shall we be saved* by his life (Rom 5:8-10).
>
> For the word of the cross is folly to those who are perishing, but to us *who are being saved* it is the power of God . . . . It pleased God through the folly of what we preach *to save* those who believe (1 Cor 1:18, 21; note also 9:22; 10:33; 15:2; 2 Cor 2:15; for other uses of "save" see 1 Cor 3:15; 5:5; 7:16).

2. *Salvation as both present and future.* Already the above texts include both present and future dimensions. Paul seems to have expected soon the end of the world and the ultimate coming of Christ; and for him there is both the *already* of what God has done in the death and resurrection of Jesus and the *not yet* of its future full implications. Paul uses salvation language further in both ways. In terms of the present, Paul speaks of our *being saved* in several texts; and to support his appeal to the Corinthians he quotes from Isa. 49:8.

> "At the acceptable time I have listened to you,
> and helped you on the day of *salvation*."
> Behold, now is the acceptable time; behold, now is the
> day of *salvation* (2 Cor 6: 2; note also in 7:10 a linkage
> to repentance—a rare term in Paul's Letters; and in 1: 6
> Paul links salvation and suffering).

In terms of the future, Paul sometimes links salvation to a future hope. With dependence on Isa 59:17, he can speak of

> a helmet the hope of *salvation*. For God has not destined us for wrath, but to obtain *salvation* through our Lord Jesus Christ, who died for us so that whether we wake or sleep we might live with him (1 Thess 8-10).

In the only place where Paul uses *savior*, it is future oriented.

> But our commonwealth is in heaven, and from it we await a *Savior*, the Lord Jesus Christ, who will change our lowly body to be like his glorious body, by the power which enables him even to subject all things to himself (Phil 3:20-21).

One other text also has this future orientation.

> Besides this you know what hour it is, how it is full time now for you to wake from sleep. For *salvation* is nearer to us now than when we first believed (Rom 13:11).

3. *Salvation and creation.* In one text Paul links our salvation in the past with the hope of future cosmic redemption. Again there is the *already* and the *not yet*:

> because the creation itself will be set free from its bondage to decay and ob-

> tain the glorious liberty of the children of God. We know that the whole creation has been groaning in travail together until now; and not only the creation, but we ourselves, who have the first fruits of the Spirit, groan inwardly as we wait for adoption as sons, the redemption of our bodies. For in this hope *we were saved* (Rom 8:21-24).

4. *Salvation and Israel.* Paul has a passionate concern for the salvation of both Jews and Gentiles, i.e. for the health of both in their relationship with God and the recognition that all people stand in need of God's salvation *from* sin (distorted relationship with God) and *for* a new life of relationship with God and with one another, both now and in the future beyond human death. It is in Romans 9-11 that Paul raises the issue of salvation for both Jews and Gentiles most pointedly.

Paul desires and prays for the salvation of his own Jewish people (Rom 10:1), and at the same time argues that their current "trespass" has led to the salvation of the Gentiles (11:11). But Paul strongly affirms that God has not rejected the Jewish people (11:1), that God's gifts and call are irrevocable (11:29), and that "God has consigned all to disobedience, that he may have mercy upon all" (11:32).

In his use of salvation language in relation to Israel in Rom 9-11, there appears to be a progression in his argument. Note the following three texts.

> And Isaiah cries out concerning Israel: "Though the number of the sons of Israel be as the sand of the sea, only a *remnant* of them *will be saved* " (9:27).

> Inasmuch then as I am an apostle to the Gentiles, I magnify my ministry in order to make my fellow Jews jealous, and thus *save some* of them. For if their rejection means the reconciliation of the world, what will their acceptance mean but life from the dead? (11:14).

> I want you to understand this mystery . . . a hardening has come upon part of Israel, until the full number of Gentiles come in, and so *all Israel will be saved* (11:25-26, followed by supporting Old Testament references).

Paul has moved from "remnant" to "some" to "all" in his understanding of salvation for Israel; and coupling this with his affirmation of God's "mercy upon all" (11:32), Jew and Gentile, Paul embraces a universal understanding of God's salvation, of God's health, for the world.

5. *Salvation, believing, confessing.* Within Romans 9-11 is a section that deals with responses to God's deed-word in Christ, but we need to keep in mind that Paul's purpose is to conclude

> there is no distinction between Jew and Greek; the same Lord is Lord of all and bestows his riches upon all who call upon him. For "everyone who calls upon the name of the Lord *will be saved*" (Rom 10:12-13).

Just preceding this is a concern for believing and confessing.

> The word is near you, on your lips and in your heart (that is, the word of faith which we preach); because, if you confess with your lips that Jesus is

> Lord and believe in your heart that God raised him from the dead, you *will be saved*. For one believes with his heart and so is justified, and he confesses with his lips and so *is saved* (10:7-10).

What is striking about this text is that salvation here involves a double response: one internal and individual, one external and communal. The inner response of believing (i.e. entering into the gift of God's word in Christ) makes right (i.e. justifies) one's relationship with God. But this cannot remain only internal and individual; it involves also verbally confessing that word in Christ (i.e. "Jesus is Lord," probably an early Christian baptismal confession), and such confession is external and communal, i.e. other persons are involved as a confessing community. It also means that salvation involves living one's total life, individual and corporate, private and public, with Jesus as Lord. This is what Paul wants for both Jew and Gentile; and here again Paul supports his view with a reference to the Hebrew scriptures.

> The scripture says, "No one who believes in him will be put to shame" (10:11).

6. *Salvation as a process.* One very interesting text occurs in Philippians, sounding at first glance almost unpauline. It occurs immediately after what we have come to know as the Christ-hymn (Phil 2: 6-11).

> Therefore, my beloved . . . work out your own *salvation* with fear and trembling; for God is at work in you, both to will and to work for his good pleasure (2:12-13; note other uses of salvation language in 1:19, 28).

This is not a text that supports a working out of one's own self-salvation; no, *God is at work in you,* but not without some human response as part of the process. It ties in well with the "pressing on" of another Philippian text (cf.3:12-14).

Summary of salvation understandings in Paul.

We can see from our look at salvation language in Paul's Letters that it is multifaceted. A few points stand out.

The center of Paul's understanding of salvation is God's deed in the death and resurrection of Jesus Christ. God's love in the cross and God's power for new life in Jesus' resurrection lie at the heart of God's *saving,* whole-making, relationship-creating, reconciling purpose intended for all people, Jew and Gentile. In this purpose God's salvation is universal.

For Paul the preaching of this message calls for response in terms of both believing and confessing. Salvation is not only internal and individual and a matter of the heart; it also is external and communal and a matter of public confession, as well as of life lived under the lordship of Jesus Christ, i.e. as expressive of God's love in him in all of life. For Paul the intent of God's salvation is universal, but it is not coercive and calls for a believing and confessing response.

Salvation for Paul is both present and future. God's love in Jesus Christ *already* has put us in a new relationship with God and with one another, but the full realization of all that this means remains a *not yet*. Furthermore, God's salvation involves not only human beings; it includes also ultimately the health of the whole creation.

For Paul, salvation involves a process. Affirming God's saving deeds in Israel's history and in Jesus Christ and working it out, we have been saved, we are being saved, and we shall be saved.

IV. EPHESIANS

Many scholars understand Ephesians as written in Paul's name in the generation after his death. Though this is not the place to develop the reasons (e.g. vocabulary, style, historical setting, theological emphases), it is interesting to note one comparison with Paul.

> For no other foundation (*themelios*) can any one lay than that which is laid, which is Jesus Christ (1 Cor 3:11).
>
> So then you are no longer strangers and sojourners, but you are fellow citizens with the saints and members of the household of God, built upon the foundation (*themelios*) of the apostles and prophets, Christ Jesus himself being the chief cornerstone (Eph 2:19-20).

In light of the fact that in Corinthians Paul has an utterly singular understanding of Christ as the foundation, it is difficult to imagine Paul as regarding himself as foundation. But it is not at all difficult to see how someone in the next generation, looking back upon the first, could regard the first apostles and earliest Christian preachers (i.e. prophets) as foundational figures.

Here we want only to deal with the five times this writing uses salvation language and to see its emphases, recognizing both its dependence upon Paul and its own particular thrust in this later second Christian generation. We note first:

> In him you also, who have heard the word of truth, the gospel of your *salvation*, and have believed in him, were sealed with the promised Holy Spirit (Eph 1:13; note also that, like Paul, the writer can use the image "helmut of *salvation*") in 6:17; cf. 1 Thess 5:8; Isa 59:17).

Though the phraseology may not be Pauline, the content is akin to passages like Rom 1:16 and 2 Cor 1:22.

However, the context indicates that "the gospel of your salvation" in linked closely with God's purpose in Christ "as a plan for the fulness of time, to unite (literally "to head up") all things in him, things in heaven and things on earth" (Eph 1:10). Thus for Ephesians salvation includes an emphasis on both a cosmic and ecclesiastical unity in Christ, a perspective similar to Colossians (though Colossians never uses salvation language).

Though Paul's Letters also have a concern for Christian unity, a second generation writing like Ephesians appears to have heightened this concern appreciably and linked it more strongly with a cosmic unity.

Another text also bears a connection to Paul's understanding of faith, but it also has its own distinctive perspective.

> But God, who is rich in mercy, out of the great love with which he loved us, even when we were dead through our trespasses, made us alive together with Christ (by grace *you have been saved*), and raised us up with him, and made us sit with him in the heavenly places in Christ Jesus, that in the coming ages he might show the immeasurable riches of his grace in kindness toward us in Christ Jesus. For by grace *you have been saved* through faith; and this is not your own doing, it is the gift of God (Eph 2:4-8).

What is distinctive here is the reference to being raised up with Christ. Nowhere do we find any such references in Paul's seven Letters. *Our* being raised is for Paul always in the future. Though for Paul Christ's resurrection is the basis for walking in newness of life, we *shall be raised* (note Rom 6:4-5). Thus for Ephesians salvation includes having already been raised up with Christ, another thrust shared with Colossians (note Col 2:12; 3:1). Why is there this emphasis?

Though there is a future dimension in Ephesians in both of our cited Ephesians texts, unlike Paul there is no expectation of a *near* end. That expectation has been disappointed and given up, but what was to have been part of that near expectation, namely the resurrection of the dead, has been made part of Christian existence in the present. For Ephesians, Christians do not have to wait for some future resurrection. Already they participate with Christ in it. That is here a distinctive part of salvation.

In a final Ephesian salvation text we note a reference to "Christ as the head of the church, his body, and is himself its *Savior*" (Eph 5:23). Again, there is both a dependence on Paul and a distinctive thrust. Paul can speak of the church as the body of Christ, but nowhere in Paul's seven Letters does he ever refer to Christ as the head of the body. For Ephesians Christ is Savior as head of the body.

This understanding is linked with the strong emphasis in Ephesians on Christ as the exalted "head over all things for the church" (Eph 1:22)—the cosmic Christ; and the task of the church is "to grow up in every way into him who is the head, into Christ" (Eph. 4:15). Here is another distinctive thrust of Ephesians which this writing incorporates into its understanding of salvation (Colossians also can speak of Christ as head of the body; note Col 1:18; 2:10, 19).

Summary of Salvation understanding in Ephesians

A later time exhibits an ongoing theological process. In Ephesians, salvation includes a) cosmic unity, b) resurrection already, and c) growth up into Christ as head.

V. LUKE

No New Testament writer uses salvation language more than the writer of Luke-Acts. In the last decade or two of the first century, he uses it some forty-seven times (*savior* four times, *salvation* thirteen times, and *save* thirty times), quite evenly distributed between his Gospel of Luke and the Acts of the Apostles (though there is more use of it in relation to physical healing in the Gospel). What this indicates is that for Luke the work of the Holy Spirit in Jesus (as witnessed to in the Gospel) and in the early church (as witnessed to in Acts) both relate to Luke's understanding of salvation. We now shall proceed to delineate that undertstanding.

1. *Savior and salvation in the infancy narratives.* In the infancy narratives Luke uses *savior* twice, once with reference to God and once to Jesus. In Mary's Magnificat:

> My soul magnifies the Lord,
> and my spirit rejoices in *God my savior* (Luke 1:46-47; cf. 1 Sam 2:1).

And in the angelic message to the shepherds:

> Be not afraid; for behold I bring you good news of a great joy which will come to all the people; for to you is born this day in the city of David a *Savior, who is Christ the Lord* . . . (Luke 2:10-11; note also the reference to Jesus as *Savior* in Acts 5:31 and as linked to David in Acts 13:23).

Simeon's song identifies Jesus as salvation for all peoples:

> Lord, now lettest thou thy servant depart in peace,
> according to thy word;
> for mine eyes have seen thy *salvation*
> which thou hast prepared in the presence of all peoples,
> a light for revelation to the Gentiles,
> and for glory to thy people Israel (Luke 2:29-32; cf. Isa 52:10; Luke 3:6 extends an Isa 40:3-5 quotation to include, "all flesh shall see the *salvation* of God").

The Savior God of Israel now is at work to save all people in the *Savior,* Christ the Lord. The link to Israel's heritage occurs also in his use of *salvation* in Zechariah's song (see Luke 1:69, 71, 77). Thus, for Luke, there is no way to understand Jesus as *Savior* without its roots in Israel's God and scriptural heritage.

2. *Salvation as healing.* Luke shares with Mark and Matthew a number of parallel texts that relate salvation language to Jesus' healing ministry.

> And he (Jesus) said to her, "Daughter, your faith has made you well (*has saved you*); go in peace" (Luke 8:48; similar texts include Luke 6:9; 7:50; 8:36,50; 17:19; 18:42, though not all of them explicitly link healing with faith).

Acts also can employ salvation language to healing but now in a distinctive witness to the post-crucifixion-resurrection setting of the early church.

> Then Peter, filled with the Holy Spirit, said to them, "Rulers of the people and elders, if we are being examined today concerning a good deed done to a cripple, by what means this man *has been healed,* be it known to you all, and to all the people of Israel, that by the name of Jesus Christ of Nazareth,

> whom you crucified, whom God raised from the dead, by him this man is standing before you well . . . " (Acts 4:8-10; note also a healing text in 14:9 and the use of "name" linked to salvation language in Acts 2:21 and 4:12 with two different name references, one to God— from Joel— and one to Jesus).

3. *Salvation and the self.* Though Luke links salvation language to physical and psychic healing, he has an even stronger emphasis on the saving of the self, the life of the total person, in relation to the message/word of God's good news in Jesus. Strikingly, the one who *saved* others cannot *save* himself (Luke 23:35, 39); yet there is also the saying:

> "For whoever *would save* his life will lose it; and whoever loses his life for my sake, he *will save it*" (Lk. 9:24).

Believing, i.e. entering into God's reign, and losing oneself in the purpose of that reign as expressed in Jesus, brings *salvation* (Luke 8:12; 18:26), wholeness to lost selves, "For the son of man came to seek and to *save* the lost" (Luke 19:10; cp. 13:23).

This salvation of the self is proclaimed also in Acts, but understandably with more explicit references to believing in the crucified and risen Jesus (note Acts 2:40, 47 in the context of Peter's speech, 2:22-40). It is a saving message that breaks through to Gentiles (Acts 11:14; 15:11; 28:28), as well as being for "the family of Abraham" and those who fear God (Acts 13:26). For Luke it is a message of God's health and wholeness for all. In Luke's witness to the words of Barnabus and Paul, words from Isaiah that point also to Israel's purpose, we find:

> For the Lord has commanded us, saying, "I have set you to be a light for the Gentiles, that you may bring *salvation* to the uttermost parts of the earth" (Acts 13:47).

Since repentance and the forgiveness of sins are major terms in Luke-Acts, it is important to note that occasionally Luke links them directly with salvation language (see Luke 1:77; Acts 5:31; note other uses of salvation language in Acts 7:25; 27:20,31,34).

4. *Salvation and public life.* Two texts, one from the Gospel and one from Acts, conclude our discussion of Luke. In the story of Zacchaeus (Luke 19:1-10) Jesus reaches out to an outcast tax collector to bring him *salvation.* That *salvation* does include Zaacchaeus' personal relation to Jesus and apparently also his home and family; but it includes also a new perspective on his work, as well as a public concern for the poor. It is after all of these in the story that Jesus says, "Today *salvation* has come to this house, since he also is a son of Abraham" (Luke 19:9). The outcast tax collector is transformed in his person, his home, his work, his public life; and now he is a true "son of Abraham," ready to fulfill the promise to Abraham that in you all the families of the earth will be blessed" (Gen 12:3).

In the story of Paul and Silas, the slave girl, and the Phllippian jailer (Acts 16:16-40), the not-to-be-silenced girl proclaims repeatedly about Paul and Silas, "These men are servants of the Most High God, who proclaim to you the way of *salvation.*" But this "way of *salvation*" includes both the personal relation of believing in Jesus Christ (vss. 30-31) with its accompanying speaking of the word, washing of wounds, baptizing, eating, rejoicing (aspects of life within a believing community, vss. 32-34), as well as the public deliverance of a demented slave girl from personal and economic bondage (vs. 18), suffering because of the collusion of economic, political, and police powers (vss. 19-24), the shaking of the foundations of penal injustice (vss. 25-26), and the calling of public officials to accountability (vss. 37-38). There is no New Testament text that combines more fully a personal and public understanding of salvation, the internal and external life of a believing community, the saving relationship to God in Jesus Christ and the saving mission in human society.

Summary of Luke's view of salvation.

Luke affirms the saving God and scriptural heritage of Israel, now coming to fulfillment in God's saving, i.e. all-inclusive, outreaching, relationship-creating deed of great joy in Jesus Christ.

That salvation includes physical/psychic healing, as well as the wholeness of relationship with God, in both personal faith within the life of a believing community, as well as in public witness that cares for the poor, frees persons from personal and economic bondage, and calls religious and governmental officials to accountability.

Luke's view of salvation seeks to embrace both Jews and Gentiles in God's one human family; and though Luke like Mark and Matthew can use salvation language in relation to the future coming of the Son of man (see Luke 9:23-27), with a deemphasis on the timing of the end Luke's emphasis falls far more on God's salvation at work *in this world* as good news of a great joy for all people now.

VI. JOHN

Though the Gospel of John uses all three forms of salvation language, its use (as compared with Luke) is not nearly so extensive (*save*, six times; *salvation* and *savior*, one time each). However these uses are distinctive and important to consider.

1. *Salvation is present through God's love in Jesus.* We see this in one of the most well known and well beloved texts from John's Gospel.

> For God so loved the world that he gave his only Son, that whoever believes in him should not perish but have eternal life. For God sent the son into the world, not to condemn the world, but that the world *might be saved* through him (John 3:16-17; note also 12:47).

God's word in Jesus is not a sentence of condemning judgment but of saving love, a love that restores relationship with God and brings eternal life, a life lived out of that love already in the present (cf. John 5:24, 34).

Among the seven "I am" metaphors in John, one is linked to salvation language.

> I am the door; if anyone enters by me, he *will be saved*, and will go in and out and find pasture (John 10:9).

In the Lazarus story the disciples say to Jesus:

> "Lord, if he has fallen asleep, he will *be saved* (the RSV reads "will recover," John 11:12).

The presence of him who is "resurrection and life" (vs. 25) brings salvation already, not only (as Martha expected) in the future (vs. 24).

But the one in whom God's saving love reaches its climax on the cross does not initially seek to save himself. There is no cry (as in the Synoptic Gospels) that seeks to escape the cross.

> "Now is my soul troubled. And what shall I say, 'Father, *save* me from this hour'? No, for this purpose I have come to this hour. Father, glorify thy name." (Jn. 12:27).

In John the love of God in the cross (cf. John 3:16) is not a prelude to the glory of the resurrection; it is the glory of God itself. God's glory is the glory of self-giving love, and it is this that reigns from the cross to save all people (note John 12: 31-33) and to draw all to respond and enter into that love.

2. *Salvation is linked to the Jewish heritage.* The Gospel of John probably received its final shape toward the end of the first century at a time when there was conflict between the Johannine community and the synagogue (note John 9:22; 12:42). Yet for John the coming of Jesus is linked inseparably to the Jewish heritage back to creation (note John 1:1-3). Images from that heritage help to elucidate Jesus and his ministry (e.g. lamb, water, bread, light, shepherd, life), and in John Jesus' relationship to Passover occurs three times (not once as in the Synoptic Gospels). Thus John can write: "*salvation* from the Jews" (John 4:22). For John, God's saving deeds in Israel's history are not negated; they reach a climax in Jesus.

But that *salvation* no longer is limited either to Israel or the Samaritans and their respective localizations of worshlp (John 4:20-21). That *salvation,* rooted In the Hebrew heritage, now becomes universal in Jesus with "worship in spirit and truth" (John 4:24). The love of God in Jesus breaks through (in the story of the Samaritan women) the barriers of geography, gender, race, and religion to bring living water to all the world.

3. *Jesus as Savior of the world.* Already we have seen this implicitly in other texts, but in the Samaritan story the woman's own people finally say to her:

> "It is no longer because of your words that we believe, for we have heard for ourselves, and we know that this is indeed the Savior of the world" (John 4:42; cf. 1 John 14).

Such a statement is not an abstract generalization; it is a confession of those who "have heard for ourselves" and who have known one who has come to them to break through all human barriers to save and include them in a new relationship with God in loving community. Jesus is *Savior of the world* because he *saves* people from an old barrier-ridden existence for a new life, born and nurtured in God's love for all the peoples of the world.

Summary of John's view of salvation.

John's understanding of *salvation* centers in God's outreaching love for the world in Jesus that climaxes on the cross. That *salvation* has its roots in God's saving deeds in Israel's history, but in Jesus it becomes universalized as the Savior of the world. To respond to this *salvation* is to enter into (i.e. believe) God's love in the present ("eternal life" is now, as well as future) and let that love be the reigning power in all of life.

A Note: Jesus is way, truth, life (John 14: 6), not because he is the way *to God*, but because he is God's way *to us* and to the whole world. He is not the exclusive way to God; rather, for John he expresses God's inclusive *saving* way to the world, a way that is to be received, believed, and lived with love and joy.

VII. THE PASTORAL EPISTLES

Most scholars regard 1-2 Timothy and Titus as written in Paul's name (perhaps in the second generation after Paul), thereby letting '"Paul" speak to a different situation some forty years or so after his death. It will be interesting to see how these writings that build on Paul may reflect their own distinctive understanding of salvation (*save*, seven times; *savior*, ten times; *salvation*, three times).

1. *A Savior God.* It is striking to note that the Pastoral Epistles use *savior* far more than any other New Testament writing. Dominant is the reference to God as *Savior* (1 Tim 2:3; 4:10; Tit 1:3; 2:10; 3:4), though other texts refer to Jesus as *Savior* (2 Tim 1:10; Tit 1:4; 2:13; 3:6). The language of God as *Savior* distinguishes it from almost all other references to *savior* that we have examined. *God* is the *Savior* of all people (1 Tim 2:4; 4:10; Tit 2:11) in *Jesus* as *Savior.*

2. *Salvation in Jesus' appearing.* The Pastorals can link salvation language to both Jesus' first and final appearing.

> Do not be ashamed then of testifying to our Lord . . . who *saved* us, not in virtue of our works but in virtue of his own purpose and the grace he gave us in Christ Jesus ages ago, and now has manifested through the appearing of our *Savior* Christ Jesus, who abolished death and brought life and immortality to light through the gospel (2 Tim 1:8-10) .

> But when the goodness and loving kindness of God our *Savior* appeared, he *saved* us, not because of deeds done by us in righteousness, but in virtue of his own mercy, by the washing and regeneratlon and renewal in the Holy Spirit, which he poured out upon us richly through Jesus Christ our *Savior*, so that we might be justifled by his grace and become heirs in hope of eternal life. The saying is sure (Tit 3:4-8; note also the familiar saying in 1 Tim 1:15).

In the above quotations God's saving grace and mercy are at work in Jesus' first appearing, though with future implications for immortality and eternal life. What follows embraces his first appearance but moves to the final appearing with ethical implications in between.

> For the grace of God appeared for the *salvation* of all people, training us to renounce irreligion and worldly passions, and to live sober, upright, and godly lives in this world, awaiting our blessed hope, appearing of the glory of the great God and our *Savior* Jesus Christ who gave himself for us to redeem us from all iniquity and to purify for himself a people of his own who are zealous for good deeds (Tit 2: 11-14; note also 2 Tim 2:10 and 4:18 for other future references linked to salvation language).

3. *Salvation, scripture, and teaching.* The Pastorals place strong emphasis on sound teaching (the term *didaskalia* occurs fifteen times, only five in the entire rest of the New Testament) and link salvation language to both teaching and the sacred writings. For the Pastorals these participate in the process of salvation.

> Take heed to yourself and to your teaching; hold to that, for by so doing you *wlll save* both yourself and your hearers (1 Tim 4:16).

> But as for you, continue in what you have learned and have firmly believed, knowing from whom you learned it and how from childhood you have been acquainted with the sacred writings which are able to instruct you for *salvation* through faith in Christ Jesus (2 Tim 3:14-15).

4. *Salvation, slaves, and women.* We have little difficulty in resonating with the above *salvation*-related Pastoral Epistle texts. But we do with what follows. One text has to do with slaves.

> Bid slaves to be submissive to their masters and to give satisfaction in every respect; they are not to be refractory, nor to pilfer, but to show entire and true fidelity, so that in everything they may adorn the doctrine of God our Savior (Tit 2:9).

New Testament writings generally do not challenge the institution of slavery directly, and the Pastorals are concerned that Christians live a quiet, peaceable, godly, respectful life in their society (cf. 1 Tim 2:1-2). Here in this text the submissiveness of slaves even is portrayed as adorning the doctrine (*didaskalia*) of God our *Savior*. It obviously is a text we no longer employ to support slavery.

Another text is a part of 1 Timothy that denies women the right to pray (the men pray, 2:8), silences women in all submissiveness (2. 11), denies them the right to teach or have any authority over men (2:12), makes women reponsible for the entrance of transgression into the world (2:14), and finally says:

> Yet woman *will be saved* through bearing children, if she continues in faith and love and holiness with modesty (1 Tim 2:15).

Such a text is most degrading to women; and it stands in conflict with other affirmations in the Pastorals that speak of *salvation* in terms not of works but of God's grace and mercy. Someone once sald, "None of us is entirely useless; even the worst of us can serve as horrible examples." This is one text that is a horrible example of bad theology in the early church.

The authenticity and authority of scripture is that it includes such texts too as a true reflection of one kind of theologizing that went on in the early church, but (like the slaves' text) it cannot be a prescription for the way we are to understand the place of women in the church today, especially when other New Testament texts make women full partners with men in the life and ministry of the early church.

VIII. CONCLUSION

Where has our look at the use of salvation language in a number of biblical writings led us? It has led us to see that there can be no simplistic understanding of what *salvation* means; rather, biblical writings present a rich variety of meanings. What do they include? Though the following list is not exhaustive, it does serve to indicate some of the multiple dimensions of God's *salvation*.

1. Salvation from political/economic bondage, as well as from personal adversaries.
2. Salvation of the poor, needy, weak, oppressed, and those threatened by death.
3. Salvation from a sense of personal anguish and the sin of a rebellious distortion of relationship with God.
4. Salvation that challenges idolatry and military solutions and that is the hope of all peoples.
5. Salvation that embraces justice and righteousness for all nations and all generations.
6. Salvation as God's gift of a new relationship with God through God's love in Jesus Christ, present already now, but whose full realization is in the future.
7. Salvation that includes the future health of all of creation.
8. Salvation that is universal for both Jews and Gentiles to which people are to respond in personal belief and communal confession.
9. Salvation as something to be worked out because God is at work in us.
10. Salvation that involves the cosmic unity of all things, being raised with Christ, and growing up into him as the head of the body, the church.
11. Salvation that ties the Hebrew heritage and God's good news in Jesus Christ firmly together.

12. Salvation that involves physical and psychic healing, as well as the relationship of the whole self with God.

13. Salvation that includes integrity in work, public concern for the poor, deliverance of people from economic enslavement, and calling public officials to accountability.

14. Salvation in Jesus as the *savior* of the world who breaks the barriers of geography, gender, race, religion.

15. Salvation that involves sound teaching and scripture to present the content of faith in Jesus Christ.

This paper has not developed in any sustained way homiletical concerns with our texts. What it has done is to present some of the multiple aspects of biblical understandings of *salvation* that may feed into the process of selecting and preaching from biblical texts with *salvation* themes embedded in them. In that homiletical-interpretive process may such interpretation of scripture make "our hearts burn within us."

DOUBLE GRACE: JOHN CALVIN'S VIEW OF THE RELATIONSHIP OF JUSTIFICATION AND SANCTIFICATION

JONATHAN H. RAINBOW

The question of the relationship of justification and sanctification is one that continues to exercise Christian theologians and exegetes. Theologically it is a question of the connection of the forgiveness of sins and moral renewal; exegetically it is primarily a question of the meaning of "justification" in Paul. It becomes, in the end, a church question, and a question for the preacher, who must both proclaim remission of sins through Jesus Christ and exhort the people of God to holy living.

It is my purpose in this essay, not to do either theology or exegesis, but to provide some historical background through a study of the Reformer John Calvin's approach to the question of the relationship of justification and sanctification. Calvin was a strong spokesman for the concept of justification that emerged out of the first era of the Reformation, on which there was, according to Alister McGrath, a "broad consensus," and which included three essential elements: first, the understanding of justification as a *forensic declaration*, a change in the sinner's status rather than in the sinner's nature; second, a *systematic distinction between justification and sanctification*; and third, the identification of the *alien; imputed righteousness of Christ* as the immediate cause of justification.[1] As we shall see, Calvin spoke for this Reformation consensus.

The value of taking a close look at Calvin's thought on the present topic derives in part from the current state of Pauline scholarship. The Reformation doctrine of justification was, in exegetical terms, a theological interpretation of Paul, and especially of Romans. It continues to find support from exegetes of Paul.[2] A significant portion of New Testament scholarship today, however, would consider the classic Reformation distinction between justification and sanctification to be inadequate as an interpretation of Paul's doctrine of justification. Indeed, the influential scholar Ernst Käsemann, in his commentary on Romans, rejects the justification-sanctification distinction, almost as if it were not worthy of serious consideration, and insists throughout his exposition that in Paul's thought justification is both *gift and power* (i.e., to use traditional theological language, forgiveness and sanctification).[3]

If this is the trend in New Testament scholarship, it will be helpful to hear once again what Calvin says about justification and sanctification, if for no other reason than to know exactly what is being left behind.

It is also worth bringing up the old question: does the Reformation doctrine of justification really make Christian obedience superfluous? Calvin was a working pastor, and the majority of his preaching and teaching was aimed, not so much at convincing people to believe the Reformation doctrine of justification, but at moving those who believed it to holy living. Like Luther, Calvin often bemoaned what he perceived to be the sad moral state of the reformed churches. So it was essential for him that Christian obedience rest on solid theological ground. It is on this pastoral background that his effort to integrate justification and sanctification theologically should be understood.

I. HUMANITY'S DOUBLE PLIGHT

Calvin's thinking about salvation through Jesus Christ is rooted theologically in his analysis of human fallenness, which we find most clearly laid out in the discussion of original sin in the *Institutes* 2.1. Tracing the human disaster back to Adam, Calvin finds that it actually has two aspects: guilt and corruption. "For since it is said that we became subject to God's judgment through Adam's sin. . , he is said to have made us guilty. Yet not only has punishment fallen upon us from Adam, but a contagion imparted by him resides in us, which justly deserves punishment." Fallen humanity then stands before God with two distinct but connected problems, legal liability and the moral corruption of human nature. Humanity has a legal problem and a personal problem, which together constitute the sin problem.

The sin problem in both of its aspects goes back to Adam, and from Adam flows to every descendent of Adam. There is in Calvin no effort to salvage something pleasing to God from the catastrophe of the Fall. The little baby in the womb, so apparently innocent, is for Calvin a "rotten branch" from a rotten root. "For, even though the fruits of their iniquity have not yet come forth, they have the seed enclosed within them. Indeed, their whole nature is a seed of sin; hence it can be only hateful and abhorrent to God."[5] And if the little baby is already condemned and corrupt, how much more those who have had years to cultivate their sinfulness. So there is no question about the severity and thoroughness of Calvin's doctrine of original sin. "Original sin, therefore, seems to be a hereditary depravity and corruption of our nature, diffused into all parts of the soul, which first makes us liable to God's wrath . . . . "[6] Humanity stands in a helpless plight before its Maker both in the forensic-legal sphere, where we find ourselves guilty and condemned, and in the personal-ethical sphere, where we find ourselves dead and corrupt. Jesus Christ saves humanity from both guilt and corruption of nature; in Christ there is justification and sanctification.

II. JUSTIFICATION: CALVIN WAS A LUTHERAN

Calvin teaches that justification is wholly a legal-forensic transaction, the imputation of the alien righteousness of God to the unrighteous sinner, through faith alone, for the sake of Christ. Calvin is on this point as "Lutheran," as emphatic, and as polemical as

Luther. As Luther had said that justification is the article of the standing or falling church, so Calvin can say that it is the "main hinge on which religion turns."[7] It would be hard to find a clearer, more uncompromising exposition of justification by faith alone in all the literature of the Reformation—the writings of Luther included—than that which occupies the *Institutes* 3.11-18.

It is worth emphasizing again, with Calvin, the exact point at which the struggle for the Reformation doctrine of justification needs to be waged. It is not that justification is by grace. Certainly the reformers believed that; but so did Augustine, and so did the Jansenists. The belief that justification is by grace alone does not make one a Protestant. Nor does the assertion that justification is by faith alone make one necessarily a Protestant. Nor does the assertion that it is the righteousness of God that justifies the sinner make one automatically a Protestant. The key to the Reformation doctrine of justification is the concept of imputation. Justifying righteousness is imputed righteousness. That takes justification decisively out of the realm of good works, regeneration, and ethical renewal, and puts it in the divine court of law. It also isolates justifying faith from all the other virtues that otherwise accompany faith. It severs justifying righteousness and justifying faith from any personal ethical behavior.

This is Calvin's doctrine everywhere in his writings, from the beginning of his career as a reformer to its end. "Therefore we explain justification simply as the acceptance with which God receives us into his favor as righteous men. And we say that it consists in the remission of sins and the imputation of Christ's righteousness."[8] In defending the doctrine, he is no respecter of persons. He polemicizes, naturally, against the Roman Catholic doctrine which was formulated emphatically at the Council of Trent and which stated that good works are necessary for justification. He polemicizes against the "Anabaptists," believing that their call for a pure and regenerate church involved the compromising of justification. And he does not hesitate to wield his sharp scalpel even against those whom might be considered closer to home.

There is, for example, Calvin's long dismantling, in the *Institutes*, of the doctrine of the "Lutheran" revisionist theologian Osiander. Calvin gives this summary of Osiander's position: "For in this whole disputation the noun 'righteousness' and the verb 'to justify' are extended in two directions; so that to be justified is not only to be reconciled to God through free pardon but also to be made righteous, and righteousness is not a free imputation but the holiness and uprightness that the essence of God, dwelling in us, inspires."[9] Calvin's critique is that Osiander sees justification not only as imputed righteousness but also as infused righteousness. Osiander teaches that God justifies "not only by pardoning but by regenerating."[10] Osiander "laughs at those men who teach that 'to be justified' is a legal term; because we must actually be righteous. Also, he despises nothing more than that we are justified by free imputation."[11] Osiander, in short, is scandalized by God's justification of the ungodly; he cannot imagine that God would declare a person righteous if that person were not, in some degree of actually, righteous.[12] So Osiander must speak of "double righteousness," which includes both imputation and transformation. This Calvin harshly rejects. Justification is by imputation alone. "The benefits of Christ—sanctification and righteousness—are different. From this it follows that not even spiritual works come into account when the power of justifying is ascribed to faith."[13]

Nor does Calvin hesitate to take issue even with Augustine, whose treatment of justification is not substantially different from Osiander's. Calvin—perhaps inconsistently—treats Augustine with respect where he had treated Osiander with scorn, but his evaluation amounts to the same thing: "Augustine's view, or at any rate his manner of stating it, we must not entirely accept. For even though he admirably deprives man of all credit for righteousness and transfers it to God's grace, he still subsumes grace under sanctification, by which we are reborn in newness of life through the Spirit."[14] Augustine defended God's grace, but he allowed transforming grace to intrude into the realm of justifying grace, and this Calvin cannot allow—even when Augustine does it!

Where, then, is transforming grace?

III. JUSTIFICATION AND SANCTIFICATION: ALWAYS IN TANDEM

For Calvin, transforming grace is always in tandem with justifying grace. For guilt and corruption, though distinct problems, are always together, and both must be solved for the sinner to see the face of God.

The God of grace meets humanity's double plight with a "double grace: namely, that being reconciled to God through Christ's blamelessness, we may have in heaven instead of a Judge a gracious Father; and secondly, that sanctified by Christ's spirit we may cultivate blamelessness and purity of life."[15] There is, in other words, both forensic grace and transforming grace. Calvin sometimes designates these as "forgiveness" and "repentance," as when he says that "the whole of the gospel is contained under these two headings, repentance and forgiveness of sins," and that "each grace is grasped by faith."[16] Or he can call them "remission" and "sanctification": "By the word grace, we are to understand both parts of redemption—the remission of sins, by which God imputes righteousness to us,—and the sanctification of the Spirit, by whom he forms us anew unto good works."[17]

It is clear from these statements that transforming grace, by whatever name (sanctification, renewal, repentance) is not for Calvin an afterthought or a footnote to justification, but a theological equal. Believers must "learn to embrace him [Christ], not only for justification, but also for sanctification, as he has been given to us for both these purposes, lest they rend him asunder by their mutilated faith."[18] The same faith that appropriates imputed righteousness also appropriates "the sanctification of the Spirit."[19] "The grace of regeneration is *never disjoined* from the imputation of righteousness."[20]

Salvation consists of the double grace of justification and sanctification, forgiveness and repentance, pardon and renewal. It is with this conception that Calvin meets the objection of Trent, and of Osiander, that imputed righteousness must destroy Christian ethics. Forgiveness of sins stands on its own ground, the ground of imputed righteousness, and the renewal of obedience to God stands on its own ground, the ground of regeneration and sanctification by the Holy Spirit. The double aspects of God's grace do not overlap or interpenetrate, but they always come together, inseparable. It should be carefully noted also that Calvin's "double grace" is not at all the same as Osiander's "double righteousness." Osiander wanted to speak of an infused righteousness which formed part of the basis on which God pronounces justification, Calvin will have no part in that. Calvin is willing to call God's transforming work "grace," but not "righteousness."

Sanctification, then, is not simply an outgrowth of justification, but a work of divine grace in its own right. Calvin's careful emphasis on this point distinguishes his thinking on sanctification from that which sees moral renewal and Christian obedience growing *out of* justification. This latter approach is more characteristic of Luther; it is also to be seen in the Heidelberg Catechism (originating in the Palatinate, 1563), which lays out the whole Christian life under the theme of "thankfulness" for justification. In Calvin, justification and sanctification are not root and branch, but two branches from a common root.

IV. THE COMMON SOURCE OF JUSTIFICATION AND SANCTIFICATION: THE REDEMPTIVE WORK OF JESUS CHRIST

For Calvin the common root of both justification and sanctification is the redemptive work of Jesus Christ. The clearest expression of this doctrine comes in his exposition of the words "crucified, dead, and buried" in the Apostles' Creed. The "whole of perfect salvation consists" in the death and resurrection of Christ;[21] though Scripture sometimes derives salvation from Christ's death, and sometimes from his resurrection, we should understand that both, as one integrated redemptive work, are included in each.[22]

Along the lines of his conception of double grace, Calvin identifies in the death of Christ two fruits or effects: first, Christ on the cross "took our place to pay the price of our redemption" (forensic grace); second, "by our participation in it, his death mortifies our earthly members, so that they no longer perform their functions; and it kills the old man in us so that he may not flourish and bear fruit . . . . Therefore, in Christ's death and burial a twofold blessing is set forth for us to enjoy: liberation from the death to which we had been bound, and mortification of our flesh."[23] The grace of the mortification of the old man also flows to us, as we should expect, from the resurrection of Christ.[24]

Sanctification does not come, as it were, from justification; it comes, like justification, straight from the cross. The double grace of salvation is integrated, not by allowing sanctification to encroach on justification, nor by relegating sanctification to second fiddle status, but by tracing both to Jesus Christ. They are integrated Christologically.

V. "THE LIFE OF THE CHRISTIAN MAN"

Before ending our look at Calvin, we should say something, if only in summary, about the actual substance of his doctrine of the Christian life. The important *locus* in this connection is Book III, chapters 6-8 of the *Institutes*.

Calvin makes it clear at the beginning of this section that his purpose is not to set out the specific ethical duties of Christian living in detail, which would "occupy a large volume,"[25], but rather to "set down some universal rule with which to determine [one's] duties."[26] In other words, Calvin is looking for the theme of the Christian life, that which binds it together. Significantly, Calvin does not find this theme in the keeping of the Ten Commandments. At this point in the *Institutes* the Ten Commandments have long since been expounded; Calvin has indeed maintained the so-called "third use of the Law," insisting that the Decalogue is directed to the justified believer as the rule of conduct, and he alludes to this once (but only once!) in the three chapters on the Christian life.[27] But Calvin's theme of the Christian life is not the law. It is Christ.

Christ is the *pattern* to which the believer must conform, "set before us as an example, whose pattern we ought to express in our life."[28] Moreover, the saving grace of Christ is a most powerful *inducement* to holiness of life; the "indicative" of salvation grounds and feeds the "imperative" of obedience for Calvin, though he does not use this terminology.[29] Coming to the "sum of the Christian life," Calvin turns to Rom 12:1, in which the Christian life is encapsulated in the metaphor of sacrifice, and argues that *self-denial* is the true ordering principle of life in Christ. There is no room for triumphalism in Calvin's thought. The believer is a pilgrim in an alien world,[30] and must, like Christ, bear a cross through it. "While he [Christ] dwelt on earth he was not only tried by a perpetual cross but his whole life was nothing but a sort of perpetual cross. . . . Why should we exempt ourselves, therefore, from the condition to which Christ our Head had to submit, especially since he submitted to it for our sake to show us an example of patience in himself?"[31]

Can it be an accident that Calvin, who traces his theological doctrine of sanctification directly to the cross, also envisions the Christian life in the shape of the cross?

We must note what Calvin intends to achieve theologically by his doctrine of double grace in Christ:

a) He protects the doctrine of justification from the destruction that he believes will occur when the transformational side of salvation is allowed to intrude upon it to any degree. With justification, it is all or nothing: either it is all of imputation, or it is no justification at all.

b) He preserves the imperative and the significance of Christian obedience, or sanctification. Sanctification is not for Calvin an afterthought, or a problem, or an implication, or a psychological human response to justification. Sanctification is *salvation,* just as much as justification is *salvation.* It is grace. Nor is it optional, or dispensible, but necessary and inevitable. Furthermore, sanctification is for Calvin Christ-centered and Christ-shaped.

c) He finds the unity of the "double grace" in the saving work of Jesus Christ. Pastorally, this means that the believer is driven to the person of Christ for both righteousness and holiness, and that the preacher's proclamation of free forgiveness and exhortation to obedience both rest upon Christ.

NOTES

1. A. McGrath, *Iustitia Dei: A History of the Christian Doctrine of Justification: The Beginnings to the Reformation* (Cambridge: Cambridge University Press, 1989) 182.

2. C. E. B. Cranfield, for example says, "There seems to us to be no doubt that *dikaious,* as used by Paul, means simply 'acquit', 'confer a righteous status on', and does not in itself contain any reference to moral transformation." *A Critical and Exegetical Commentary on The Epistle to the Romans.* Vol.1, ICC (Edinburgh: T. & T. Clark 1975) 95.

3. Ernst Käsemann, *Commentary on Romans,* trans. Geoffrey W. Bromiley (Grand Rapids: Eerdmans, 1980). "The distinction between justification and sanctification and the sequence derived from it were possible only when the gift was separated from the Giver. . ." (172). "The conclusion is unavoidable that in Paul righteousness cannot be restricted to the judgment of justification or even to the gift of the righteousness of faith" (185).

4. *Institutes* 2.1.8. Quotations are from J. T. McNeill, ed., *Calvin: Institutes of the Christian Religion,* The Library of Christian Classics Vol. XX (Philadelphia: Westminster , 1960).

5. *Institutes* 2.1.8.
6. *Institutes* 2.1.8.
7. *Institutes* 3.11.1.
8. *Institutes* 3.11.2.
9. *Institutes* 3.11.6.
10. *Institutes* 3.11.6.
11. *Institutes* 3.11.11.
12. "For he [Osiander] contends long and verbosely that we obtain favor with God not by imputation of Christ's righteousness alone, because it would be impossible (I use his words) for him to regard as just those who are not just," *Institutes* 3.11.12.
13. *Institutes* 3.11.14.
14. *Institutes* 3.11.15.
15. *Institutes* 3.11.1.
16. *Institutes* 3.3.19.
17. On Rom 6:14. Quoted from John Owen, trans. and ed., *Commentaries on the Epistle of Paul to the Romans* (Grand Rapids: Baker Book House, 1981).
18. Comment on Rom 8:13.
19. *Institutes* 3.2.8.
20. Comment on Rom 8:2, emphasis mine. Similarly, Calvin says, ". . . man is justified by faith alone, and simple pardon; nevertheless, actual holiness of life, so to speak, is not separated from free imputation of righteousness," *Institutes* 3.3.1.
21. *Institutes* 2.16.5.
22. *Institutes* 2.16.13.
23. *Institutes* 2.16.7.
24. "Further, as we explained above that the mortification of our flesh depends on participation in his cross, so we must understand that we obtain a corresponding benefit from his resurrection," *Institutes* 2.16.13.
25. *Institutes* 3.6.1.
26. *Institutes* 3.6.1.
27. *Institutes* 3.7.3.
23. *Institutes* 3.6.3.
29. *Institutes* 3.6.3.
30. *Institutes* 3.7.3.
31. *Institutes* 3.8.1.

An Announcement

North Park Theological Seminary in Chicago, Illinois is pleased to announce that the first Symposium on Theological Interpretation of Scripture will take place October 12 -14, 1990. The Symposium will start at 1:30 p.m. on October 12 in Nyvall Hall and will extend through noon on October 14.

The theme of this year's symposium will be **Prophetic and/or Apocalyptic Eschatology**. The following persons have agreed to make presentations:

Professor Klaus Koch	*Old Testament*
Professor Leslie Allen	*Old Testament*
Professor John Collins	*Intertestamental Literature*
Professor George Beasley-Murray	*New Testament*
Professor David Scholer	*New Testament*
Professor Adela Yarbro Collins	*New Testament*
Sister Agnes Cunningham	*Church History*
Professor Timothy Weber	*Church History*
Professor Gabriel Fackre	*Theology*
Professor John Howard Yoder	*Ethics*

Persons interested in attending the sessions should write before September 1, 1990 to:

Dr. Klyne Snodgrass
North Park Theological Seminary
3225 W. Foster Avenue
Chicago, Illinois 60625

Meals may be taken at North Park, and assistance will be provided in finding nearby lodging.

The Theme Of Salvation In Karl Barth's Doctrine Of Reconciliation

ALASDAIR I. C. HERON

The Gospel is the message of salvation for all who believe, first for the Jews but then also for the nations (Gentiles).

The meaning of "salvation" has been hotly debated in modern times. That should not surprise us. There are so many things, powers, forces and tendencies from which people may wish to be "saved", so many ways in which they may seek "salvation"—salvation by meditation, by physical exercise, by lowering of the blood cholesterol level, by proper social or political commitment . . . the list could go on at some length.

Do these offerings have anything to do with what the Bible and the Church mean when they speak of salvation? The straight answer is: very little! Salvation is not a matter of worldly success or achievement, nor even of *mens sana in corpore sano*. It has to do with the salvation of the world, the healing of its ills, the hope of a new heaven and a new earth, and so with the transcendent perfecting of human life in the Kingdom of God.

Let us pause to consider this perspective. The final perfecting of human life in the Kingdom of God is not realizable under the conditions of life in this world, upon this earth, for the very simple reason that human life in this world and upon this earth is provisional, passing and transient—to say nothing of its being sinful. We may achieve all kinds of things in the course of our life on earth: we may become wealthy, do good for humankind, be excellent parents, advocates of justice, splendid humanists, philanthropists, benefactors of humanity, professionally successful and the like. We may even become great theologians or respected teachers of the Church. And in all this we can gain the world and lose our soul, or even, if we are not careful, join the company of those electronic preachers so recently sadly but devastatingly exposed as charlatans and hypocrites.

Where do we go from there? The *via negativa* would consist in systematic exposure and denunciation of false hopes of salvation or of such charlatans, as assiduously and greedily practised by the American news media. But the Church has more important tasks than this critical one to fulfill. Above all it needs to reflect on what salvation really means, as the gift and promise of God to humankind, and to take its bearings from that.

And that concern and interest can bring us back to Karl Barth as a major reformed theologian of the 20th century.

But: does Karl Barth really deserve this special attention? Many voices in North American theology today would deny that he does, though that may be as significantly revealing of the character of North American theology as of Barth's. Consider the following:

a) Karl Barth sought to be a *biblical theologian.* I have recently heard it said that many American biblical scholars doubt whether "biblical theology" is a viable enterprise, and that many American theologians teaching in seminaries and universities no longer regard the Bible as relevant to their research and teaching. In this perspective, "biblical study" is a matter of linguistic archaeology and cultural history of religions; "systematic theology" one of speculative philosophical construction of ideas and concerns drawn from sundry metaphysical, religious, cultural, social or political interests, perhaps indeed vaguely "theistic" or "deistic," but scarcely necessarily biblical—or even recognizably Christian—in impulse and orientation.

b) Karl Barth's theology was a sustained undertaking of critical, lively (and frequently controversial) *questioning appropriation of the history and tradition of Western theology,* patristic, medieval, reformed and ecumenical, open to that past history, but also to the intellectual and cultural challenges of the present. As such, it was a *contextual* theology—to be more precise, a process of committed, life-long theological engagement with "the science of God" in critical dialogue with that whole tradition and the history of science, philosophy and theology which it has brought forth. By contrast, much contemporary American theology seems concerned to assert its autonomy and independence from that historical tradition, to be concerned above all else to deny these roots. Ironically enough, it does so by appealing to alternative models of largely European provenance. Whether the preferred choice be Hegelianism, Marxism, existentialism, process philosophy, psychology, political liberationism or pastoral theology: turn over the stones and you will find the European intellectual heritage staring up at you. The American Revolution brought no radical intellectual break with old Europe, only the transposition of old European concerns, interests and dreams to a new context in a wider world. A context and a world, admittedly, which presented fresh opportunities and new challenges; but it was after all not a *different* world, merely *another continent* of the same.

c) Particularly destructive and corrosive has been the description, so popular in the anglo-saxon world, of Karl Barth as "NeoOrthodox." This has made it all too easy for American theologians to regard Karl Barth as if he were a kind of European Reinhold Niebuhr. If Reinhold Niebuhr had a counterpart in European theology, that counterpart was Emil Brunner, not Karl Barth. It is perhaps no accident that Brunner has commonly been more popular and more widely read in the U.S.A. than Barth. Barth was widely perceived as dangerous and subversive. The best way to defuse his work and render its influence harmless was to categorize him as "Neo-Orthodox" or "Neo-Confessionalist." That ensured that he would not be read by "liberals" and "conservatives" alike. Many American seminaries and university faculties today are stacked with professors who designate themselves alternatively as "liberal" or "conservative" and by this expedient avoid facing up to the challenge represented by Karl Barth, who really fits neither category. But if we are concerned to trace the traditions and sources that can help to revitalize our human and Christian awareness; if we are concerned at all to discover and rediscover the roots of our human calling and our destiny in the purposes of the triune God: we can do worse than go to school with Karl Barth.

It is time now to come to our proper theme—the understanding of salvation in Barth's theology. Ideally here one should try to draw on the entire *Church Dogmatics*, for Barth's handling of all the major dogmatic themes relates implicitly or explicitly to the nature of salvation. So, for example, we could refer to his treatment of revelation and the triunity of God in volume one, of election in volume two or creation and covenant in volume three. Especially important in view of the fact that he did not reach the planned fifth volume on redemption is Barth's discussion of creaturely human being in volume three, part two, notably the sections "Real Man" (pp. 132-202), "Humanity as Likeness and Hope" (pp. 285-324) and "Ending Time" (pp. 587-640).

It is, however, in his treatment of the doctrine of reconciliation in volume four that Barth most frequently speaks of "salvation," "theories of salvation," "history of salvation" or the *ordo salutis*.. I therefore propose in the limited compass of this paper to focus on volume four, and within it on a few particularly significant passages. Before coming to them, some remarks on the style and structure of the *Church Dogmatics* in general and volume four in particular may be helpful.

The first (and sometimes only) impression left on many who try to work through any major part of the *Church Dogmatics* is that it is terribly long and slow-moving, that there seem to be many repetitions, and that a great deal of it is set in print so small as to try the eyesight of most readers over forty—especially when, as not infrequently, the small print goes on for ten or twenty or even more pages. This makes it very easy to lose sight of the forest for the trees, to miss the pattern of the whole and the way it is built up, and thus to be somewhat at a loss in seeing the relation of the various chapters and sections to each other. Attention to the overall shape can help to supply the necessary orientation, as can the realization that the passages in small print fulfill the function variously of footnote comments or of more extended exegetical, theological-historical or dogmatic *excursus*, filling out or grounding the preceding passages in normal print.

In four separate seminars in Erlangen dealing respectively with each of the four volumes of the *Church Dogmatics* I have found that careful attention to the overall structure as well as to the thrust of the various passages in small print, along with the brief summaries given at the head of each of the main sections (e.g. in volume four, part one, the sections §§ 57-63), is the best way of highlighting the contours of the whole and keeping the forest as well as the trees in view. Simply starting at the beginning and reading on from page to page is not the best method, unless one is prepared to devote as many years to reading the *Church Dogmatics* as Barth spent writing them or his hearers in Basel in listening to them as he delivered them in the form of lectures!

This is not to suggest that the length of the *Church Dogmatics* is as such excessive, nor that one should never take the trouble to follow longer passages or whole volumes from beginning to end. Had Barth not engaged so thoroughly, patiently and thoughtfully with the subject-matter as he did, he would probably not have come to the distinctive reorientations that are such a striking feature of his work. And going to school with him certainly requires taking time to think along with him at the pace at which his thought developed, or at least doing so some of the time. But it is also possible and useful to keep the total shape of this unfinished symphony and of the individual movements in view.

For a proper understanding of the *Church Dogmatics*, awareness of the fundamental axioms shaping Barth's study and reflexion is also necessary. The foundation, center and goal of his thought is *the self-revelation of God in Jesus Christ as Creator, Reconciler and*

Redeemer of humanity. Theology and anthropology, dogmatics and ethics are held together in a dynamic, dialectical but ultimately coherent vision, which is reflected, not in a theological system, but in a moving progress of theological enquiry, which itself is a challenge and invitation to share in the same journey. This is especially well illustrated by the plan of the first three parts of volume four as Barth himself lays it out in the summary at the head of § 58, 'The Doctrine of Reconciliation (Survey)' CD IV/1, p. 79), which also marks out the horizon in which his references to salvation should be seen:

> The content of the doctrine of reconciliation is the knowledge of Jesus Christ who is (1) very God, that is, the God who humbles Himself, and therefore the reconciling God, (2) very man, that is, man exalted and therefore reconciled by God, and (3) in the unity of the two the guarantor and witness of our atonement.
>
> This threefold knowledge of Jesus Christ includes the knowledge of the sin of man: (1) his pride, (2) his sloth and (3) his falsehood—the knowledge of the event in which reconciliation is made: (1) his justification, (2) his sanctification and (3) his calling and the knowledge of the work of the Holy Spirit in (1) the gathering, (2) the upbuilding and (3) the sending of the community, and of the being of Christians in Jesus Christ (1) in faith, (2) in love and (3) in hope.

The order of presentation thus outlined is then followed through in each of the first three parts of volume four, IV/1 taking up the themes signalled here by (1), IV/2 those marked (2) and IV/3 those indicated by (3). Part four of this volume, which was intended to present an ethics of the Christian life (parallel to the ethics of creation developed in III/4 under the title, 'The Command of God the Creator') was only partly completed and published as IV/4 Fragment, 'Baptism as the Foundation of the Christian Life'.

Each of these four parts of volume four of the *Church Dogmatics* contains numerous references to and discussions of salvation under various aspects, whereby (as might be expected) a good deal of repetition and reiteration can be observed. Instead of attempting to list them all —a task already completed for us by the compilers of the index volume —I have chosen here to select those passages which are of particular weight and significance. We begin with the opening chapter of IV/1, "The Subject-Matter and Problems of the Doctrine of Reconciliation" (which also serves as the introduction to the entire fourth volume), and there with § 57.1: "God with us." This is the first of three sections which together form the first part (§ 57) of the chapter under the general heading "The Work of God the Reconciler'; the second and third sections deal respectively with 'The Covenant as the Presupposition of Reconciliation" (§ 57.2) and "The Fulfilment of the Broken Covenant" (§ 57.3). (The second part of this chapter is § 58, "The Doctrine of Reconciliation (Survey)", from which we have just quoted above.)

I. "GOD WITH US"

§ 57.1 is constructed in a fashion characteristic of Barth's style of procedure. First, the theme is presented in broad outline (pp. 3-5), with a following small-print excursus on the name *Immanuel* as it occurs in Isaiah 7 and 8 and Matt 1:21-22. (pp. 5-6). Then it is articulated in a series of seven connected points (pp. 6-16) which taken together do formally say 'in rough outline . . . almost everything that has to be said about the 'God with us' as the covenant . . . fulfilled in the work of atonement" (p. 16), but not as yet 'with the concreteness with which it is said at the heart of the Christian message' (p. 16) Here now Barth introduces the name of Jesus Christ and relates all seven points to him as their core and content (pp. 16-20), concluding the section with another small-print excursus (pp. 21-22), but this time one which is dogmatic and methodological rather than exegetical.

Within this discussion—though "discussion" is not perhaps the best term to describe what is more a process of sighting the target, scanning the field and then homing in on the decisive center—the term "salvation" is repeatedly employed and in the process outlined and focussed. This can best be illustrated by some quotations, beginning with the third of the seven points developed in pp. 6-16:

> 3. From the standpoint of its meaning, the particularity of this event [sc. "God with us"] consists in the fact that it has to do with the salvation of man . . . Salvation is more than being. Salvation is fulfilment, the supreme, sufficient, definitive and indestructible fulfillment of being. Salvation is the perfect being which is not proper to created being as such but is still future. Created being as such needs salvation, but does not have it: it can only look forward to it. To that extent salvation is its *eschaton*. Salvation, fulfillment, perfect being means—and this is what created being does not have in itself— being which has a part in the being of God, from which and to which it is: not a divinized being but a being which is hidden in God, and in that sense (distinct from God and secondary) eternal being. . . . The coming of this salvation is the grace of God—using the word [sc. grace] in its narrower and most proper sense. . . . It means the redemptive grace of God (pp. 8-9).
>
> 4. In the light of this we must now try to outline this particular event with rather greater precision. According to the Christian message "God with us" means God with the man for whom salvation is intended and ordained as such, as the one who is created, preserved and over-ruled by God as man. . . . The ordaining of salvation for man and of man for salvation is the original and basic will of God, the ground and purpose of His will as Creator. It is not that He first wills and works the being of the world and man, and then ordains it to salvation. But God creates, preserves and overrules man for this prior end and with this prior purpose, that there may be a being distinct from Himself ordained for salvation, for perfect being, for participation in His own being, because as the One who loves in freedom He has determined to exercise redemptive grace—and that there may be an object of this His redemptive grace, a partner to receive it (pp. 9-10).
>
> 5. But again we must go further. "God with us" in the sense of the Christian message means God with us men who have forfeited the predetermined salvation, forfeited it with a supreme and final jeopardizing even of our creaturely existence . . . . The situation of man in this event is this. He occupies a position quite different from that which he ought to occupy according to the divine intention. He does not conduct himself as the partner God has given Himself to receive His redemptive grace. He has opposed his ordination to salvation. He has turned his back on the salvation which actually comes to him. He does not find the fulfilment of his being in participa-

> tion in the being of God by the gift of God. Instead he aims at another salvation which is to be found in the sphere of his creaturely being and attained by his own effort. His belief is that he can and should find self-fulfillment. He has himself become an *eschaton.* This is the man with whom God is dealing in this particular redemptive history: the man who has made himself quite impossible in relation to the redemptive grace of God; and in so doing, the man who has made himself quite impossible in his created being as man, who has cut the ground from under his feet, who has lost his whole *raison d'être*. . . .But it is with this lost son in a far country, with man as he has fallen and now exists in this sorry plight, that God has to do in this redeeming event. And this is what reveals the gulf . . . It is not independent reflection on the part of man, or an abstract law, but grace which shows incontrovertibly that man has forfeited his salvation and in so doing fatally jeopardized his creaturely being—which reveals his sin and the misery which is its consequence. From the redemption which takes place here we can gather from what it is that man is redeemed; from the *factum purum* of the salvation which comes to man without and in spite of his own desserts we may know the *factum brutum* which he for his part dares to set against God (pp. 10-12).

It is, we may think, a dark picture that. Barth paints here, one not exactly designed to present an encouraging view of our human existence. But such a reaction overlooks Barth's positive intention, which is far more concerned with the *factum purum* of "God with us" than the *factum brutum* of our alienation from God. It is—and that is fundamental to Barth's theology—the light of God's grace that casts into relief and makes visible to us the reality of our plight as rebellious sinners lost and wandering. And God's grace has a name and an identity in the person of Jesus Christ. So Barth goes on to focus these reflections christologically:

> We must realise that the Christian message does not at its heart express a concept or an idea, nor does it recount an anonymous history to be taken as truth and reality only in concepts and ideas. . . . But it recounts this history and speaks of its inclusive power and significance in such a way that it declares a name . . . This means that all the concepts and ideas used in this report (God, man, world, eternity, time, even salvation, grace, transgression, atonement and any others) can derive their significance only from the bearer of this name and from His history, and not the reverse . . . . They can serve only to describe this name—the name of Jesus Christ. (pp. 16-17)

Or, as Barth expresses it in the concluding *excursus* to this section:

> The Christian message is service, and the one whom it serves is at all points Jesus Christ Himself. What it says at its heart as the doctrine of the atonement is that He Himself is and lives and rules and acts, very God and very man, and that He is peace and salvation. He Himself is the whole. (p. 20)
>
> It is not, therefore, doing Him a mere courtesy when it names the name of Jesus Christ. It does not use this name as a symbol or sign which has a certain necessity on historical grounds, and a certain purpose on psychological and pedagogical grounds . . . this name is not merely a cipher . . . The peace between God and man and the salvation which comes to us men is not

> something general, but the specific thing itself: that concrete thing which is indicated by the name of Jesus Christ and not by any other name. For He who bears this name is Himself the peace and salvation. The peace and salvation can be known, therefore, only in Him and proclaimed only in His name (p. 21).

These quotations set the scene for Barth's unfolding of the doctrine of reconciliation throughout volume four of the *Church Dogmatics*. In the remainder of this article I shall highlight only a few further passages from this volume—passages which illustrate particular applications of Barth's christological and soteriological concentration.

II. CHRIST AND US

When the reality of achieved salvation is so powerfully presented as determined by God from all eternity and actualized in Jesus Christ, the question must arise of what this message has to do concretely with the ongoing history of the human race and with individual human lives. Barth was well aware of this dimension of the matter and his presentation of the meaning of salvation is characterized by a triple critical boundary: against pietistic individualism; against mystically-tinged ecclesiasticism; against mere dogmatic objectivism. Here too, it is appropriate to let him speak for himself, especially from CD IV/1 and IV/2. First, the individual Christian and the community of the Church:

> [The doctrine of reconciliation] is a matter of Christendom and of Christians, of the community ("Church") of Jesus Christ and of its members (individual Christians in their personal relationship to Jesus Christ). There cannot be the one without the other. The Holy Spirit is not a private spirit, but the power by which the Son of God (*Heidelberger Catechism* § 54) "has from the beginning of the world to the end assembled out of the whole race of man, and preserves and maintains, an elect congregation." But He assembles and preserves and maintains it, not as a pile of grains of sand or as an aggregate of cells, but as a community of those of whom each one can individually recognize and confess by His power "that I am a living member of the same, and will be so for ever.". . . Salvation is ascribed to the individual in the existence of the community, and it is appropriated by the community in the existence of the individuals of which it is composed. In the light of this correspondence it is more fitting to take the question of Christendom before that of the individual Christian.
>
> It was an intolerable truncation of the Christian message when the older Protestantism steered the whole doctrine of the atonement—and with it, ultimately, the whole of theology—into the *cul de sac* of the question of the individual experience of grace, which is always an anxious one when taken in isolation, the question of individual conversion by it [sc. grace] and to it, and of its presuppositions and consequences. The almost inevitable result was that the great concepts of justification and sanctification came more and more to be understood and filled out psychologically and biographically, and the doctrine of the Church seemed to be of value only as a description of the means of salvation and grace indispensable to this individual and personal process of salvation. We will only ask in passing whether and

> to what extent Luther's well-known question in the cloister—which was and will always be useful at its own time and place—contributed if only by way of temptation to this truncation, or whether it is simply an aberration first of [old Prostestant] orthodoxy and of the Pietism which began in it and followed it. What is more to the point is to remember (and this, too, is something we can only mention) that we will do well not to allow ourselves to be crowded again into the same *cul de sac* on the detour via Kierkegaard. (CD IV/1, pp. 149-150)

What Barth has in view here is the individualistic subjectivism which can express itself equally in pietistic, philosophical-existentialist or banal secular forms, as under the motto of "self-expression" or "minority rights," as these have recently became fashionable, more fashionable than Barth could have envisaged. We may well feel that such concerns in the development of a more democratic and more human society deserve more appreciative attention than Barth could give to them. But his warning also deserves to be heeded:

> Our theme is the reconciliation of the world with God in Jesus Christ, and only in this greater context the reconciliation of the individual man. This is what was completely overlooked in that truncation. And if it is to be brought to light again, the prior place which the Christian individual has for so long . . . claimed for himself in the dogmatics of the Christian community must be vacated again. We must not cease to stress the individual. We must not throw doubt on the importance of his problem. But!
>
> Only in the proper place. The "pillar and ground of truth" (I Tim. 3,15), the salt of the earth, the light of the world, the city set on a hill, is the community of God and not the individual Christian as such, although the latter has within it his assured place, his indisputable function, and his unshakable personal promise. It is not he but the *ecclesia una sancta catholica et apostolica* that stands (in close connexion with the Holy Spirit) in the third article of the Creed. . . It is in its existence, therefore—and only in the sphere of its existence in that of individual Christians—that the salvation ascribed to the world is appropriated by man (CD IV/1, p. 150).

These quotations well illustrate Barth's campaign against subjectivist individualism, which he saw—not without reason—as a pervasive influence in modern Protestantism. Against that subjectivism he appealed to the confession of the Creed of Nicea/Constantinople: "We believe one holy, catholic and apostolic Church." But he was equally disinclined to accept or approve of those ecclesiastical institutions which claim to incorporate the one holy, catholic and apostolic Church on earth, whether in Roman Catholic, Eastern Orthodox, Anglican or Lutheran forms. In such ecclesiasticism he diagnosed a form of collective subjectivism differing only in form, not in substance from the individualistic subjectivism of modern Protestantism. This other side of the coin (which in Barth's eyes is less *another* side than the *same* side viewed from the *opposite angle*) is addressed in IV/1, § 63.2 "The Act of Faith."

Having spelt out the nature of faith as a free act of recognition and decision involving the whole person, Barth calls for a halt. "We have come to a point in our discussion which is not entirely free from danger." (p. 767) The danger is that of failing to distinguish between divine and human action, of forgetting that the decision of faith is "a radical but not an eschatological decision" (p.767), that "even at this climax of our exposition of the recognition of faith we are speaking of most important penultimate things, but not of ultimate things" (p.767). This introduces an important *excursus* (pp. 767-769):

> One description of what is involved in the believer's knowledge concerning Jesus Christ and himself is as follows. The real event of faith in Jesus Christ consists in the fact that the event of salvation as it took place in Jesus Christ is made present or reenacted in it. The history of Jesus Christ, His death and resurrection, becomes the history of the believer. . . . If this is a true description, we have been speaking already not merely of the penultimate but of the ultimate things, of the absolute disturbance, of the eschatological decision, of the act of God in itself and as such, as these take place in faith.
>
> There have been many attempts to make the history of Jesus Christ coincident with that of the believer, and *vice versa*. The theology of the younger Luther (up to 1519) was nothing but a powerful move in this direction. But we can approve and make common cause with it neither in its earliest forms nor in that authoritatively represented today by R. Bultmann. The real presentation *(repraesentatio)* of the history of Jesus Christ is that which He Himself accomplishes in the work of His Holy Spirit when He makes Himself the object and origin of faith. Christian faith takes note of this, and clings to it and responds to it, without itself being the thing which accomplishes it, without any identity between the redemptive act of God and faith as the free act of man. . . . What takes place in the recognition of the *pro me* of Christian faith is not the redemptive act of God itself, not the presentation and repetition of Jesus Christ, not the presentation and repetition of His obedience and sacrifice and victory. What is Bultmann's conception but an existentialist translation of the sacramentalist teaching of the Roman Church, according to which, at the climax of the mass, with the transsubstantiation of the elements—in metaphysical identity with what took place then and there there is a "bloodless repetition" of the sacrifice of Christ on Golgatha? Those who regard this doctrine of the mass as basically untenable will find it impossible to make what took place *eph' hapax* in Jesus Christ coincident with what takes place in faith. With the later Luther they will understand faith as a recognition and apprehension (*comprehendere*) of Jesus Christ as the one who dies and rose again for us men and in our place, but they will not confuse it with the dying and rising of Jesus Christ, nor will they confuse the dying and rising again of Jesus Christ with what takes place in faith. Therefore when they speak of what takes place in faith, they will not speak of an absolute disturbance or an eschatological decision or the redemptive act of God.
>
> When I say this I am not looking only at Bultmann (pp. 767-768).

Why not only Bultmann? Barth has in view his friendly Roman Catholic interpreter and critic Hans Urs von Balthasar. After mentioning von Balthasar's studies of Theresa of Lisieux, Elisabeth of Dijon and Reinhold Schneider he goes on to say:

> And if I understand aright their theological content, it seems plain to me that he too (like Bultmann, but with infinitely richer material) sees from that [sc. Christological] centre which he has grasped so finely and clearly a whole field of possible and actual representations of the history of Jesus

> Christ, the repetitions or re-enactments of His being and activity by the saints or by those who achieve some measure of sanctity. And as the author sees and represents them these have taken place and do take place in history *post Christum* and in our own time with such significance, such positive and stimulating force, that the one whose being and activity is supposedly reproduced obviously fades into the background as compared with His saints. I now have an inkling of something which at first I could not understand; what is meant by the "christological constriction" which my expositor and critic urged against me in terms of mild rebuke. But we must bring against him the counter-question, whether in all the spiritual splendour of the saints who are supposed to represent and repeat Him Jesus Christ has not ceased—not in theory but in practice—to be the object and origin of Christian faith. . . . If so, it unfortunately means that this promising new beginning in Roman Catholic theology is in danger of returning to, or it may be has never left, the well-worn track on which the doctrine of justification is absorbed into that of sanctification—understood as the pious work of self-sanctification which man can undertake and accomplish in his own strength. My concern is whether this is perhaps the case. For the doctrine of the sacrifice of the mass, the archetype of the whole idea of representation, is still unshaken. . . . If only we were agreed— and this applies to my neighbour on the left as well as on the right—that the ultimate and the penultimate things, the redemptive act of God and that which passes for our response to it, are not the same. Everything is jeopardized if there is confusion in this respect. (p. 768)

The *excursus* then concludes with a further warning, anticipating the argument in IV/4 Fragment on the nature and meaning of baptism:

> That is the danger which threatens at this point and which we must here avoid. And we must see to it that we do not fall into it again by way of certain theories of baptism which are current even in Protestantism. Faith is the free act of man, and is wonderful enough in relationship to Jesus Christ as its object and origin. It is a recognition and apprehension of His being and activity for man. But it is not the repetition of it. The being and activity of Jesus Christ needs no repetition. It is present and active in its own truth and power (pp. 768-769).

This said, however, the positive relationship between "the being and activity of Jesus Christ" and our human "activity of faith as recognition and decision" still requires to be articulated.

> Faith is the free act of man. If this is secure, we cannot speak too strongly of what takes place in it as the recognition and apprehension of Jesus Christ, as the subjective realization of the *pro me*. . . . The concept which forces itself upon us is that which says neither too much nor too little, the concept of analogy (p. 769).

There is an *analogy*, a *correspondence* between the death and resurrection of Jesus Christ and the path of faithful Christian obedience, which Barth goes on to describe in the final pages of IV/1 in terms of *mortificatio* and *vivificatio* (with strong echoes in particular of Calvin). Dying and rising with Christ and therefore also from him and to him is the *leitmotif* of Christian existence. This rules out the "fantastic notion that I am a kind of second Christ" (p. 769).

> I am not the Lord who became a servant. I am not the Son who in obedience to the Father allowed Himself to be judged as my Judge and the Judge of all men. The glory of God has not been reveled in me as in His resurrection. Far from being a Saviour, I am only a proud man like other men, and as such I have fallen a prey to eternal death and perdition. I can only believe in Him as the One who is also, who is just my Saviour. And I cannot do this in my own reason or strength, but only as He encounters me in the witness of Scripture and the proclamation of His community, only as He awakens me to it by the power of His Holy Spirit. But this faith in Him, this recognition of Jesus Christ, carries with it ineluctably a recognition of myself . . . in which, without even remotely being or becoming like Him, I see myself as the man I am irresistibly determined by Him, unmistakably stamped by Him, clearly set in His light from the depth, the lowest depth, in which I find myself in relation to Him (pp. 769-770).

This analogy and correspondence between Christ and ourselves is drawn out repeatedly in IV/2, where Barth is regularly at pains to emphasize the depth of our involvement as Christian believers in God's act of salvation, in opposition to pure objectivism of the sort which would only affirm the objective, given reality of the being and activity of Jesus Christ, but leave no place for the effective outworking of that being and activity in us, whether as individuals or as members of the Christian community. The Christmas message

> is not just the supernatural indicative that there was then born an exceptional man who was God himself, a creature who was also the Creator who rules over all things, and that this remote fact is our salvation if we today will accept it. Nor is it the supernatural imperative that what took place then can and should be repeated today, God Himself being born in us, or in our soul. What it does tell us is that in the union of God with our human existence of this man, prior to our attitude to it, before we are in any position to accept or reject it, with no need for repetition either in our soul or elsewhere, we today, bearing the same human essence and living at a particular point in time and space were taken up (quite irrespective and even in defiance of our own action and merits) into the fellowship with God for which we were ordained but which we ourselves had broken; and that we are therefore taken up into this fellowship in Him, this One. The Christmas message speaks of what is objectively real for all men, and therefore for each of us, in this One (IV/2, p. 270).

> Being made man among them, He comes to His own possession (John 1.11). Whether they recognise it or not. He is their Head from all eternity. He can be more to them than an example. He can do that which He does actually do in the atonement, representing God to them and them to God. His history can be their own history of salvation. (IV/2, p. 36).

This again raises the question of the relation between the objective, universal truth, valid for all humankind, that the history of Jesus Christ is *the* (and *only*) history of salvation, and the realisation and reflection of *that* history in the obedient response of faith in human life. In terms of classical dogmatic terminology, what is involved here is the relation between *justification* and *sanctification;* it can also be seen as the relation between *dogmatics* and *ethics;* or again in terms of *the work of Christ* and *the work of the Holy Spirit.* All three of these themes are developed by Barth in detail: for example the first in § 66 "The Sanctification of Man" (IV/2, pp. 499-613); the second in § 68 "The Holy Spirit and Christian Love" (IV/2, pp. 727-840); and the third in "Baptism with the Holy Spirit" (IV/4, pp. 3-40). Space does not permit any full summary of his arguments here, but it may be useful to notice some of the points he is concerned to underline.

In § 66.1 "Justification and Sanctification," Barth devotes an *excursus* to critical examination of the idea, prominent in old Protestant dogmatics, of an *ordo salutis* ("way of salvation"). What is meant by this is a series of stages or steps in Christian life which can be distinctly identified and characterized (e.g. calling, conversion, justification, perseverance etc.).

> In its later stages the older Protestant dogmatics tried to understand *iustificatio* and *sanctificatio* as steps in a so-called *ordo salutis,* preceded by a *vocatio* and *illuminatio,* and followed by the separate processes of *regeneratio* and *conversio,* and then (in the Lutherans) by a *unio mystica* and *glorificatio.* For the most part this *ordo salutis* was thought of as a temporal sequence, in which the Holy Spirit does His work here and now in men—the outworking of the reconciliation accomplished there and then on Golgatha. This temporal sequence corresponded only too readily to that of the temporal relationship between the humiliation and exaltation of Christ as it was viewed in the Christology of the older dogmatics. A psychologistic pragmatics in soteriology corresponded to the historicist pragmatics of Christology. . . But if this [reception of the grace of Christ] consists in a series of different steps, how can it better be made apprehensible than as a series of spiritual awakenings and movements and actions and states of a religious and moral type? The greater and more explicit the emphasis on the ordo salutis understood in this way—and this was the tendency in the seventeenth century—the more clearly it was revealed by the uncertainties, contradictions and exegetical and conceptual arbitrariness and artificiality in which those who espoused it were entangled, that they were on the point of leaving the sphere of theology. And the nearer drew the time—the time of the Enlightenment which dawned already with Pietism—in which a religious and moral psychology would take over the leadership and suppress theology, first at this point, and then everywhere (IV/2, p. 502).

The fundamental error, as Barth sees it, was not merely the dissolving of theology into psychology, but the underlying dividing up of God's *act of salvation* into series of *salvific actions.* He quotes an atypical statement by Quenstedt that justification and sanctification occur simultaneously, cohere more closely than in a mathematical point and cannot be divided, then continues:

> This is inevitable if we are really thinking of the act of God as it comes to man in Jesus Christ by the Holy Spirit. If Quenstedt and that whole theology had taken this insight seriously, it would have meant that they could not have understood that *ordo* as a series of different divine actions, but only as the order of different "moments" of the one redemptive occurrence coming to man in the *simul* of the one event. This would perhaps have led to the

> collapse of the historicist pragmatic, and even perhaps of the dualism between an objective achievement of salvation there and then and a subjective appropriation of it here and now, in favour of a recognition of the simultaneity of the one act of salvation whose Subject is the one God by the one Christ through the one Spirit—"more closely united than in a mathematical point." The God who in His humiliation justifies us is also the man who in His exaltation sanctifies us. He is the same there and then as He is here and now. He is the one living Lord in whom all things have occurred, and do and will occur, for all (IV/2, pp. 502-503).

To turn now to § 68, subsection 3 "The Act of Love" deserves special attention for the way in which it deals with the hinge between the first and second commandments of love—love to God and love to the neighbour. Here too Barth speaks of the "history of salvation":

> Christian love has these two dimensions and is thus love for the neighbour. The history of salvation is both a history between God and man and also a history between man and man. It is the second as and because it is the first. That is to say, as and because it is first a history between God and a people . . . the life of this people, the common life of its members, becomes part of the event and itself the history of salvation. . . . As the history of salvation takes place vertically as the act of God's love and the corresponding act of human love for God, it also takes place on the horizontal plane where these men are together reached by the divine act and together engaged in the corresponding act (IV/2, p. 809).

> The first commandment is always the first. But it is a matter of confirming its primacy in the fulfillment of the second commandment. As there can be no above without a below, no before without an after, so there can be no divine revelation without a human history of witness, no history of salvation between God and man without its reflection and repetition in a history between man and man. The one without the other would necessarily prove to be a mere mythology and illusion in the form of a "positivism of revelation." But its reflection and repetition can take place only as the men who are loved by God and love him in return enjoy and make use of the freedom to love one another (IV/2, p. 818).

Finally, in IV/4 Barth directly poses the question of how "the divine change effected in the history of Jesus Christ" can also be "the origin and beginning of the Christian life" responding in faith and free obedience (p. 18).

> What has this Other, who there and then was born in Bethlehem and died on Golgatha, what has He to do with me? What has the freedom of His life as very Son of God and very Son of Man to do with my necessary liberation to be a child of God . . .? How can that which He was and did *extra nos* become an event *in nobis*? (IV/4, p. 18).

Barth observes that "any solution is artificial in which the contrast in the unity between Christ and the man who becomes a Christian is eliminated" (ibid.). This rules out alike "what might be called a christomonist solution" (p.19) and an "anthropomonist view" (p. 19). On the first of these views

> the *in nobis,* the liberation of man himself, is simply an appendage, a mere reflection, of the act of liberation accomplished by Jesus Christ in His history. Jesus Christ, then, is fundamentally alone as the only subject truly at work. The faithfulness of the man who is distinct from Him cannot be an answer to the word of divine faithfulness spoken in His history. It is not man's free action. . . . It is simply a passive participation of man in that which God alone did in Jesus Christ (IV/4, p. 19).

On an anthropomonist view, the situation is merely reversed:

> it is Jesus Christ, and what took place in His history, *extra nos,* which is regarded as a mere predicate and instrument, cipher and symbol, of that which truly and properly took place only *in nobis,* the subject being none other than man himself (IV/4, p.19).
>
> Common to both these obvious but distorted solutions is the fact that they approach the data—that is why they are artificial —from outside and with the aid of an alien concept of unity. They do not allow the matter to be its own interpreter. Hence both of them conjure away the mystery which confronts us in it. But if we conjure away the mystery and imprison it in one or other of the two monistic formulae (or perhaps alternately in both), we falsify the matter itself and let it slip from our gaze. . . . One must accept the first riddle if one is to see how the matter interprets itself, how the riddle is solved from within (IV/4, p. 20).

The "solution of the riddle from within" is offered by Barth in three steps (pp. 20-30). The first step is to'"follow the singular movement of New Testament thinking" (p. 20), which is two-sided. "The matter explains itself, not only from above downwards, but also from below upwards." (p. 21) "From above downwards" we see:

> The history of Jesus Christ is different from all other histories. In its particularity, singularity and uniqueness it cannot be compared or interchanged with any other . . . as the history of the salvation which God in His free grace has ascribed, addressed and granted to all men, it is from the very first a particular story with a universal goal and bias. . . . It is a fruitful history which newly shapes every human life. Having taken place *extra nos,* it also works *in nobis,* introducing a new being of every man. It certainly took place *extra nos.* Yet it took place, not for its own sake, but *pro nobis: qui propter nos homines et salutem nostram descendit de coelis.* This *pro nobis* or *propter nos* is to be taken literally and strictly. As the true Son of God, and hence as the true Son of Man, Jesus Christ was not merely faithful to the faithful God . . . He was also faithful to us as His brethren . . . . (IV/4, pp. 20-21).

That is the dynamic of the matter seen "from above"; but the New Testament witnesses also see it "from below," "always present it also with reference to the Christian. As Jesus Christ takes the place of man, does there what he [sc. man] does not do, and is faithful to God in the stead of the unfaithful, He, or God through Him, liberates man for faithfulness to God on his own part" (p. 22).

> What, then, does it mean for us who are not Jesus Christ that His history,

> which took place *extra nos*, took place *pro nobis*, that this *pro nobis is* efficacious, and that it thus includes the fact that, as it took place then and there, as the history of that One, it also takes place here and now, *in nobis*, in the life of the many? Obviously . . . it means that the God at work in that history, while He does not find and confirm a direct relation between Himself and us, does create and adopt this relation . . . He is now present to us, not at a distance, but in the closest proximity, confronting us in our own being, thought and reflection. . . . The change which God has made is in truth man's liberation. It comes upon him wholly from without, from God, Me-vertheless, it is his liberation. The point is that here, as everywhere, the omnicausality of God must not be construed as His sole causality. The divine change in whose accomplishment a man becomes a Christian is an event of true intercourse between God and man. . . . [Man] is taken seriously as an independent creature of God. He is not run down or overpowered, but set on his own feet. . . . The history of Jesus Christ, then, does not destroy a man's own history. . . . The faithfulness to God to which he is summoned is not, then, an emanation of God's faithfulness. . . . As there must be in this matter no subjectivism from below, so there must be no subjectivism from above. As there must be no anthropomonism, so there must be no christomonism (IV/4, pp. 22-23).

That, then, is the first step towards the "solution of the riddle"—and one which shows how far off the mark those critics of Barth are who accuse him (as so many do) of "christomonism." The second step is one of methodological reflection, taken in a concentrated paragraph on p. 23, which also supplies the transition to the third step. Essentially, this paragraph asks what is the nature of the "event" by which, '"viewed from above," "the history of Jesus Christ becomes once in time the origin and commencement of the reorientation and refashioning of the life of a specific man," and by which, "seen from below," "once in time a specific man" is liberated for the reorientation and refashioning of his life in the history of Jesus Christ as his origin and commencement." We have to do here with what is "truly an event, not a timeless or supratemporal relation. In other words, what the statements describe is a concrete and dynamic, not an abstract and static relation." The question is therefore: what is the event, or: what are the events, which on the one hand establish Jesus Christ in his unique history as the origin of Christian life, and on the other incorporate Christian life in that history of its own salvation?

The third step answers these questions by reference a) to the resurrection of Jesus and, b) to the work of the Holy Spirit.

> To put it first in a single sentence: There is manifested in the resurrection who Jesus Christ was in His history and what He did therein—He who was born for us men at Bethlehem and crucified and put to death for us on Golgatha. In His resurrection, then, His temporal history was not transcended and outmoded by another history. It was not made past history. On the contrary, it herein showed itself in its totality to be, not past and transient history, but history which, because it happened once-for-all, is present to all later times and indeed to all earlier times, cosmically effective and significant history (IV/4, p. 24).

> To put it again in a single sentence: In the work of the Holy Spirit the history manifested to all men in the resurrection of Jesus Christ is manifest and

present to a specific man as his own salvation history. (IV/4, p. 27)

Here this study must break off and come to an end. I hope it may serve to indicate how many-sided Barth's account of the nature and meaning of salvation is, and how his thought combines consistent christocentrism with a thoroughly wakeful eye for human individuality and responsibility. Let me conclude with two final quotations which characteristically sum up the heart of the matter as he invites us to see it.

> What [Christian witness] has to attest is the light which has broken into the world in Jesus Christ, not the darkness into which it falls in order to dispel it. For the same reason its concern cannot be merely with human questions longings and hopes for an expected alteration of the world, but only with that which is already accomplished in Jesus Christ, which is already reality, and which hastens towards its full and definitive manifestation. For the same reason again it cannot be concerned only with abstract doctrines, principles, ideas and ways of salvation. It has to attest the crucified and risen Jesus Christ who in His person is salvation and its self-declaration (IV/3, p. 835).

> [The resurrection of Jesus] has the character of peace. Its origin is the reconciliation of the world with God as it is resolved in God's eternal will and fulfilled in time at Calvary. This reconciliation and therefore this peace are revealed in the resurrection of Jesus Christ from the dead. Their power, therefore, is the power to spread peace; to spread on earth the peace which is resolved in heaven, and which is now concluded on earth. Following the biblical usage, we might just as well call it the power of salvation. But salvation consists in the occurrence of reconciliation, and therefore in a healing; in a healing of the rent, a closing of the mortal wound, from which humanity (and openly or secretly every man) suffers. It consists in the removal of antitheses; the antithesis between God and man; then the antithesis between man and man; and finally the antithesis between man and himself. In this sense salvation means peace (IV/2, p. 314).

BE NOT FAR

A Reflection on the *Lifework* of Jesus Christ

JOHN WEBORG

I. THESIS

This essay in soteriology seeks to remove the conjunction "and" between Jesus Christ's person *and* work, incarnation *and* crucifixion. The term "lifework" is a unit and as such seeks to speak of the "lifework" of Jesus Christ as one phenomenon encompassing his birth, life, death, and resurrection. What took place on Good Friday cannot be separated from Christmas; the cross may be distinct but it is not separate from the cradle; the incarnation includes Jesus' passion, and when seen retrospectively, entails the cross. Because of Jesus' identification and solidarity with humankind he represents and embodies God's project of reconciling the world to Godself and at the same time, represents and embodies the condition of humankind before God. This representation may include substitution, but only because representation is the ground of substitution and may be propitiatory, but only indirectly so since whatever is entailed by propitiation is so because of the incarnation, and because of the incarnation, entails a cross.

The lifework of Jesus is to announce and enact the news that God is not far away. God's name is Immanuel, which means, "God with us."

II. CLASSICAL QUESTION: *CUR DEUS HOMO*?

When Athanasius was confronted with that question, he posed two others. The first was, "What is not fitting for God to do in response to human sin?" The second was, "What is fitting for God to do?"

His responses to the first question were that God could not go back on God's word that the soul that sins should die; that the goodness of God could not let God's creatures be brought to nothing through the deceit of the devil; that death should triumph; that the work of God should finally disappear.[1] By contrast, what was fitting was that God offer Godself as a substitute for all and pay the debt humankind owed; that God recreate the likeness of the image in humankind by reversing the powers of corruption and death; that God destroy the work of Satan, especially death; that immortality be given back to humankind.[2]

All of this grounds Athanasius' statement that repentance itself is not a sufficient means to salvation. The reason is that more than a trespass is involved in sin. Death and corruption are entailed. Hence none other than God who creates can redeem and launch a new creation. *Cur Deus Homo*? Only the one who created out of nothing in the first place can recreate humankind and save humankind from being consumed by nothingness.[3] The self-same Word who created the world is the redeemer of the world.

Anselm found these questions serviceable as well. But the answers are considerably different. Sin means to rob God of God's honor and hold God up to contempt. This means that so long as honor is not restored, humankind remains at fault, adding insult to injury. One needs to offer compensation, not just for what has been robbed, but for the anguish caused when one suffers from contempt.[4] What to do?

It is not fitting to put away sin by compassion alone. To do so is to cancel sin without compensation or punishment and to obliterate the difference between the guilty and not guilty. If injustice is cancelled by compassion alone, it is more free than justice.[5] Neither is it fitting that God should take back sinful people without satisfaction and atonement.[6] It is necessary that something greater has to be restored to God than what was taken because God suffered loss and contempt.[7]

The problem is that human beings who owe both satisfaction for the robbery and merit for the contempt cannot pay this. The only fitting response is the person Jesus Christ who is fully God and fully human. Jesus Christ, the free and perfect human, can offer satisfaction for us whose debt is beyond payment and Jesus Christ, fully God, who never exposed his Father to contempt, also contributes the overage.[8] Thus, as by human beings God suffered loss, so by a human being must the loss be recovered, but since a sinner cannot justify another sinner, the perfect one is needed.[9] That one is Jesus who satisfies all of the requirements of justice and who shows that by his death, justice is not collapsed into compassion thereby making sin of no consequence. In this manner, Anselm argued, the dignity of God and human beings was upheld and order was maintained in the universe so that genuine happiness is more than a false euphoria. Happiness is contingent on justice.

How could this classical grid serve in understanding the question, *Cur Deus Homo*? in feminist theology, to take but one contemporary line of inquiry? Using the work of Ann Carr, I will take it as exemplary, not exhaustive, of the issues involved.

For Carr, sin is characterized as a lack of pride, lack of self-esteem, lack of ambition or personal focus.[10] This is in contrast to sin as understood in male terms as pride, overriding self-esteem, or ambition.[11] By implication at least, sin includes an overriding sense of self-blame for failing to assume responsibility for one's life and to "drift into decision according to familial or societal expectation."[12] Weakness and passivity can be just as destructive of relationships as pride.[13]

What is not fitting is that the passive roles of victim, scapegoat, and subordination be used as descriptions of Jesus in order to engender a passivity of person and immobility of place in human life and service.[14] Further, it is not fitting that Jesus' death be viewed as a necessary act of sacrifice required by God since that destroys the notion of Jesus' free choice of loving service and reinforces the image of passivity and victimiztion.[15] Finally, it is not fitting to construct an ontology that makes maleness intrinsic to the work of the redeemer.[16]

It is fitting to speak of "God's plan," i.e. the "necessity" for a work of salvation if we conceive of it in the sense that God willed that Jesus live a truly human life. In the living of his days, Jesus' life and words, given in freedom and love, led to his death. Human beings, not God, determined Jesus' death. It came to be understood as the *redemptive* event because, as the culmination of Jesus' life, the scandalous character of Jesus' death has also to be reflected upon in light of the resurrection. Hence this Jesus was vindicated and put at the center of Christian proclamation as God's solidarity with all people.[17]

While maleness is not ontologically intrinsic to the work of the redeemer, there may yet be a fittingness to Jesus' maleness. Given the sociology of Jesus' time, Jesus' life and demeanor as a male was subversive to every form of patriarchy known in that period of history.[18] Jesus' work as a servant is a reversal of expected roles, and as Carr says, "It is the man Jesus who enacts the women's role as servant."[19] What makes Jesus a fitting example in Carr's view is the "free agency" Jesus exercised in being a servant, in breaking out of preconceived ways of speaking, doing, and living. And since Jesus fostered free agency in those whom he called to himself—women, lepers, outcasts, and other public sinners—Jesus is also the source of free agency for women today.[20] *Cur Deus Homo*? To establish emancipative solidarity with all who are oppressed by life, and by death, and by vindication in the resurrection, to foster free agency in persons by means of continued emancipative solidarity.[21] God continues to be near.

III. CENTRAL MOTIF: FRIENDSHIP AND FUNDAMENTAL TRUST

In my view, the basic character of sin is the violation of trust, accompanied by estrangement and alienation. The prohibition not to eat of the one tree in the garden was given to inexperienced people. They had no idea of the consequences of human deeds, no notion that sin has cumulative effects, no sense of posterity. God's command was in a way, a revelatory, an informing command. It implied that, if the fruit of that tree was eaten, some major consequence would ensue, but of course, there was no experiential framework by which to know the wisdom of that command. In other words, the prohibition was not meant to be a sheer prohibition or a test of obedience. It had in mind the long haul of history, not the short-term life of two people.

Trust in God's wisdom was violated. A relationship was devastated, not only with God but between the man and woman. Intimacy was replaced by intimidation, freedom by shame, accessibility by hiding, and life turned into a game of "who was the least wrong." Somewhere in Saul Bellow's writing there is a line to the effect that the need for self justification makes geniuses of all of us! Who can break the downward spiral of dehumanization and demoralization? This downward spiral is nothing other than Athanasius' descent into non-being where finally the human being counts for nothing in anyone's eyes: God's, others', and one's own. This is corruptibility with a vengeance. God seeks to reverse it and recreate the person. How?

By friendship. Indirectly, God's friendship is shown in the way God approached the man and woman as they hid from God and each other. God's questions are not direct, intimidating, and embarrassing. "Where are you?" God asks. It is an invitation to conversation. No "Yes" or "No" answer will work. The invitation to converse *intimates* that God will listen. But to *know* that, one must trust and act on the intimation (Gen. 3:9). The next question is also indirect: "Who told you that you were naked?" (Gen 3:11). Only the final question is direct: "Have you eaten of the tree I commanded you not to eat?" (Gen 3:11). Friends know how to converse, how to evoke trust. This can be true even in the case of a heinous crime. God's first question to Cain, "Why are you angry and why is your countenance fallen?" is meant to intercept and reverse Cain's downward spiral into the intolerable situation of plotting the murder of his brother (Gen 4:5). Even after the murder, the first question is indirect, namely, "Where is Abel your brother?" (Gen 4:9). Only the final question is direct: "What have you done?" (Gen 4:10). This is the astounding pattern of friendship-making between God and the persons who have broken trust. A basis for trust resides only in friendship, even with sinners and enemies. God tries to makes friends, and is not far off.

The explicit Old Testament instance of divine friendshipmaking is in reference to Abraham. "But you, Israel my servant, Jacob whom I have chosen, the offspring of Abraham, my friend . . . ." (Isa 41:8). Israel, in the words of 2 Chron 20:7, understood itself as the descendants of Abraham, God's friend. In James 2:23, Abraham's friendship with God is rooted in the declaration of his righteousness by God and received in faith. The point, I take it in all of this, is that Abraham became God's friend at God's initiative. God makes friends, as the poignant intimacy of God's conversation with Moses also shows (Exod 33:11). Friends speak face to face.

The New Testament explodes with a new sense of divine friendship as this is shown in the life and ministry of Jesus Christ. Moltmann says that what Jesus does is to break the "peer and parity principle" and to make friends with those who are most unlike him.[22] This results in Jesus' "open friendship,"[23] making friendship the concrete concept of freedom.[24] Moltmann's critique of the "exalted titles" of Christ, as he calls them, is that they do not express what Christ does for people, especially that of bringing all sorts and conditions of persons into fellowship with God through himself by means of meals, home visits, and by being called the friend of publicans and sinners (Luke 7:35).[25] The exalted titles of Jesus fail to account for Jesus' public and personal ministry of friendship-making. This is a key thought for Moltmann because, as he points out, in Old High German, "friend" and "enemy" were public and political terms, not private terms regarding one's personal relations. The implication is that Jesus' friendship with sinners was a public, political act because he crossed boundaries between Jews and Samaritans, Jews and Romans, and between the several distinctions among Jews themselves, e.g. with lepers and tax collectors.[26] Friendship can be a costly form of identification with those on the margins of life. Sometimes implicitly, sometimes explicitly, the political character of friendship comes out.

There is also a subtle side to Jesus' friendship-making and in this, Jesus replicates the *indirectness* of God's effort at building trust. In Mark 2 there is a description of Jesus healing the paralytic whose sins Jesus had also forgiven. When the Pharisees objected, Jesus asked, "Why do you question thus within your hearts?" On the night of the betrayal Jesus asked, "Judas, would you betray the Son of Man with a kiss?" (Luke 22:48). To the man paralyzed for thirty-eight years, Jesus asked, "Do you want to be healed?" (John 5:6). To Peter, after the resurrection and with vivid memories of the denial on his mind, Jesus asked three times, "Do you love me?" (John 21:15-19). When the disciples asked if they could sit, one on Jesus' right and one on Jesus' left in the glory to come, Jesus asked, "Are you able to drink the cup I drink, or to be baptized with the baptism with which I am baptized?" (Mk 10:35-40). Like the God whom Jesus called Father, Jesus built trust in the same way: he initiated conversation and identified with the people with whom he conversed. The weakness of people was never exploited, the concern of people was never trivialized, the need of people was never minimized. Questions are an invitation to conversation with the One who is not far.

According to Sallie McFague, it is precisely because friendship is a freely chosen relation that mutual trust and loyalty are at its center. Thus the paradoxical union of freedom and bonding gives friendship its distinctive character and when trust is violated, it is the profoundest kind of betrayal. Because friendship is a freely chosen relation, it has, says McFague, the capacity to be the most inclusive. This destroys the elitist and exclusive character of the "peer and parity" qualities noted by Moltmann. Finally, says McFague, friendship requires the maturity associated with adulthood to be enduring and true to form. This is because mutuality and reciprocity are at the heart of friendship so that, while there is a sense of responsibility for one another, there is to be no type of neurotic dependency on the one hand, and a domineering demeanor on the other.[27] Friendship is a free and freeing act.

I have used the term "fundamental trust," a term I owe to Hans Küng and David Tracy. "Fundamental trust is a task,"[28] says Kung because "apart from taking the risk of an encounter in trust, there is no knowledge of the ultimate trustworthiness of the other person. But the encounter in trust changes the image of the other person and the image of the world."[29] Since trust has the enormous power to open a person out,[30] it is understood as a gift which enables the task of trusting and opening to another.[31] It is precisely at this point that Tracy is most helpful because it could be argued that to refer to God and to Jesus Christ as friends sentimentalizes them and robs them of their transcendent character. While that can be a danger, Tracy points out that friendship entails a dialectical understanding of itself. True friendship requires critique and suspicion, if rightly understood. Such a healthy suspicion is not a neurotic, perpetual "taking of the pulse of the relationship" but rather is the kind that when it suspects a friend is anxious, is tending to go back on a commitment, is withdrawing into some kind of isolation, can inquire whether or not such processes are going on.[32]

That is precisely what happens when the Jesus of the Gospels asks questions of us. However destabilizing the questions may be, however dangerous the memories of Jesus are, they are meant to liberate us to trust Jesus completely because Jesus' friendship with us is not vulnerable to compromise and expediency.[33] Friendship and fundamental trust imply each other and are at the heart of the gospel. After all, salvation is by grace through faith so that by grace, mediated by the divine friendship, the faith that is required for salvation is made available. The gospel is that God in Christ makes God trustable, for God is not far off. In Christ, God drew near. What does that mean?

IV. EXEGETICAL MOTIF: THE INTERCHANGE IN CHRIST

Acknowledging my indebtedness to James Dunn,[34] C. F. D. Moule, [35] D. E. H. Whiteley,[36] and Morna Hooker,[37] among others, I will cite briefly the work of Ms. Hooker as providing a suggestive case for a representative view of the atonement, based on the interchange that takes place in Christ, that does not drive a wedge between Jesus' person and work and the incarnation and crucifixion. Irenaeus furnishes her a well-known thesis: "He (Jesus) became like us so that we might become like him."

In Phil 2:5-11 one finds a classic incarnational text. Incarnation (made in human likeness) and crucifixion are together. So far, it pertains to Jesus alone. But in 3:17-21, the human participation in Jesus is taken up, especially the change into the likeness of Jesus, and so the interchange. The reason for Jesus' likeness to us is so that we might become like him. In fact, in 3:21, the major words of 2:5-11 dealing with the form and humility of Christ are virtually repeated, this time in relation to humankind, showing that our lowly bodies will be made like Jesus' glorious body, effected through Christ's humiliation.

In Romans 8 there is the mysterious assertion that "God . . . sending his own Son in the likeness of sinful flesh and for sin. . . condemned sin in the flesh in order that the righteous decree of the law might be fulfilled in us who walk not according to the flesh but according to the Spirit" (vss 3-4). After vs. 14 we are told that we have the Spirit by means of adoption whereby we can cry "Abba," and that if we can call God Father, then we are children of God, heirs of God, and will share in the glory of Christ (vss 16-18), thus constituting an interchange.

The parallel between this text and Gal 4:4-7 is unmistakable. There Paul teaches that Christ was born of a woman, born under the law that we might receive adoption as children of God and receive God's Spirit with the result that we are no longer slaves but heirs. By implication, is it not the case that Jesus became as a slave so that we might become heirs?

In fact, this text may throw light on another. It has already been noted that in Rom 8:3 Paul avers that Jesus was made in the likeness of sinful flesh, although he was not made a sinner. Ms. Hooker proposes that 2 Cor 5:21 be read in a similar way. Jesus was made sin so that in him we might become the righteousness of God. Her proposal is that, read in the light of Rom 8:3, 2 Cor 5:21 might also refer to the incarnation and not just to the crucifixion.

Viewed this way, might not Gal 3:13 ("Christ redeemed us from the curse of the law having become a curse for us—for it is written, 'cursed be everyone who hangs on a tree' ") be read similarly? While Lightfoot[38] and Duncan[39] take pains to point out that Paul does not say that Jesus was accursed, Ridderbos, stressing the penal character, does and calls it a "personal judgement of God."[40] Hans Dieter Betz attempts no explanation[41] but Bruce does. He notes that Paul omits "by God" after "cursed" since such a view would "conflict with his conviction that Christ's enduring of the cross was a supreme act of obedience (Rom 5:19) and that in Christ God was reconciling the world to himself."

Bruce then notes that Paul's initial hostility to Christians was rooted in the identification they made between the crucified Jesus and the Messiah. To call the cursed one, since he had hung on a tree, the Messiah, was blasphemous. What Paul came to see was that Christ had endured the curse on his people's behalf in order to redeem them from the curse pronounced on those who failed to keep the law.[42] The reason I suggest that Gal 3:13 might be read similarly to 2 Cor 5:21 is that according to Gal 3:10 anyone is cursed who does not keep the law, thereby hinting perhaps that being under the curse is inclusive of more than hanging on a tree. Jesus had been identified as a law breaker during his ministry and identified freely with those who were. In this way the curse of the lawbreakers became his so that, as Gal 3:14 teaches, the blessing of Abraham might come to the Gentiles and that we might receive the promise of the Spirit, the same "in order that" phrase that occurs in Gal 4:4-7. Hence Jesus has identified with Jews and Gentiles alike since both are obligated to keep the law (Rom 2:12-16) and both are offered the benefits of Jesus having borne the curse that belongs to any who do not keep the law. While other texts such as 2 Cor 8:9, Romans 5, and 1 Thess 5:10 could be explored, what has been done is sufficient to indicate a line of thought.

Can such an exchange be found in the Gospels? Perhaps not in the structural sense that appears in Paul but narratively, I think so. Luke, for example, early in his Gospel records the angel's address to Mary: "The Lord is with you." This address, rather than the subjunctive, "The Lord be with you," is noted by Brown[43] and Fitzmeyer[44] to mean a declaration of divine assistance. The Gospel comes to a near climax in the words of Jesus to the penitent thief: "Today, you should be with me in Paradise." It is the only time in the "Amen" sayings in Luke the "you" is in the singular,[45] making the sayings to the thief as direct a declaration as was made to Mary. Robert Karris calls this text "the Gospel within the Gospel" and says that it epitomizes Luke's soteriology of "withness,"[46] namely that Jesus is with people in order to be for them. But what is striking to me is what I suggested at the beginning of this paragraph, namely, that narratively, an exchange does take place. In the beginning, the Lord is with Mary; in the end a thief is with Jesus. The Lord is with humankind in order that humankind might be with the Lord. Luke's narratives are full of surprises. The mighty who are cast down from positions of power (1:52) are prayed for by Jesus on the cross, when he said, "Father forgive them for they know not what they do" (23: 34).[47] Jesus the righteous one is called a friend of gluttons and drunkards (7: 34), which in Deut 21:18-21 is virtually proverbial for being an apostate.[48] A Samaritan comes to the aid of a Jew, transcending years of institutionalized and theologically legitimated prejudice. An interchange and reversal of another sort often happens at meals where Jesus was a guest. John Koenig points out that in the pericope 7: 35-50, where Jesus is the guest of Simon the Pharisee, there is a shift and Jesus becomes the host of both Simon and the sinful woman who has intruded and anointed Jesus' feet. What is remarkable is that such unlikely people are "guests" simultaneously and almost before they realize what was taking place. This is the surprise of the kingdom. Koenig points out that similar role reversals are found in 5:29-39; 10: 38-42; 11:27-28; 14:1-24; 19:127; 24:13-35. All but the first passage are unique to Luke. [49] Within the confines of this interchange an entirely new configuration of relating takes place.

These narratives provide cogency to Karris' contention that the episode of the conversion of the thief on the cross is the gospel within the Gospel. At that moment, Marshall says, "Jesus acts as the Messiah who has the kingly right to open the doors of paradise to those who come into fellowship with him."[50] But implicitly, Jesus' table contact with people showed his kingly right to admit all sorts and conditions of people to the messianic feast without regard for "peer and parity." Those acts of open friendship, portrayed as one narrative, are the interchange in which Jesus came to be with us that we might be with him. This was his lifework. He was not far from any who called upon him, and he called upon them to come near.

The biblical material cited above makes it plausible for me to suggest that incarnation and atonement and the person and work of Jesus cannot be separated. Jesus is a lifework. Jesus bore crosses before the cross and his passion lasted longer than six hours. Heb 5:7 says that "In the days of his flesh, Jesus offered up prayers and supplications, with loud cries and tears, to him who was able to save him from death, and was heard for his godly fear," and no doubt pertains to more than the suffering Jesus endured in Gethsemane, as F. F. Bruce has shown. Bruce refers especially to the influence of Psalm 22, which in Heb 2:12, has application to the entire life of Jesus. While Gethsemane may be a telling episode of Jesus' intense suffering and prayer, it is not the exclusive referent of this text. The intensity may not have been the same, yet the temptation in the wilderness at the beginning of Jesus' ministry was likewise a fierce encounter with the temptation to resort to miraculous deliverance just as Jesus could have had such recourse in Gethsemane.[51]

Given good ground then for saying that the incarnation and life of ministry was part of the passion, I think we can literalize the Kähler statement to the point of absurdity: the Gospels are passion stories with long introductions.[52] This will be so until the introductions cease being introductions and become the story. I would argue further that such sentiment has produced the situation Edward Dowey, Jr. lamented in his commentary on the Confession of 1967 of the Presbyterian Church, U.S.A., namely, that the Jesus of the ministry has received little or no hospitality among creed writers.[53] The leap from Christmas Day to Good Friday gives one pause to wonder what the connection is between the people among whom Jesus was born and the people for whom he died, an issue that Anselm seems to bring in only at the end of *Cur Deus Homo*.[54] I turn now to the constructive task of giving my own response to the question, *Cur Deus Homo?*, particularly so that the interchange which took place in Jesus (He became like us so that we might become like him) can be the basis for understanding Jesus as our representative.

V. CONSTRUCTIVE MOTIF: REPRESENTATION

The idea of representation needs to be nuanced if it is to be of service to my agrument.[55] The political idea of an elected representative is of little help since saviors are seldom elected to office. The idea of a legal representative comes closer to being of help, especially in the role of advocacy, but it is only so if it is shorn of business agreements of salary for services rendered.

Lech Walesa is also a type of a representative. This kind of representative emerges in a movement as he or she has the courage of conviction and love of people to the point where he or she, as one of the people, steps forth to speak for the people, to represent the people in such a fashion as to become a virtual substitute.

On the grounds of solidarity and mutual identification, i.e. an interchange, an *inclusive substitution* occurs.[56] In many such cases, tyrannical governments think that if they can kill the symbol, i.e., the representative, they can kill the movement. Conceived of in this way, the substitution is grounded in and contingent upon, the representation embodied in such a figure. In some fashion, tyrannical governments treat such persons as virtually interchangeable with the movement they represent.

This phenomenon is not limited to political and social movements. Elie Wiesel writes, speaking particularly of life in concentration camps or of other severely suppressed conditions, "Even if only one free individual is left he will be proof that the dictator is powerless against freedom. But a free man is never alone; the dictator is alone. The free man is one who, even in prison, gives to the other persons their thirst for, and memory of, freedom."[57] Interestingly, in 1988 when Wiesel met Walesa at Auschwitz, he said to him, speaking of his lifework in Poland, "You will remain here as our representative and we shall be yours all over the world . . . ."[58] Some form of interchange is presupposed in Wiesel's telling comment, "You will remain here as our representative and we shall be yours . . . . "

In the same vein, Irina Ratuskinskaya, who, as a releasee from a Russian Gulag, served as a poetess in residence at Northwestern University, wrote, "It is the condition of every totalitarian system to, first of all, kill independent people who are able to speak for all the people . . . . When people lose their fear and begin to speak honestly it is the beginning of the end" (of the totalitarian system).[59] The pattern of *one* more or less free or "independent" person, who steps forth as a representative, is no longer one. He or she is now "the many," who at the same time remains "the one," yet not as a solitary but as an "inclusive substitute."

In the lifework of these three persons, a twofold process was set in motion. On the one hand, all of their compatriots had a spokesperson, a symbol, a representative of their hopes, fears, and bondage, and, on the other, because the representative, the inclusive substitute, now had become a bit "larger than life," or more powerful than the government had realized, the respective representatives embodied a new force, a transcendent power of some kind that could keep faith, hope, and love alive. In the representative and inclusive substitute, something came from the people and something came to the people. What came from the people in terms of despair, lack of will, and loss of nerve was exchanged via the representative and inclusive substitute for hope, renewed determination, and courage. The three persons whose lifework I have highlighted *freely* took up this vocation, no doubt without really knowing where it would lead. In this freely chosen lifework, they resemble the more or less charismatic prophets of whom perhaps Luke writes, who arise for a season, who are often unlikely prospects for such a vocation, but who are graced with an inner person capable of enduring loneliness, having great capacities to bear the pain of others, and whose courage allows them to articulate the conceptualized diagnoses they have made of the times in which they live.[60]

Walter Kasper of Tübingen has argued that the freedom of the many presupposes the freedom of one, and the freedom of one is the necessary condition for the freedom of the many. When one person exercises his or her freedom in becoming a representative and then an inclusive substitute, the freedom for the many that he or she embodies, is, in many of these cases, only so eschatologically. The iron gates do not fall immediately. Oppressors are not easily and quickly transformed. But in a sense, *in principle,* when one of these representatives, at great personal cost, becomes larger than life, the possibility of change is suggested. What the representative does, in effect is, in the face of incredible odds, power, and cruelty, to create, however haltingly and minisculely, the possibility for an order of, and zone for, freedom.[61] Thus, in the freedom of the one, the representative, the inclusive substitute, the others see and know their own freedom, even if only proleptically.

Jesus of Nazareth lived in solidarity with human beings. By an act of the Holy Spirit he was incarnate of the Virgin Mary and made a human being with us. But that did not obviate the fact that Jesus had to choose not to be far away from those who had need of a friend, of a spokesperson, and of one who could deal with them as persons made after the image and likeness of God. Jesus' open friendship and violation of the "peer and parity principle" brought him into solidarity with companions who, ironically, would be his downfall. Jesus' friendships were fatal to himself but lifegiving to his friends. How else is there to build fundamental trust, to open people out, as Küng said, in order to take up the task of trusting, and therefore become more open.

The incarnation is divine identification and solidarity with humankind in the profoundest way possible. When the "word was made flesh," Jesus the word became part of that humankind that God had consigned to disobedience, in order that God might have mercy on all (Rom 11:32; Gal 3:22). He was "born in the likeness of sinful flesh," "made sin for us who knew no sin," and "was made a curse for us." To be in solidarity with humankind meant also to live under and with the conditions of human existence, which, according to Rom 1:18-23, means to live in circumstances that are under the wrath of God. The consequences of human sin were not intercepted by God and nullified nor were they winked at. The lack of trust that spawned sin in the first place was now compounded and seemed beyond any kind of arrest. "God gave them up . . . . " So it became Jesus' lifework to put an end to this downward spiral and to recreate an order and zone of trust and freedom by means of solidarity and friendship.

When God gave Jesus *to* the world Jesus gave himself *for* the world. The Incarnation is foundational to a representation that emerges in the course of ministry so that when it is "expedient for one to die for the sake of the nation," the substitution that takes place does so because the solidarity and identification implicit in the incarnation becomes explicit in the way Jesus became the representative of the people. Jesus is "interchangeable" with all "those people." On the one hand, he is a solitary figure; on the other hand, he is the inclusive substitute for all of those whom he represents and with whom he is in solidarity. Jesus is no longer the one but the many. After all, he was made in their likeness so that through him they might be like him and share his relation to God. The freedom of the one, Jesus of Nazareth, is the precondition for the freedom of the many and the freedom of the many presupposes the freedom of the one. Jesus came from those for whom he lived and died, in some respects like the charismatic prophets whose origins and authority were mysterious and suspect, but whose freedom to be for others was so threatening that it could not be tolerated. The cross is the culmination of Jesus' ministry, a distinct form of suffering, but not separate from his lifework of being the representative and therefore eventually the inclusive substitute for the people whom he loved.

Krister Stendahl has remarked that the longer he lives, the more he likes plurals![62] While that can be a haven for sloppy thinking, it can also point to the mystery of something that is better described than defined. I think that pertains to the *hilastērios* family of words, cognates, and meanings. Raymond Brown,[63] Donald Guthrie,[64] I. Howard Marshall,[65] and C. K. Barrett, to name but a few, form a consensus on the point that this family of words entails both propitiation and expiation. While Barrett favors the meaning of expiation, he writes that it has "the effect of propitiation: the sin that might justly have excited God's wrath is expiated (at God's will), and therefore no longer does so."[66]

This language suggests that God must act toward sinners and sin in such as way as to be self-consistent. In such texts as Rom 3:25; 8:28-39;1 John 2:1-4; 4:7-12; Heb 2:10-11; and 2 Cor 5:18-21, God is the subject of what happens in Christ and yet perhaps an object as well. But I would argue that God is the object only as a result of what God does as the subject of the work accomplished in Christ and therefore only indirectly the object. Using an illustration, let us say that a parent punishes a child by sending the child to his/her room, as was promised if the child did not obey. As Athanasius and Anselm said, one cannot go back on one's own word without negatively affecting the credibility of one's word. To relent is not only to be inconsistent, it is to minimize the seriousness of the act. Discipline and punishment are epistemological: they reveal the gravity of a deed. The parent can spend the night with the child, thereby remaining consistent, acknowledging the seriousness of the deed, and yet be *for* the child. In this way the parent is both the subject and object of his/her action. The parent is not far.

To acknowledge the wrath of God is not to posit rage or hatred but it is to say that the opposite of love is not hate but indifference. The act of atonement preserves God's integrity, permits identification with sinners, and portrays the grievous end of sin and God's judgment on it: death. At the incarnation Jesus came under the wrath of God by becoming part of humankind which had to live with and under God's wrath. Hence he bore wrath more indirectly than directly, but foundationally, not because of the cross but because of the incarnation. While the cross was the climax of Jesus' lifework it should not be used to subvert the suffering, wrath, and pain of love he knew as one of us. Nor should one overlook the pain of God in Jesus' death, for God is the subject-object of this act minus the conjunction "and" as in "subject and object," thereby implying a split. It is fitting that love and justice intertwine; that righteousness and peace kiss; that neither wrath nor mercy cancel each other; that grace and truth serve each other, but at terrible cost, to both God and Jesus, for they are neither far from each other nor from us.

VI. *CUR DEUS HOMO*? TO OVERCOME HISTORY WITH HISTORY

Grace is an event. I was made aware of a family whose child had been murdered. In the midst of a long and painful process of grieving they were given the grace and courage to ask about their responsibility to the murderer. It was a question formed and informed by a long association with scripture, knowledge of Christ, and church teaching. The claims of all of these on their lives had moved from the diffuse level of consciousness to a definite matter of conscience. While not knowing the rest of the narrative I am moved by the grace to entertain the question and to be open to such a monumental claim on one's life. To follow the claim leads to the inevitable encounter between victims and victimizer and the possibility of the nearly unheard of opportunity for some kind of reconciliation. But let it be noted that such an opportunity is created by those who have suffered dearly yet acted freely.

At the concentration camp in Ravensbruck, 92,000 women and children died. Near the body of a dead child, written on a scrap of paper, a prayer was found, but without a name. This graced person prayed:

> O Lord,
> remember not only men and women of goodwill, but also of ill will. But do not only remember the suffering they have inflicted on us, remember the fruits we brought thanks to this suffering—our comradeship, our loyalty, our humility, the courage, the generosity, the greatness of heart which has grown out of all of this. And when they come to judgement let the fruits that we have borne be their forgiveness. AMEN. AMEN. AMEN.[67]

These narratives land us in the middle of a daring question posed by Nicholas Berdyaev. According to Robert McAfee Brown Berdyaev once noted that while we have God's question to the killer, "Cain, Cain, where is your brother Abel?" (Gen 4:9), human morality begins with another question. This one fits the narrative of the parents and the prayer at Ravensbruck: "Abel, Abel, where is your brother Cain?"[68]

For one such as myself—privileged, educated, never having been a refugee, never having been a victim—to comment on such a question appears irreverent. Yet the very actions of these persons and the attitude of the prayer invite one into the mystery of suffering, the just for the unjust, that reconciliation of some sort might stand a chance. The creation of such a possibility, initiated by victims, is part of the mystery of atonement, rooted in a human solidarity that has the capacity to transcend but not negate pain, grievance, hostility, maybe even hate, fear, prejudice, and whatever else there is that ruptures the human community. This is the care and the courage of the question, "Abel, Abel, where is your brother Cain?"

"Fundamental trust" cannot be developed except by such vulnerabilities. Gestures of grace, a reaching out, make grace an event. But what characterizes grace is its freedom, a kind of absolute freedom. It has the structure of an "uncaused cause," if I may use Aristotelian language. Whereas acts of prejudice, crime, deceit, gossip, abuse, injury, intimidation, caricature, stereotype, and whatever else, tend to generate a response in kind, namely revenge, a getting even, and reciprocal threats, grace breaks that very cycle. The response of grace is not in kind but is the total opposite of these destructive acts. In fact, grace is out of character, and on the surface at least, unrelated to the issues it seeks to address and redress. Epistemologically, it defies understanding. It is novel.

The novelty is the freedom to be for Cain. As to its source, it is inexplicable to me. But it is the freedom of the victims to be for the victimizer that is the precondition of the latter's freedom. Their freedom presupposes the freedom for the victimizer, as is true in the case of the parents of the murdered child as well. The interchange takes place when the victims consider the pain of the victimizer worse than their own and in effect, by grace, change places. One cannot really describe how fundamental trust can be built to the point that the victimizer, who in the torment of unworthiness, could receive such grace and let the reality of such an interchange obtain. For such interchanges are not automatic and involuntary.[69] Neither do the parties share equally. While they do "change places," the giver gives up everything and the receiver receives all of it, gratis, yet the giver is not empty. Fundamental trust, built by open friendship, can lead to personal reception of such grace and thus by faith, let the giver be what he or she in their freedom want to be, namely a redeemer. Jacob Handel's (1550-1591) *O Admirabile Commercium* sings it this way:

> O wondrous exchange! The Creator of mankind
> Taking a living body is worthy to be born of a Virgin;
> Issuing forth as a man unbegotten. He has bestowed on us
> his Godhead.

Whatever it is that overcomes sin must be an event not only of superior power but also that which is sin's opposite. It must have the capacity to engender a trajectory of power that not only counters but conquers sin. The event of sin is overcome by the event of grace which is the theological version of overcoming history with history. The writer to the Hebrews says that "Christ has appeared once for all at the end of the ages to do away with sin by the sacrifice of himself" (9:26). It is not obvious that sin has ended. But sin has found its end in Jesus Christ, for he does not return sin for sin thus intensifying the downward spiral of sin. Jesus' freedom in this regard is his freedom to be for us, victim for the victimizer, counting our pain worse than his and thus offers to change places. By putting an end to sin—literally it stopped with Jesus—atonement has been accomplished. By raising Jesus from the dead, the life of the one "made sin for us," the one "having become a curse for us," God vindicated him as the one in and through whom sin and death find their end. Jesus' end is our beginning. O admirable exchange!

Cur Deus Homo? The fitting way is to overcome history with history, to conquer sin by grace, and death by dying and being raised. The incarnation was an event of God's friendship and solidarity with sinners.[70] In the freedom of open friendship, God seeks to establish the ground for fundamental trust out of which and in the framework of which, saving faith can emerge. In this act of enfleshment, God came under God's own sentence, so to speak, thereby keeping faith with truth while at the same time being truly faithful to God's creation. God was not far. The lifework of Jesus was meant to show that. And that is the lifework of Christians, who are to be "little Christs."[71]

NOTES

1. St. Athanasius, *On The Incarnation,* trans. A. Religious of C.S.M.V., 2d., rev. ed. (Crestwood: St. Vladimir's Orthodox Theological Seminary, 1954) 2.6-7.

2. Ibid. 2.7; 4.20; 4.25-5.27.

3. Ibid. 2.7.

4. St. Anselm, *Basic Writing,* trans. 5. W. Deane , 2d. ed. (La Salle: Open Court , 1962), *Cur Deus Homo*? 1.11.

5. Ibid. 1:12 and 24.

6. Ibid. 19.

7. Ibid. 1.21.

8. Ibid. 2.7-8.

9. Ibid. 1.23.

10. A. Carr, *Transforming Grace* (San Francisco, et al.: Harper and Row, 1988) 58. See V. Saiving, "The Human Situation: A Feminist View" in *Womanspirit Rising,* ed. by C. P. Christ and J. Plaskow (San Francisco, et al.: Harper and Row , 1979) 25-42.

11. Ibid. 58, 119.

12. Ibid. 129.

13. Ibid. 186.

14. Ibid. 163, 174.

15. Ibid. 174.

16. Ibid. 187.

17. Ibid. 188.

18. Ibid. 187. At this point Carr cites the work of J. O'Connor, "Feminism and Christology," *News Letter of the Currents in Contemporary Christology Group of the AAR* (Fall, 1986), 14.

19. Ibid. 175.

20. Ibid. 58, 176, 186.

21. Ibid. 188. See also J. Sobrino, *Christology at the Crossroads,* trans. John Drury (Mary Knoll: Orbis Books, 1978) 201-235.

22. J. Moltmann, *The Passion For Life,* trans. M. D. Meeks (Philadelphia: Fortress , 1978) 58-61 and *The Church In the Power of the Spirit*, trans. by Margaret Kohl (New York et al.: Harper and Row Publishers, 1977) 120.

23. Moltmann, *Passion* , the title of chapter 4.

24. Ibid. 52 and with obvious use of Hegel.

25. Ibid. 55 and *The Church* , 114-115.

26. Moltmann, *The Passion* , 61.

27. S. McFague, *Models of God* (Philadelphia: Fortress , 1987) 162-167.

28. H. Küng, *Does God Exist?*, trans. by E. Quinn (Garden City: Doubleday, 1980) 453.

29. Ibid. 459.

30. Ibid. 457 and David Tracy, *The Analogical Imagination* (New York: Crossroad, 1981) 430.

31. Küng, *Does God Exist?*, 451 and Tracy, *Imagination*, 432.

32. D. Tracy, *Plurality and Ambiguity* (San Francisco: Harper and Row , 1987) 112. While I have cited but one page, the entire work is most relevant since it deals with the hermeneutics of conversation.

33. Tracy, *Imagination*, 330.

34. J. D. G. Dunn, "Paul's Understanding of the Death of Jesus" in *Reconciliation and Hope,* ed. by R. Banks (Grand Rapids: Eerdmans, 1974) chapter 8.

35. C. F. D. Moule, *The Origin of Christology* (Cambridge, et al.: Cambridge University Press, 1977) chapter 4.

36. D. E. H. Whiteley, "St. Paul's Thought on The Atonement," *Journal of Theological Studies* 8 (1957) 240-255.

37. What follows is based on three works by Ms. Hooker, namely, "Interchange and Atonement," *Bulletin of the John Rylands Library* 60 (1977-78) 462-481; "Interchange and Suffering," in *Suffering and Martyrdom in The New Testament,* ed. by W. Horbury and B. McNeil (Cambridge: Cambridge University Press, 1983) 70-83; and "Interchange In Christ," *Journal of Theological Studies* 22 (1971) 349-361. My summary uses the last citation most directly.

38. J. B. Lightfoot, *The Epistle of St. Paul to the Galatians,* 3d reprint ed. (Grand Rapids: Zondervan, 1962) 140.

39. G. S. Duncan, *Galatians,* Moffatt Commentary Series (New York: Harper and Row, n.d.) 100.

40. H. Ridderbos, *The Epistle of Paul to the Churches of Galatia,* NICNT (Grand Rapids: Eerdmans, 1956) 127-128.

41. H. D. Betz, *Galatians,* Hermeneia (Philadelphia: Fortress,1979) 150-151.

42. F. F. Bruce, *The Epistle to the Galatians,* NICNT (Grand Rapids: Eerdmans, 1982) 164-167.

43. R. Brown, S. S., *The Birth of the Messiah* (Garden City: Doubleday , 1977) 288.

44. J. Fitzmeyer, S. J., *The Gospel According to Luke,* I-IX, AB (Garden City: Doubleday, 1981) 346.

45. J. Fitzmeyer, S. J., *The Gospel According to Luke,* X-XXIV, AB (Garden City: Doubleday, 1985) 1510 and for further reference, J. C. O'Neill, "The Six Amen Sayings In Luke," *The Journal of Theological Studies,*10 *(1970) 1-9.*

46. R. J. Karris, *Luke: Artist and Theologian,* Theological Inquiries (New York, et al: Paulist Press, 1985) 121.

47. Ibid, 6.

48. Ibid. 57-60.

49. J. Koenig, *New Testament Hospitality,* Overtures to Biblical Theology (Philadelphia: Fortress , 1985) 90-91.

50. I. H. Marshall, T*he Gospel of Luke,* NIGNT (Grand Rapids: Eerdmans, 1978) 865.

51. F. F. Bruce, *The Epistle to the Hebrews,* NICNT (Grand Rapids: William B. Eerdmans, 1964) 97-102.

52. M. Kähler, *The So-Called Historical Jesus and the Historic Biblical Christ,* (Philadelphia: Fortress Press, 1964) 24.

53. E. A. Dowey, Jr., *A Commentary on the Book of Confessions* and an *Introduction to the Book of Confessions* (Philadelphia: Westminster, 1968) 43.

54. *Cur Deus Homo,* 2.19.

55. Some exponents of a representative view of the atonement are C. Braaten, *The Future of God* (NewYork, et al.: Harper and Row Publishers, 1969) chapter 3 and "The Christian Doctrine of Salvation," *Interpretation,* 35 (1981) 125-126; Soelle, *Christ the Representative,* trans. D. Lewis (Philadelphia: Fortress, 1967); W. Pannenberg, *Jesus–God and Man,* trans. L. F. Williams and Duane Priebe (Philadelphia: Westminster, 1975) 195-208.

56. Pannenberg, *Jesus–God and Man,* 263-65 for an exposition of this expression.

57. *Chicago Tribune: Parade* (December 27, 1987), 9. 58. *Chicago Tribune* (January 18, 1988) Section 1, p.5.

59. "An Interview with Irina Ratuskinskaya, " *Northwestern Perspective* (Winter, 1988) 38-39.

60. J. Koenig, *New Testament Hospitality,* 95-103.

61. W. Kasper, *Jesus The Christ,* trans. B. Green (New York: Paulist Press and London: Burns and Oates, 1976) 222, but see the entire context of this discussion, 215-225.

62. K. Stendahl, *Meanings* (Philadelphia: Fortress , 1984) 1 .

63. R. Brown, *The Epistles of John*, AB (Garden City: Doubleday, 1982) 3 217-222.

64. D.Guthrie, *New Testament Theology* (Downers Grove: InterVarsity Press, 1981) 469.

65. I. H. Marshall, "The Death of Jesus in Recent New Testament Study," *Word and World* 3 (1983) 16.

66. C. K. Barrett, *The Epistle to the Romans*, HNTC (New York: Harper and Brothers, 1957) 77-78.

67. Quoted in *The Lord of the Journey*, ed. R. Pooley and P. Seddon (London and Blackburn, Austria: Collins Liturgical Publicans, 1986) 349. The source is untraced.

68. R. Mc. Brown, *Elie Wiesel: Messenger to All Humanity*, rev. ed. (Notre Dame: University of Notre Dame Press, 1989) 239-244.

69. Hooker, "Interchange and Suffering," 71 and "Interchange and Atonement," 479.

70. That friendship has a component of interchange has been shown by R. M. Adams, "Christian Liberty" in *Philosophy and the Christian Faith*, ed. by T. V. Morris (Notre Dame: University of Notre Dame Press, 1988) 161.

71. This paper first emerged as a discussion piece at a Faculty Colloquium at North Park Theological Seminary and was refined further for presentation at the Evangelical Theology Section of the American Academy of Religion in November, 1988. My thanks to colleagues whose questions and suggestions enriched this work, which now is a total rewrite and enlargement.

SALVATION: A MISSIOLOGICAL PERSPECTIVE

DAVID J. BOSCH

Salvation is undoubtedly a key notion in every religion. It therefore came as no surprise that, about a decade ago, the Roman Catholic journal *Studia Missionalia* devoted two consecutive volumes (1980 and 1981) to the theme of salvation in world religions. In addition to studies on salvation in Christianity, the volumes contain examinations of the notion in Islam, Buddhism, Hinduism, and African traditional religions. On the basis of these studies it would not be wrong to say that every religion is a religion of salvation. Indeed, it is arguable that the quest for salvation constitutes the fundamental theme of all religions. As far as Christianity is concerned, the response to this quest is, in a sense, the test for the relevance of the Christian faith as such; the conviction that God has decisively wrought salvation for all in and through Jesus Christ stands at the very center of the Christian faith.[1] After all, the very name "Jesus" means "Savior."

It would also be correct to say that—to a significant extent—the entire Christian *missionary movement* was motivated by the idea of mediating salvation to those still outside the Church. The "soteriological motif" may indeed be termed the "throbbing heart of missiology" since it concerns the "deepest and most fundamental question of humanity."[2] It therefore makes sense that international missionary conferences would be devoted in their entirety to this theme. One may refer, for instance, to the 1973 Bangkok conference of the WCC's Commission on World Mission and Evangelism (CWME), the theme of which was "Salvation Today." More recently in October 1988 the Roman Catholic "Congregation for the Evangelization of Peoples," meeting at the Urban University in Rome, devoted a week-long consultation to the same subject. That these were *missionary* consultations makes eminent sense, since one's theology of mission is always closely dependent on one's theology of salvation, one's soteriology; it would therefore be correct to say that the scope of salvation—however we define salvation—determines the scope of the missionary enterprise.

Of course, salvation is and has always been an elusive concept. How does it differ from near-synonyms like redemption, eternal bliss, justification, liberation, eternal life, the new birth, new creation, *shalom*, freedom, the forgiveness of sins, reconciliation, attaining perfection, and the like? Does salvation have to do with this world, or with

God's future world, or perhaps with both? Where does salvation occur: in the individual, the Church, or society? How does salvation relate to well-being? Is it identical to socio-political and economic liberation? Are all religions effective ways to salvation? And how does salvation (*Heil*) relate to "unsalvation" (*Unheil*)?[3] These and similar questions are, and have always been, of crucial importance for the theory and practice of the Christian mission.

In what follows, I will first attempt to trace the idea of salvation in the history of Christian missions. Next, I wish to survey, briefly, the inadequacies inherent in the various definitions. Finally I shall attempt—however tentatively—to outline a responsible way of interpreting and communicating the salvation idea in mission.

I. SALVATION IN CHRISTIAN MISSIONARY HISTORY

Christians' understanding of salvation is usually being shaped by their interpretation of the gospel, their personal experience, and the context in which they find themselves. The message of salvation is always understood as *good* news over against the *bad* news the individual or the society has experienced. This contextual dimension of the way in which salvation is perceived is and has always been of crucial importance.

Nineteenth century Protestant theology suggested that the interpretation of salvation went through three phases: from a *mystical* view of salvation in the (Greek) Patristic church, via a *juridical* understanding of salvation in the Western Church, to a more *subjective* and *ethical* interpretation in the modern period.[4]

1. *The Greek Patristic Mission*

It was to be expected that the early Christian mission, when it penetrated the Greek linguistic and cultural world, would have absorbed many elements from that tradition. Two elements are of particular importance for our theme: the fact that traditional Greek ontology did not really find it possible to draw a qualitative distinction between God and humans, and that Greek thinking and culture was dominated and permiated by the idea of *paideia,* of the gradual upward "education" of human beings.[5] It was therefore more or less natural that salvation, as proclaimed by the Christian Church, would find expression particularly in the idea of the divinization or the *theosis* of the believer.

In the second and subsequent centuries the ardent eschatological expectation of the early church declined. Apocalyptic ideas began to play the role of inherited pieces of furniture: they were handed on to the next generation and may not be discarded, but they were no longer functional. Faith in the immortality of the soul replaced faith in the eschatological intervention of God. The host in the Eucharist now became a *pharmakon athanasias*, a "medicine of (or unto) immortality." The aim of mission was the transfer of *life*, especially *eternal life*.[6] The content of the proclamation to nonbelievers was "a word of life unto life."[7] Christ did not come primarily to conquer people's sin but to repair in them the image of God and give them life, for "they are called to participate in his glory."[8] This happens in a unique way in the *theosis*. The phrase "heaven on earth," familiar to each Orthodox believer, gives expression to the realization, in *this world*, of the *eschaton*. Not the cross of Christ stands at the center but his incarnation, particularly as instrument of the divine *paideia*.[9] As Athanasius put it: "He became human, in order that we may be divinized."

This theological "model" of salvation was eminently successful.[10] Within just a few centuries the Christian church, cast in this mold, spread and took root throughout Eastern Europe, the Western parts of Asia, the North-Eastern corner of Africa and eventually also in Russia.

2. *The Interpretation of Salvation in the Western Church*

In the Western (Latin) church salvation gradually acquired a different meaning. One should not underestimate the differences between the two major "wings" of the Church—differences which would eventually lead to the schism of the year 1054. The Byzantine church was theocentric, the Latin church cosmo- and anthropocentric. In the East, salvation was a process by which human nature, via a "pedagogical" progression, would in the course of time be taken up into the divine nature; the West emphasized the devastating effect of sin as well as the restoration of the fallen individual by means of a crisis experience. The theology of the Eastern church was incarnational: the emphasis was on the "origin" of Christ, on his preexistence and the contribution of his incarnation to exalting human beings; the theology of the Western church, by contrast, was staurological (from *stauros* cross): it put the emphasis on Christ's substitutionary death for sinners.[11] The Church Father Augustine played a decisive role in this entire development. His personal experience of divine grace as well as the traumatic event of the sacking of Rome by the Goths under Alaric, provided important building blocks for the Western-church's understanding of salvation, as did his conflict with the Donatists on the one hand and with Pelagius on the other. Some elements of the missionary understanding of salvation which flowed from this are of particular importance.

First, there was a tendency in the Western church to reduce salvation to the salvation of *souls*. The relationship between the body and the soul was increasingly seen as a kind of unhappy marriage and the body as a prison in which the soul was held captive. Only when the body dies and decays will the immortal soul be released. The Neoplatonic interpretation of "soul" was hereby without ado imputed to the New Testament. So effective was this almost complete limitation of salvation to the redemption of the *soul* that it remained the dominant soteriological emphasis, even when the Gospel was proclaimed among the Germanic and Slavonic peoples. Hans-Dietrich Kahl[12] has shown that the traditional religions of these peoples were entirely this-worldly and quite concretely concerned with matters like fertility, growth, plentiful harvests, and political security. Still, among these peoples the Christian mission proclaimed, with remarkable success, its message of salvation only for the soul. Centuries later the process would repeat itself in respect of the traditional religions of Africa and elsewhere: once again a material interpretation of salvation had to give way to an interpretation in which only the eternal soul was featured.

Secondly, in the Western church salvation was *individualized*. Not without reason Krister Stendahl called Augustine "the first truly Western man."[13] Augustine's fundamental question was, "Where does one find eternal bliss?" The answer was formulated in such a way that conversion was understood entirely in individualistic categories. In this way salvation became a private affair between God and the individual soul; redemption was the inward experience of grace which the individual subjectively made his or her own.[14] The individual stood alone before God. Augustine could therefore write, "I only desire to know God and my soul, nothing else." This interiorization and privatization of salvation was, as far as Catholicism is concerned, advocated particularly by the School of Münster and, in Protestantism, by Pietism and various contemporary evangelical groupings.[15]

Along with the individualization of salvation there was, thirdly, a tendency to interpret salvation entirely in otherworldly or supernatural categories. In the case of Augustine, his dependence on Neoplatonism and this philosophical movement's deprecating attitude toward everything material played a further important role.[16] And even though withdrawal from the world never became a dominant characteristic of Western theology it is true that—since salvation was viewed as something that happened exclusively between God and the individual—the world was understood as a neutral area on which the drama of the individual's salvation or damnation played itself out.[17] According to this vision, says Adrio König, salvation was defined entirely as *celestial* salvation; as a matter of fact, earth and salvation stood over against each other, and the place really to look forward to was heaven where salvation would be complete. A radical distinction was made between a "higher" and a "lower" realm, between heaven and earth, between the spiritual and the material.

Fourthly, during the Middle Ages the world was viewed as an orderly and well balanced structure; every interference with and questioning of this divine *ordo* was viewed as evil *(perversio)*. Salvation was the *restoration* of the *ordo*. In contradistinction to the situation in the early church people no longer expected salvation from a dynamic future; rather, it was defined retrospectively as the restoration or recreation of the order that had once been but was ruined by human sin. Restoration could only take place if somebody—who had to be both truly divine and truly human—were to do reparation on behalf of all people for the terrible devastation of sin. This is what Christ achieved who–by vicariously suffering death on the Cross–appeased God *(the satisfactio vicaria* of Anselm of Canterbury). Through his substitutionary death Christ had, therefore, already objectively secured salvation. All that remained to be done was for people to appropriate it subjectively. The salvation wrought by Christ was a kind of reservoir upon which converts could draw.[18] In this entire process a high premium was placed on the subjective *assurance* of *being saved.*

The consequences of this understanding of salvation were far-reaching, also for mission.

First, it led to grace being rendered independent: it became a divine power directly given by God to renew people. In a sense, grace took the place of the Holy Spirit, a process which began as early as Augustine. Greshake quotes O. H. Pesch in this respect: "Augustine says grace where Paul talks about the Spirit. The believer's new conduct which Paul identifies as the 'fruit of the Spirit,' Augustine refers to as the effect of the new power of grace in the soul."[19]

Since the "person" and "work" of Christ were increasingly detached from each other and treated as separate themes, soteriology gradually became unhinged from Christology. Eventually Christology was made subservient to soteriology, since the emphasis was laid, more and more, on the subjective experience of redemption.[20] And since salvation could only be mediated sacramentally (in Catholicism) or mainly through proclamation (in Protestantism)—that is, in both cases, exclusively through the Church soteriology contributed to an ever greater isolation of the Church from society.

A second consequence of the prevailing interpretation of salvation has to do with the way in which Gods "salvific" activities were increasingly distinguished from his "providential" activities in respect of the well-being of individuals and society. Never, at any stage, was there any doubt that Christians were called to serve others and practice charity. Likewise, it went without saying that, from the earliest period onward, the Christian mission rendered a remarkable service in respect of the care of the sick, the poor, orphans, and other victims of society, as well as in respect of education, agricultural instruction, and the like. This was true of Orthodox, Catholic, and Protestant missions alike. Early Pietist mission, for instance, consciously proceeded from the presupposition that the *Dienst der Seelen* (service to souls) should go hand in hand with the *Dienst des Leibes* (services to human bodies).[21] And after the Evangelical Awakenings in the Anglo-Saxon world, missionaries and mission agencies went out of their way to effect the uplifting of the populations in the traditional "mission fields."

Because of the positivistic attitude toward the status quo and the powers that be it very seldom happened, however, that missionaries—as an integral part of their agenda—challenged the unjust societal structures which in many cases were responsible for social and other evils. Rather, in most cases a strict distinction was maintained between "horizontal" and "external" emphases (charity, education, medical help) on the one hand and the "vertical" or "spiritual" elements of the missionary agenda (such as preaching, the sacraments, church attendance, etc.). Only the latter had a bearing on the acquisition of salvation. The other projects, by contrast, were often identified as "auxiliary services" and not as mission in themselves. Their purpose was to dispose people favorably toward the gospel, to "soften them up" and thereby prepare the way for the work of the *real* missionary, namely the one who proclaimed God's word about eternal salvation. Even the so-called "Comprehensive Approach"—which gained prominence in missionary circles from the 1920s until after World War II—as well as the development projects which were in vogue particularly during the 1960s, proceeded, in the final analysis, from a dualistic view of humanity and separated salvation from well-being.

To summarize: in the Western church humans were consistently viewed from the perspective of the Fall and no longer also from the perspective of the (good) creation of God. Human beings were, above all, *lost* beings in whom the image of God was, admittedly, not completely destroyed, but nevertheless severely impaired. Humans really stood only in a "vertical" relationship, as individuals, before God. And salvation—which exclusively had to do with the saving of one's immortal soul in the hereafter—could only be achieved via a strictly religious route. This attenuated definition of salvation inevitably led to a preoccupation with narrowly defined ecclesiastical activities, which, for their part, severely complicated the believers' involvement in society since such involvement had nothing to do with salvation except to draw people toward the Church where they might get access to salvation proper.

3. *Salvation in the Modern Era*

The theological constellation outlined above could only survive unscathed as long as people lived in the context of Christendom and felt themselves to be completely dependent on the comprehensive, transcendent activity of God as the sole explanation for everything that happened in the world. With the advent of the Enlightenment in those countries where Christianity had for many centuries been the dominant religion this entire interpretation of salvation came under severe pressure, with the result that traditional soteriology was increasingly being challenged.[22] Human experiences which had hitherto operated within the *religious* understanding of salvation now shifted to the area of the observable and analyzable; virtually all problems encountered by people could now be solved through human capabilities. On this side of death the possibility of determining the future expanded exponentially, as it were. Interest in the "last things"—particularly the redemption of the soul in eternity—made way to interest in the "penultimate," *this* life, and what people should make of it.

The triumphal progression of scientific developments invariably led to people freeing themselves from the ties that had bound them to God. Sin as guilt before God, forgiveness of sin as coming only from God, eternal life only through and with God, communion with God, profound dependence upon God for every step one took—all these elements which had enveloped and determined the life of the medieval person from the cradle to the grave, were no longer part and parcel of the modern person's experience of reality. The idea of salvation coming from outside, from God, totally out of reach of human power and capability, had become extremely problematic.[23] The modern human being had, after all, come of age, was autonomous, personally responsible for what had to be done, and no longer dependent upon others dictating to him or her—even if it were God himself. Thus the overpowering characteristic of the modern age was its radical anthropocentrism, modern history was, *par excellence,* a history of human freedom and emancipation.

The modern critique of religion took its point of departure here. Religion as expression of total dependence upon God and as eternal salvation in the hereafter was an anachronism and remnant of humankind's period of childhood. Salvation now meant liberation from religious superstition, attention to human welfare and the moral improvement of humanity. An alternative soteriology emerged: an understanding of salvation in which humans were the active and responsible agents which employ science and technology in order to effect material improvements and induce sociopolitical change in the present. In this respect, the critique of religion became, in essence, the critique of soteriology: salvation would not arrive via religion, but via human accomplishments.[24] Salvation remained the motivating force in the life of modern people, but it was redefined radically.

The reaction of Church and mission to the challenge of modernism was—very generally put—twofold.

The first reaction has, in fact, already been identified. It amounts to the Church continuing to define salvation in traditional terms, ignoring, as it were, the challenges of the Enlightenment, and proceeding as if nothing has changed. In Roman Catholic circles this usually takes the form of a return to and a holding on to a scholastic definition of salvation on the basis of the traditional *extra ecclesiam nulla salus*.

In Protestantism the traditional interpretation is upheld especially by those groups which call themselves "evangelicals" and even more specifically among various Holiness, charismatic, Pentecostal and fundamentalist groupings. A strict dualism between body and soul is often being championed. Salvation involves only the soul. It is purely spiritual and otherworldly. It has nothing to do with the socio-political dispensation; to change the structures of society is therefore optional. In these circles people tend to adopt a neutral attitude toward the powers-that-be, since a major purpose of mission is to prepare humankind for Christ's *parousia.* With respect to this dispensation, there is widespread apocalyptic pessimism: the time left before the *parousia* leaves room only for witness and suffering. There is an extremely negative attitude toward every manifestation of liberation theology since it is viewed as an attempt to define salvation in purely mundane, horizontal and political categories.

The second reaction is to attempt to take the challenges of modernism seriously, also with respect to its understanding of salvation. Those who pursue this route refuse to accept the relativism of the Enlightenment and contend that religion–more specifically the Christian religion–has a vital role to play in the world and is indeed able to offer people salvation. One way in which Christianity is being "salvaged" is to reject the view according to which Jesus died a substitutionary death for humankind and thereby propitiated God. Jesus was, rather, the ideal human being, an example to emulate, a moral teacher. Not the *person* of Jesus is at the center but the *cause* of Jesus; the *ideal*, not the One who embodies the ideal; the *teaching* (particularly the Sermon on the Mount), not the Teacher; the *kingdom* of God, but without the King?[25]

People still need salvation–not because they have sinned against God, but because they fail to live according to God's intentions. Primarily, guilt and salvation no longer primarily divide and unite God and humans, but humans among themselves. Luther's cry, "Where do I find a merciful God?", is changed to "How can we be merciful neighbors to each other?" God's "vertical" coming into this world manifests itself in changed, felicitous, "horizontal" relationships; the saving relationship of the human with God is being concretized in the conversion of the human being to his or her brother and sister, to reconciliation between people. Sin is—in categories borrowed from Marx—alienation between humans. Salvation does not come via change in individuals but via the termination of perverted and unjust structures.[26] Conversion—as a document in preparation for the Uppsala Assembly of the WCC put it—occurs not so much on the individual/personal level, but on the corporate level in the form of social change.

Since salvation is no longer viewed as coming exclusively from God and does not occur by God changing sinful human beings (Jesus is, after all, only an example!), it goes without saying that it lies within human competence to effect it. An optimistic view of humanity is typical of the modern era.[27] The apocalyptic pessimism of fundamentalism is refuted with the aid of evolutionary optimism. It is believed that people will soon be freed from *every* form of servitude to ignorance, hunger, misery and oppression. The "paradise of the future" is being painted in vivid utopian colors.

The guidelines for the new theology were devised in the theological ivory towers of nineteenth century Europe; its first large-scale practical application would, however, be worked out in the United States of America, in the shape of the "Social Gospel." Salvation, defined in the American way, had to be exported to the "mission fields." Around the turn of the century, and in the spirit of the time, James Dennis devoted three massive volumes to the theme *Christian Missions and Social Progress.*[28] In this paradigm, sin is defined preeminently as *ignorance*. People only had to be *informed* about what was in their own interest. The Western mission was the great educator which would mediate salvation to the unenlightened. And this salvation was increasingly understood in this-worldly categories. "Is anything in the whole universe of God, when rightly understood, supernatural?" asked W. B. Brown.[29] The supernatural was eliminated and replaced by professionalism, efficiency and scientific design. The reign of God was a matter of technique and planning rather than religious devotion. The key concepts were natural continuity and social progress. God was, above all else, a loving and benign being, little more than the embodiment of all ideal human attributes, "the God who exists for the sake of human life and morality," "the synthetic unity of goodness, truth, and beauty."[30]

After World War II the theological renewal associated with the name of Karl Barth terminated the hegemony of European liberal theology and the American "Social Gospel." By the end of the 1950s, however, the Barthian influence was rapidly waning. This coincided with a tremendous upsurge in interest in the writings of Dietrich Bonhoeffer and his idea of humans having come of age, able to live and act "as if there were no God" (*etsi Deus non daretur*). A new era of optimism dawned, this time because of the global penetration of secularization, which was hailed as a fruit of the Christian mission. By the beginning of the 1960's there was increasing talk, particularly in missionary circles, about God being active *outside* the Church. Put differently, the apostolary turning to the world, which characterized the Church's understanding of mission until the 'fifties became a diaconal orientation in the 'sixties.[31] For Johannes Hoekendijk, the goal of mission was no longer eternal bliss for the soul, but *shalom*, because, he says, "*Mission begins beyond religion*."[32] With this, Hoekendijk proposed a fundamental and total restructuring of the world. *Shalom* was a *theo-political* concept, indeed, "a *secularized* concept . . , a *social* happening, an event in inter-human relations, a venture of co-humanity."[33] Shalom was, Hoekendijk suggested, a more comprehensive notion than salvation, and if one had to choose, it was by no means self-evident that one would choose *salvation*. After all, we impose an antiquated anthropology upon our contemporaries if we continuously act as if they have to be on the look-out for a merciful God who could forgive their sins.[34]

A most crucial conference for the debate about salvation was the 1966 consultation on Church and Society, held in Geneva. Here there surfaced, for the first time, the fundamental difference between what Charles West[35] referred to as the "technological humanists" and the "revolutionary humanists." At the conference the two most important advocates for the two positions were Emmanuel Mesthene and Richard Shaull. Both agreed that *this* world was the main arena of God's activity and the (only?) place where salvation could be effected. Where Mesthene's frame of reference was the modern industrialized and secularized West and where he saw the solutions to the world's problems in technological progress, Shaull's frame of reference was the Third World, more particularly its experience of injustice, exploitation and poverty. Mesthene's theology attempted to respond to the challenges of the Enlightenment, Shaull's to the challenges of Karl Marx and colonial exploitation. For Mesthene, salvation meant the large-scale encouragement of technological development so that all may get a share in the wealth of the West; for Shaull, salvation meant liberation, which could be achieved only by overthrowing the existing order.

The next general assembly of the WCC (Uppsala 1968) attempted, in a sense, to reconcile these two positions. Two reports on the "Structures for Missionary Congregations" were prepared for the meeting.[36] The European report took its cue from Hoekendijk's *shalom* concept, the North American report, however, from the idea of *humanization*. The latter report put it as follows:

> We have lifted up humanization as the goal of mission because we believe that more than others it communicates in our period of history the meaning of the messianic goal. In another time the goal of God's redemptive work might best have been described in terms of man turning towards God . . . . The fundamental question was that of the true God, and the Church responded to that question by pointing to him. It was assuming that the pur-

> pose of mission was Christianization, bringing man to God through Christ and his Church. Today the fundamental question is much more that of true man, and the dominant concern of the missionary congregation must therefore be to point to the humanity in Christ as the goal of mission.[37]

In light of all these developments it was almost a matter of course that the theme for the next conference of CWME (Bangkok, 1973) would be "Salvation Today." It had to be determined, once and for all, what salvation was and what it was not. Uppsala's (and Hoekendijk's) negative assessment surfaced in some of the preparatory documents for Bangkok. It almost appeared as if the classical Roman Catholic adage, "*outside* the Church no salvation," had been turned into its opposite: "inside the Church no salvation." A Canadian study on the theme "Salvation Today" put the question, "Is the Church not arrogant in thinking it can offer man salvation?"[38]

The "spirit" of the conference itself, it seems, emerges where salvation is defined exclusively in this-worldly terms. Section II depicts salvation in four dimensions: it manifests itself in the struggle for 1) economic justice against exploitation; 2) human dignity against oppression; 3) solidarity against alienation; and 4) hope against despair in personal life.[39] In the "process of salvation," we must relate (only?) these four dimensions to each other.[40]

Meanwhile, developments in Catholic missionary thinking parallelled those in Protestantism. In 1959 Pope John XXIII announced the Second Vatican Council. The vision of the Council, in the Pope's words, was to "identify the 'signs of the times,'" in order to enable the Church to contribute meaningfully to the solution of the problems of the modern world. Since then an impressive number of Catholic publications on the "signs of the times" have appeared; in fact, the expression has become crucial to contemporary Catholic thinking. As in Protestantism, it is believed that the God of mission is at work not only in the Church, but also in the structures of society outside the Church. By implication this means that salvation cannot be defined only in "religious" (or "ecclesial") terms but also in terms of what happens elsewhere. The Council's Pastoral Constitution on the Church in the Modern World, *Gaudium et Spes*, devoted particular attention to this (e.g. in its paragraph 4). It was, furthermore, especially in Roman Catholic liberation theology that a wider interpretation of salvation emerged.

The doyen of liberation theologians, Gustavo Gutiérrez, devotes an entire chapter to the relationship between liberation and salvation.[41] He portrays salvation in two forms. First, since salvation is intimately linked to creation (creation is "the first salvific act") and since creation is universal, salvation also has to be universal. Secondly, "salvation is not something otherworldly" but is an "intrahistorical reality."[42] These views are similar to those which the Latin American Bishops' Conference adopted as its own at its meeting in Medellin, Colombia (1968). The similarities with ecumenical Protestant views are striking. The optimism is also similar. In the introduction to the Medellin document,[43] for instance, it is said, "Latin America is obviously under the sign of transformation. . . ." The document proceeds:

> . . . we are on the threshold of a new epoch in this history of Latin America. It appears to be a time of zeal for full emancipation, of liberation from every form of servitude, of personal maturity and of collective integration.

To sum up: there can be no doubt that the interpretation of salvation which emerged in the recent ecumenical theology of mission and in liberation theology has introduced elements into the definition of salvation without which it would have been dangerously narrow and anaemic:

a) We have learnt, that it is totally untenable to limit salvation to the individual and her or his personal relationship with God. We live in a world in which people are dependent on each other and every individual exists within a web of interhuman relationships. Hatred, injustice, oppression, war, and other forms of violence are manifestations of evil; concern for humaneness, for the conquering of famine, illness and meaninglessness is part of the salvation for which we hope and labor.

b) We have learnt that—when we talk about salvation—our reference point must be the reign of God and that this reign must also become a reality on earth. After all, we pray, "Your kingdom come, your will be done *on earth* as it is in heaven" (Matt 6:10). Salvation is thus indeed being realized on earth, in history, in the here and now; the *earth* is the *locus* of the Christian's calling and sanctification.

c) We have discovered that much of our traditional narrowing of salvation to the individual has closed our eyes to the far-reaching anthropocentrism of traditional theology: to a large extent, and in spite of the emphasis the Church had put throughout on *God* being the source of everything, it was largely a case of pious individuals occupying themselves with their own salvation and of Christ playing the role of the One who had to save lost souls. Hence the fact that, in this tradition, Christology was made subservient to soteriology.

II. CRISIS IN THE MODERN UNDERSTANDING OF SALVATION

1. *A Critique*

Even before the middle seventies of our century the "secularist" as well as the "liberationist" definitions of salvation had come under pressure. By the time the WCC held its fifth Assembly (Nairobi, 1975) the general atmosphere had become more sober and the pronouncements more moderate than those which had characterized the conferences in Geneva (1966), Uppsala (1968) and Bangkok (1973). The same was, on the whole, true of the sixth Assembly of the WCC (Vancouver 1983) and of the two most recent gatherings of CWME (Melbourne 1980 and San Antonio 1989). During the past two decades there has, in addition, been a tremendous resurgence of fundamentalist and charismatics groupings, most of which, sometimes with aggression, depict salvation in otherworldly and eschatological categories. Perhaps even more important: it has gradually become clear that the "horizontalist" model was riddled with inconsistencies, both theological and practical. Let me highlight some of the elements of criticism of the modern salvation model.

a) The idea that it lies within people's capability to usher in utopia has been dealt a devastating blow. It was self-deception to begin to think and act as if salvation lay in our grasp, was at our disposal, or something we could bring about. We realize, once again, that no human project can be equated with the fullness of God's reign, that (in spite of the deeply rooted heretical conviction that we can bring about salvation through our own good works) even Christians have no ready-made answers to the needs of society. Many Christians have discovered that they had promised themselves too much, for instance at Uppsala and Medellin (both in 1968), when many statements were made to the effect that within the foreseeable future *all* injustice, *all* poverty, and *every* form of servitude would be something of the past. Thomas Wieser, the WCC staff member responsible for coordinating the "Salvation Today" project, sounds the following sobering warning:

> The task of identifying God's saving purpose in the midst of historical events requires solid theological criteria on the basis of which critical judgments can be made. Here an important task remains to be undertaken in order to ensure that the Church's credibility will not again be lost in a dash for short-lived "relevance."[44]

The fact is that history is and remains ambiguous and that it is therefore risky to universalize from the presuppositions of any particular historical period; a few years later, says John Taylor, such a perspective may appear "strangely naive and questionable."[45]

b) During the past two decades we have also become conscious of the "limits of growth." Unchecked technological development has become nonsensical, since earth's non-renewable resources are being exhausted, while the rich become richer and the poor poorer. Even if humans could live by bread alone, there is simply no longer enough bread for all, because of structures which appear to be unalterable. We have, in addition, become conscious of the real possibility that our technological and scientific know-how may lead to our irreversibly ruining the ecosystem. We are, reluctantly, arriving at the conclusion that not everything that is technologically possible should be manufactured. The modern story of success tends toward becoming a story of catastrophe, and some people even try to withdraw into an illusory pretechnological world. Meanwhile the dreams about the "paradise of the future" disappear in the smoke of interminable wars and, much worse, in the radioactive winds of nuclear explosions which threaten to destroy all life on earth. The optimism and euphoria of the 'sixties are indeed no longer part of our experience. Five years after the Bangkok Conference on "Salvation Today," John Taylor reflects on it in the following words:

> . . . the euphoric sense of a break-through which the members of the Assembly experienced at the time was in some ways deceptive. The ringing statements about the meaning of salvation actually raised more questions than they answered.[46]

c) Christians are today also forced to ask whether the tendency to allow theology and mission to be submerged in social ethics must not unavoidably lead to a relativizing of the person of Jesus Christ in Christianity. Wolfgang Beinert rightly remarks in this respect, "The indispensable christological element of soteriology is not (always) made sufficiently clear."[47] The inescapable result of much of the modern paradigm is that the world's needs and solutions are being portrayed in terms which, at least to a certain extent, are independent of Jesus Christ.[48] The Church, however, is called, in its mission, to give witness to what God has "once for all, absolutely new, unrepeatably and finally done in Jesus Christ for the sake of the salvation of the world."[49] A recent Memorandum of the Roman Catholic Church has put it unequivocally:

> Jesus Christ accomplishes all salvation. No one can complete his work if he does not achieve it himself . . . .[50]

d) There is an implicit suggestion in the modern interpretations of salvation that people may partake in this salvation without a personal inward renewal based on the new birth in Jesus Christ, without repentance and the forgiveness of sins, without faith and justification. Traces of universalism are noticeable in this thinking. A document in preparation for the Uppsala meeting of the WCC stated *inter alia* that every human being already is a member of the new humanity, because of the resurrection of the new man, Jesus Christ.[51] The only difference, so it appears, would be that some people are not yet aware of the fact that they are saved whereas others already know it. In a study described as "a contribution to a reorientation of the theology of mission," P. G. Aring drew the logical consequences from this: since Easter the world is already the reconciled world of God; as a matter of fact, it is totally impossible to picture God without his reconciled world. It is therefore preposterous to view mission work as the announcement of something that still has to happen. After all, it is not *our* duty to "articulate" God to the world; God "articulates" himself, without humans having to pave the way for him through mission work or in any other way.[52] The question is, however, whether, in light of God's revelation as Christians confess it, we can subscribe to such a view.

To summarize: salvation and well-being, even if they are very closely interlocked, do not coincide completely. Unless we distinguish between salvation and well-being, salvation exhausts itself in earthly happiness. The Christian faith is a critical factor, however, the reign of God a critical category, and the Christian gospel not identical with the agenda of modern emancipation and liberation movements.[53] A completely "secularized" church has little to offer the world.

2. *A Return to the "Classical" Position?*

Might the solution lie in simply exchanging the modern interpretation of salvation for the traditional position as it had taken shape in the Western church?

This is the route followed by various so-called "evangelicals." And, indeed, there is much to say for this understanding of salvation. It upholds and defends the Church's unique role as mediator of salvation, by proclaiming the Word, administering the sacraments, and calling people to repentance and discipleship. It is based on the conviction that there will be no new humanity until there are, first, individuals who have experienced renewal through a personal encounter with the living Lord and who live according to the Gospel. In his Apostolic Exhortation, *Evangelii Nuntiandi* (paragraph 5), Pope Paul formulated it as follows:

> (Evangelization) is the duty incumbent on (the Church) by the command of the Lord Jesus, so that people can believe and be saved. This message is indeed necessary. It is unique. It cannot be replaced. It does not permit either indifference, syncretism or accommodation. It is a question of people's salvation. . . . It is truth.

Still, in spite of its positive elements, serious objections have to be raised against the traditional perspectives on salvation, particularly as they are being continued in some evangelical groups.

a) In many instances the meaning of salvation has been dangerously and indefensibly narrowed, as if it referred only to people's spiritual needs and personal problems; as if the purpose of mission were just to prepare people for the return of Christ and for eternity; as if salvation comprised only the forgiveness of sins, escape from the wrath of God, and the encounter of the individual soul with God; as if our mission should prepare people only for a heavenly abode; as if salvation could be summarized as liberation *from* this world a liberation that only becomes a reality when, at the moment of death, the soul escapes and proceeds to its real home in heaven.

b) The "evangelical" approach leads to too sharp a distinction being made between creation and re-creation and therefore between salvation and well-being. Such a strategy almost always spawns an absolute dualism as well as a contrast between spiritual and physical, heaven and earth, the eternal and the temporary, religion and politics, salvation and humanization. Donald McGavran articulates this view in the following words:

> . . . the reformation of the social order (rightly emphasized) should not be substituted for salvation. . . . Salvation is a vertical relationship . . . which issues in horizontal relationships . . . . The vertical must not be displaced by the horizontal. Desirable as social ameliorations are, working for them must not be substituted for the biblical requirements of/for "salvation."[54]

This watertight separation between the doctrines of creation and redemption is untenable. This world is God's creation en route to its consummation. In our mission we do not only encounter a world which has been alienated from God because of sin, but also a world, a humanity, which God loves. Any extreme two kingdoms doctrine is in conflict with the heart of the Gospel. Redemption is never salvation *out* of this world *(salus e mondo*) but always salvation *of* this world (*salus mundi*).[55] Salvation in Christ is salvation in the context of human society *en route* to a whole and healed world. The Church's concern for salvation thus has a universal dimension and, with that, a physical and political dimension.[56]

c) The "evangelical" interpretation of salvation leads to an imagined neutrality in respect of society. Mission is limited to the communication of a religious message, the "principles" of which may then be applied to society as an optional second step; it is a message which refers to conversion to God without at the same time touching upon conversion from one human being to another. Our involvement in the existential needs of others is then, at best, an ethical consequence of our faith and not an expression of that faith. The result of all this is that the emphasis on salvation in the hereafter in effect separates and alienates us from our neighbors, thus giving credence to the accusation that religion is the opiate of the people. In the face of this it must be forcibly maintained that precisely our understanding of salvation compels us to take sides in society, and to do this in favor of the poor and the oppressed.

III. TOWARD COMPREHENSIVE SALVATION

The challenges of the modern world to the mission of the Church in respect of the interpretation of salvation cannot simply be ignored. New challenges call for new responses. We are forced by circumstances to reflect anew on this entire matter.

It is not, however, a case of having to start from scratch in order to establish what salvation is. Rather, contemporary challenges should help us to look with new eyes at the tradition from which we come so that we may be enabled to penetrate to an understanding of salvation which transcends both the classical answers of the Eastern and Western church and those of the modern church which has made the responses of the Enlightenment its own. The fact of the matter is that all these responses have limited salvation by interpreting it *either* in individual *or* in social categories, *either* transcendent *or* immanent, *either* for this life *or* for the hereafter. In both instances the variegated witness of Scripture has been made subservient to one, preconceived agenda.

1. *The Witness of Scripture*

If we now, in light of the fact that all traditional and current definitions of salvation seem to have failed, turn to Scripture, we note that a mosaic of interpretations of salvation appear to emerge.

For Israel salvation stands in the most intimate relationship to its faith in God as Creator. Creation is, as it were, God's "first salvific act" (Gutiérrez). In the older parts of the Old Testament God's saving activities are apparently *mundane* through and through. His liberating deed *par excellence* was to save Israel from slavery in Egypt. Salvation has to do with this earth. Salvation is *shalom*: peace, safety from one's enemies, plentiful harvests, a large family, a good king, sound interpersonal relations, social justice, a long life. None of these aspects of salvation may, however, be seen in isolation from Israel's relationship to Yahweh. After all, Israel stands in a *covenantal* relation to God: to Israel has been entrusted the Torah. Religion and society overlap. Salvation is comprehensive, but its parameters remain essentially life on earth.

The understanding of salvation does not remain static, however. The ordeal of the Babylonian captivity leads to a deepening of the experience of both misfortune and salvation. In Second Isaiah, in particular, salvation is linked to God's saving justice as well as to the hope for a new creation. In other words, a clear eschatological dimension is added. In the harsh, cheerless present Israel learns to look toward the future, including the future beyond death, yes, even toward a resurrection of the dead and a new life with God. This does not, however, mean that salvation forfeits its mundane character. *Shalom* will return to this *earth*; the lion and the lamb will lie down together.

When Jesus of Nazareth commences his ministry, his name for this condition of salvation or *shalom* is the *basileia tou Theou*. And this reign is both present and future. Moreover, it is indissolubly tied to the person of Jesus. He does not only *mediate* salvation, he is salvation, the reign of God in person, the *autobasileia* (Origen). In his earthly life, in his preaching and healing, his bestowing forgiveness of sins upon people, his compassionate identification with the outcast and the oppressed, salvation becomes a reality. It includes the experience of liberation from sin and death, incorporation into the *koinonia* of those who practice peace, and participation in the work of justice in the reign of God.

All these dimensions of salvation are simultaneously social and personal, "secular" and religious. Even so, there are different nuances among the various New Testament authors who wrote about salvation. Let me refer only to Luke and Paul.

One could, with van Unnik, say that salvation is the dominant theme in Luke.[57] Two aspects are of importance here. First, Luke uses salvation language in respect to a very wide spectrum of human circumstances: the termination of poverty, discrimination, illness, demon possession, sin, and so forth—or as Scheffler puts it: in respect to economic, social, political, physical, psychological, and spiritual suffering.[58]

Secondly, for Luke salvation is, above all, something that realizes itself in *this* life, *today* (see, in particular, Jesus' sayings in 4:21; 19:9; 23:43).[59] In Luke, salvation is *present* salvation. [60]

In Paul the accent appears to be elsewhere.[61] He puts a greater emphasis on the *inchoative* nature of salvation: it only *begins* in this life. Salvation is a *process*, initiated by one's encounter with the living Christ; real, complete salvation is still outstanding. The Holy Spirit given to us is only God's first gift (Rom 8:23). We are saved in hope (8:24). Reconciliation (a key concept in Paul) indeed occurs here and now, but Paul normally refers to *salvation* in the future tense: "For if while we were enemies we *were* reconciled to God . . , much more, now that we *are* reconciled, shall we be saved by his llfe" (Rom 5:10). These delicate nuances certainly have to do with the fact that Paul thinks in apocalyptic categories and wishes to emphasize that comprehensive salvation is reserved for the coming triumph of God.[62] In the present Paul still *awaits* Jesus Christ as Savior (Phil 3:20).

All of this does not, however, detract from the reality of radical renewal—both personal and social—which the believer may already experience. Through the Spirit who empowers us to shout "*Abba*!" we are already children of God (Rom 8:14-15). Nowhere has Paul articulated this fundamental renewal in stronger language than the words he uses in 2 Cor 5:17, "When anyone is united to Christ, there is a new world; the old order has gone, and a new order has already begun" (New English Bible). This "new order" has tremendous implications, also on the horizontal level *inter alia* for the relationship between Philemon and his runaway slave.[63] Present salvation also has significance for politics in a wider context. When Paul calls Christ *Kyrios* or *Soter*, he is doing it in the face of the confession that Caesar is Lord and Savior. Thus he wishes to say that the first coming of Jesus has indeed relativized all other political power and authority, and that henceforth it would be impossible to ascribe absolute authority to earthly rulers. The coming triumph of God already casts its rays into our present world, and while it beckons us toward comprehensive salvation, it inspires us to let this salvation become a reality here and now, in the structures of society.[64]

2. *Integral Salvation*

The *rélecture* of the biblical notions of salvation has exposed the inadequacies of all three historical models. For its understanding of salvation the Greek Patristic mission was oriented to the origin and beginning of Jesus' life: his preexistence and incarnation. The orientation of Western mission was toward the end of Jesus' life: his death on the Cross (formulated classically in the Anselmian satisfaction theory). In both instances salvation was located on the edges of the life of Jesus.[65] The third model, that is, the ethical interpretation of salvation, was oriented to Jesus' earthly life and ministry. It introduced a more dynamic element into our understanding of salvation, but in such a way that, in the final analysis, it made Jesus himself redundant.

What we stand in need of, is an interpretation of salvation which operates within a *comprehensive* christological framework, which makes the *totus Christus*—his incarnation, earthly life, death, resurrection, and *parousia*—indispensable for Church and theology. All these christological elements taken together constitute the *praxis* of Jesus, the One who both *inaugurated* salvation and provided us with a *model* to emulate; the salvation we have been *granted* must again and again be *practiced* by us.[66]

It, therefore, makes sense that in missionary circles today, but elsewhere as well, the mediating of "comprehensive," "integral" "total" or "universal" salvation is increasingly identified as the purpose of mission, in this way overcoming the inherent dualism in the traditional and more recent models.[67] Missionary literature, but also missionary practice, emphasizes that we should find a way beyond every schizophrenic position and minister to people in their *total* need, that we should involve individual *as well as* society, soul *and* body present and future in our ministry of salvation.

Never before in history was people's social distress as extensive as it is in the twentieth century. But also, never before were Christians in a better position than they are today to do something about this need. Poverty, misery, sickness, criminality and social chaos have assumed unheard of proportions. On an unprecedented scale people have become the victims of other people; *homo homini lupus*: the human being is a wolf to other human beings. Marginalized groups in many countries of the world lack every form of active and even passive participation in society; interhuman relationships are disintegrating; people are in the grip of a pattern of life out of which they cannot possibly wrench themselves free; marginality characterizes every aspect of their existence.[68] To introduce change, as Christians, into all of this, is to mediate *salvation;* after all, "the joy and hope, the grief and anguish of the men of our time, especially of those who are poor or afflicted in any way, are the joy and hope, the grief and anguish of the followers of Christ as well" *(Gaudium et Spes* 1). Precisely because our concern is *salvation* we may no longer regard ourselves or others as prisoners of an omnipotent fate; in its mission the Church constitutes a resistance movement against every manifestation of fatalism and quietism.

On the other hand, since we may never overrate our own or others' capabilities, we have to ask critical questions in respect to all current theories of human self-redemption. Final salvation will not be wrought by human hands, not even by Christian hands. The Christian's eschatological vision of salvation will not be realized in history. For this reason Christians should never identify any specific project with the fullness of the reign of God. We are, at best, erecting bridgeheads for the reign of God.[69]

We therefore hold on to the transcendent character of salvation also, and to the need of calling people to faith in God through Christ. God's reign does not come but along the route of repentance and personal faith commitment.[70]

The integral character of salvation demands that the scope of the Church's mission be more comprehensive than has traditionally been the case. Mission is as coherent, broad and deep as the needs and exigencies of human existence. Mission means being involved in the ongoing dialogue between God who offers his salvation and the world which craves that salvation while being, at the same time, enmeshed in all kinds of evil.[71] "Mission means being sent to proclaim in deed and word that Christ died and rose for the life of the world, that he lives to transform human lives (Rom 8.2) and to overcome death."[72] From the tension between the "already" and the "not yet" of the reign of God, from the tension between the salvation *indicative* (salvation is already a reality!) and the salvation *subjunctive* (comprehensive salvation is yet to come!) there emerges the salvation *imperative* (get involved in the ministry of salvation!).[73] Those who know that God will one day wipe away all tears will not accept with resignation the tears of those who suffer and are oppressed *now*. Anyone who knows that one day there will be no more disease can and must actively anticipate the conquest of disease in individuals and society *now*. And anyone who knows that the enemy of God and humanity will be vanquished will already oppose him *now* in his machinations in family and society.[74] For all of this has to do with *salvation*.

NOTES

1. Cf. D. Wiederkehr, *Glaube an Erlösung Konzepte der Soteriologie vom Neuen Testament bis heute* (Freiburg: Herder,1976) 9-10; *idem*, "Die ganze Erlösung," *Theologische Quartalschrift* 162 (1982) 329-30; W. Beinert, "Jesus Christus, der Erlöser von Sünde und Tod: Überblick über die abendländische Soteriologie" in *Schuld, Sühne und Erlösung* ed K. J. Rivinius, SVD (St. Augustin: Steyler Verlag, 1983) 217-18; G. Greshake, *Gottes Heil–Glück des Menschen* (Freiburg: Herder, 1983) 15.

2. J. D. Gort, "Onheil, heil en bemiddeling" in *Oecumenische inleiding in de Missiologie* ed F. J. Verstraelen, A. Camps, L. A. Hoedemaker, & M. R. Spindler (Kampen: Kok, 1988) 203 (my translation).

3. In the Germanic languages, for instance German, the opposite of *Heil* (salvation) is *Unheil* (cf. Gort, ibid). The opposite of the English "salvation", "religiously" speaking, includes evil, perdition, damnation, doom, lostness, eternal punishment, and the like. The Germanic word group tends, however, to have a wider range of meanings.

4. Cf. Greshake, *Gottes Heil*, 51-52.

5. Ibid. 57, 62.

6. Cf. G. W. H. Lampe, "Early Patristic Eschatology" in *Eschatology* (Scottish Journal of Theology Occasional Papers, No. 2; Edinburgh: Oliver & Boyd, 1957) 30-33.

7. E. Voulgarakis, "Orthodoxe Mission," *Lexikon missionstheologischer Grundbegriffe*, ed K. Müller & T. Sundermeier (Berlin: Dietrich Reimer, 1987) 359-60.

8. A. Yannoulatos, "The Purpose and Motive of Mission," *International Review of Missions* 45 (1965) 285.

9. Cf. W. Lowe, "Christ and Salvation" in *Christian Theology: An Introduction to its Traditions and Tasks*, ed P. C. Hodgson & R. H. King (Philadelphia: Fortress, 1982) 200; Beinert, "Jesus Christus," 204.

10. My very brief summary of the interpretation of salvation in the Greek church cannot possibly do justice to the theological wealth and depth of the Orthodox position. Furthermore, it should be pointed out explicitly that what we have here is not just an "accommodation" to the pagan Greek spirit. In decisive respects the Greek church broke radically with the spirit and culture of the age. The *historical* character of salvation, the rootedness of the Christian faith in God's history with Israel, and the centrality of the resurrection were maintained throughout, in the face of Gnostic and other heresies.

11. Cf. Beinert, "Jesus Christus," 203-205.

12. "Heidnisches Wendentum und christliche Stammesfürsten," *Archiv für Kulturgeschichte* 44 (1962) 88-102.

13. *Paul among Jews and Gentiles* (Philadelphia: Fortress, 1976) 16.

14. Cf. Greshake, *Gottes Heil*, 68-73.

15. See, for instance, T. Ohm, *Machet zu Jüngern alle Völker: Theorie der Mission* (Freiburg: Erich Wewel Verlag, 1962) 276-288. See also W. Weber, "Mission als Befreiung zum universalen Heil" in ". . . *denn ich bin bei Euch*" (Mt 28,20): *Perspektiven im christlichen Missionsbewusstsein Heute*: FS J. Glazik und B. Willeke, ed H. Waldenfels (Einsiedeln: Benziger Verlag, 1978) 85-86. Catholic thinking on salvation emerges, *inter alia*, in the twentieth century missionary encyclicals prior to Vatican II, especially *Maximum Illud* (1919), *Rerum Ecclesiae* (1926), *Evangelii Praecones* (1951) and *Fidei Donum* (1957). In the first of these encyclicals, for instance, missionaries are referred to as people who "open the way to heaven for souls that are hurtling to destruction." During the first half of the twentieth century the two leading missiological "schools" in Catholicism were those of Münster and Louvain. The first understood the aim of mission to be the *conversion* of pagans, the second formulated it as the *incorporation* of converts into the only church that guarantees salvation. The differences between the two schools were not as far-reaching as might have appeared at first glance: also the School of Münster never for a moment doubted that converts could only be

saved via membership of the only saving church. In Protestantism the second accent—church planting as goal of mission—was not always explicitly emphasized; the first, however, was always (and still is today) a most important element of the Protestant definition of mission and salvation. With some qualifications one could say that, in both traditions, salvation was primarily seen as the salvation of souls whilst membership of the church indicated the *way* along which souls could obtain salvation. In Catholicism, however, the church tended to play a more vital role.

16. Cf. Greshake, *Gottes Heil*, 70.

17. Cf. A. M. Aagaard, "Missio Dei in katholischer Sicht," *Evangelische Theologie* 34 (1974) 428.

18. Cf. Wiederkehr, *Glaube*, (1976), 68-70; Lowe, "Christ and Theology," 201-205; Beinert, "Jesus Christus," 203-209; Greshake, *Gottes Heil*, 64-73.

19. Greshake, *Gottes Heil*, 20 (my translation); cf 19, 71.

20. Cf. Lowe, "Christ and Salvation," 219; Greshake, *Gottes Heil*, 19-20, 72-73; Beinert, "Jesus Christus," 202, 205, 208.

21. Cf. H.-W. Gensichen, "'Dienst der Seelen' und 'Dienst des Leibes' in der früheren pietistischen Mission" in *Der Pietismus in Gestalten und Wirkungen*, ed H. Bornkamm *et al* (Bielefeld: Luther Verlag, 1975).

22. Cf. Wiederkehr, *Glaube*, 77-122; "Erlösung," 331-336.

23. Cf. Beinert, "Jesus Christus," 209; Greshake, *Gottes Heil*, 26, 74.

24. Cf. Wiederkehr, "Erlösung," 331-333.

25. Cf. Greshake, *Gottes Heil*, 76.

26. Cf. Greshake, *Gottes Heil*, 26-29; cf. also J. Gründel, "Sünde als Verneinung des Willens Gottes: Zur Frage nach dem Ursprung von Leid, übel und Bösem" in *Schuld, Sühne und Erlösung*, ed. K. J. Rivinius (St. Augustin: Steyler Verlag, 1983) 113-115, 122.

27. Cf. Gründel, "Sünde als Verneinung," 106.

28. *Christian Missions and Social Progress: A Sociological Study of Foreign Missions* (Edinburgh & London: Oliphant, Anderson & Ferrier, 1897, 1899, 1907).

29. Quoted by James H. Moorhead, "The Erosion of Postmillennialism in American Religious Thought," *Church History* 53 (1984) 66.

30. H. Richard Niebuhr, "The Social Gospel and the Mind of Jesus," *The Journal of Religious Ethics* 16 (1988) 121.

31. H. Berkhof, *Christian Faith* (Grand Rapids: Eerdmans, 1979) 413.

32. J. C. Hoekendijk, "Notes on the Meaning of Mission(ary)" in *Planning for Mission: Working Papers on the New Quest for Missionary Communities*, ed. T. Wieser (New York: The U.S. Conference for the World Council of Churches, 1966) 43 (emphasis in the original).

33. Ibid.

34. Hoekendijk, *Kirche und Volk in der deutschen Missionswissenschaft* (Münich: Christian Kaiser, 1967) 348.

35. *The Power to be Human Toward a Secular Theology* (New York: The Macmillan Company, 1971).

36. *The Church for Others: Two Reports on the Missionary Structure of the Congregation* (Geneva: World Council of Churches, 1967).

37. Ibid, 78.

38. Quoted in T. Wieser, "Report on the Salvation Study," *International Review of Missions* 62 (1973) 176 .

39. *Bangkok Assembly 1973. Minutes and Report of the Assembly of the Commission on World Mission and Evangelism of the WCC* (Geneva: WCC, 1973) 89.

40. Ibid. 90.

41. *A Theology of Liberation* (15th Anniversary Edition with a new introduction by the author; Maryknoll: Orbis, 1988) 83-105.

42. Ibid, 84-87.

43. Quoted in Gutiérrez, *Liberation* xvii.

44. Wieser, "Report on the Salvation Study," 177.

45. "Bangkok 1972-1973," *International Review of Mission* 67 (1978) 368.

46. Ibid, 368.

47. Beinert, "Jesus Christus," 215 (my translation).

48. Cf. Lowe, "Christ and Salvation," 220.

49. J. Glazik, *Mission—der stets grössere Auftrag* (Aachen: Missio Aktuell Verlag, 1979) 160 (my translation).

50. " Memorandum from a Consultation on Mission, " *International Review of Mission* 71 (1982) 459.

51 . Reference in J . Triebel, *Bekehrung als Ziel der missionarischen Verkündigung* (Erlangen: Verlag der Ev.-Luth. Mission, 1976) 110, 278 .

52. P. G. Aring, *Kirche als Ereignis: Ein Beitrag zur Neuorientierung der Missionstheologie* (Neukirchen: Neukirchener Verlag, 1971) 24, 28, 88.

53. Cf. Gort, "Onheil," 213-14. See also Beinert, "Jesus Chrustus, " 214-15 .

54. "Salvation Today" in *The Evangelical Response to Bangkok,* ed. R. Winter (South Pasadena: William Carey Library, 1973) 31.

55. Cf. Aagaard, "Missio Dei," 429-431.

56. Cf. Glazik, *Mission,* 160.

57. W. C. van Unnik, " L'usage de *sozein* 'sauver' et des dérivés dans les évangiles synoptique"in *Sparsa Collecta: The Collected Essays of W. C van Unnik* (Leiden: Brill, 1973) 32; cf. also D. Stanley, "Jesus, Saviour of Mankind" in *Studia Missionalia* (29) 78 .

58. Cf . E. H. Scheffler, *Suffering in Luke's Gospel* (University of Pretoria: Unpublished Doctoral Dissertation, 1988). See also D. J. Bosch, "Mission in Jesus' Way: A Perspective from Luke's Gospel," *Missionalia* 17 (1989) *passim.*

59. Cf . Stanley, "J esus," 74 -75 .

60. This is not, however, always and under all circumstances the case. The parable of the rich man and Lazarus (16:23-26) seems to suggest that the loss of *earthly* life is not the greatest catastrophe a human being can encounter; apparently we should pay more attention to life in the hereafter than to life here, without forgetting, however, that the decisions about the hereafter are being made here and now. And again, according to Luke these decisions have to do with our relationship to both Jesus Christ and our neighbor.

61. Cf . Stanley, "Jesus "63-69.

62. Cf. J. C. Beker, *Paul's Apocalyptic Gospel* (Philadelphia: Fortress, 1984) .

63. On this, cf. D. J. Bosch, "Paul on Human Hopes, " *Journal of Theology in Southern Africa* 67 (June 1989) passim.

64. Cf. Beker, *Gospel,* 10, 51f, 58, 111 .

65. Cf. Wiederkehr, *Glaube,* 34; Beinert, "Jesus Christus," 211 .

66. Cf. Wiederkehr, *Glaube,* 39-43.

67. Cf . H . Waldenfels, "Mission als Vermittlung von umfassendem Heil" *Zeitschrift für Missionswissenschaft und Religionswissenschaft* 61 (1977); K. Müller, "'Holistic Mission' oder das 'umfassende Heil'" in " . . . *denn ich bin bei Euch (*Mt 18,20), ed H. Waldenfels (Einsiedeln: Benziger, 1978); Weber, "Mission"; "Memorandum." In a sense, it is tautological to add any adjective to the noun "salvation": salvation is, in the nature of the case, comprehensive and integral or it is not salvation.

68. Cf. Müller, "'Holistic Mission,'" 90, who quotes H. Kramer in this respect.

69. Cf. C. Geffré, "Reflections on a New Age of Mission," *International Review of Mission* 71 (1982) 490; Beinert, "Jesus Christus," 215, 218; Beker, *Gospel,* 86-87; Gort, "Onheil," 213.

70. Cf. Wiederkehr, "Erlösung," 334; Geffre, "Reflections," 492. Cf. Gort, "Onheil," 209.

71. Cf. Gort, "Onheil," 209.

72. "Memorandum," 459.

73. Gort, "Onheil," 214.

74. W. J. Hollenweger, in an unpublished paper, entitled "Where no Nightingales are Singing . . . A Dialogue with Ignazio Silone".

SIN AND SALVATION: AMADEUS IN THE LIGHT OF ROMANS

ROBERT JEWETT

For I have already charged that Jews as well as Greeks are all under sin

As it is written,
"There is none righteous, not one;"
"there is no one that understands,
there is no one that seeks God.
All turn aside,
together they are corrupted;
there is no one that does what is proper,
there is not a single one."
"An open grave is their throat,
their tongues deceive."
"The poison of asps is under their lips."
"Whose mouth is full of curses and bitterness."
"Their feet are quick to shed blood,
ruin and misery are in their paths,
and the path of peace they do not know."
"There is no fear of God before their eyes."[1]
(Romans 3:9-18)

For the wrath of God is being revealed from heaven
against all impiety and wickedness of humans who by
wickedness suppress the truth.[2]
(Romans 1:18)

I. INTRODUCTION

In an effort to relate Biblical texts to American culture, seeking to develop an indigenized hermeneutic, I have turned in recent years to films, novels and short stories that enjoy broad popularity.[3] The method is to find a cultural artifact that resonates at a deep level with a particular Biblical passage and then to interpret both the passage and the artifact so that each throws light on the other. The goal of this interactive hermeneutic is to allow the ancient text to become accessible to the contemporary audience by correlating it with a modern text or artifact whose appeal is demonstrable. In the case of Pauline texts, whose interpretive trajectories have been so completely dominated by European modes of abstract thought, I am particularly interested in the indigeonizing and enlivening potentials of this method.

The correlation with a contemporary artifact or text, particularly with one that resonates deeply with the audience, allows a Pauline text to strike to the heart rather than merely to the mind. The contemporary life situation is thereby addressed by the text in ways that may be somewhat analogous to the original impact on Paul's initial audience. The powerful collective experiences to which Paul's Letters allude, involving alienation, conversion, transformation, ecstasy and suffering, may sometimes be more adequately replicated in contemporary experience through mass entertainment than through reading theology. There are some artifacts of contemporary entertainment that find lodgement in the same arenas of the human psyche that the gospel seeks to address. The method of correlation allows an inspired Biblical text to enter a depth dimension of contemporary life that ordinary abstract discourse has difficulty in penetrating.

The Academy Award winning film, *Amadeus*, is an ideal candidate to develop a correlation with Paul's theory of sin and forgiveness. This is one of those rare and inspired films that embodies truth beyond the grasp of filmmaker and playwrite, conveying a distinctive aspect of the theology of Romans. This dimension of *Amadeus* dawned on me slowly, however, and was not caught by any of the reviewers that I have read. The first time I saw the film, the conventional sense of sin as indecency seemed to match Wolfgang Amadeus Mozart pretty well. The film depicts Mozart as an arrogant and uncouth genius who was admired but ultimately hated by the court composer, Salieri. Mozart's foulmouthed jokes, his sexual irresponsibility, his inability to live within the limits of his income or time, his chronic abuse of alcohol—all of these made him irritating to conventional morality.[4]

His father was depicted as furious with his irresponsibility; his archbishop was disgusted at his arrogance; and the advisors of Emperor Josef were alarmed at the young composer's blithe violations of political conformity and social etiquette. According to the dictionary definition of sin as "the willful or deliberate violation of some religious or moral principle," Mozart would seem to qualify as a rake of the first order. He was a prodigal son for whom anger and jealousy by a type of elder brother would be predictable. When I saw the film for the first time, as a matter of fact, I was predisposed to view it this way because a colleague had referred to *Amadeus* as a form of the classic parable of the Prodigal Son and the Elder Brother.

The second time I saw the film was with my wife and daughter, and a different perspective began to surface. Perhaps it was because they are both musicians and perhaps it was because I was thinking more about the themes of Paul's Letter to the Romans. In fact, a very different perspective emerges when one views *Amadeus* in the light of Romans 1 and 3. It is the character of Mozart's well placed and highly successful competitor, the composer Salieri, that reveals a deeper, and ultimately more pervasive and serious level of sin. By correlating the argument of Romans with this powerful story, the abstraction becomes embodied in a provocative and potentially transforming fashion.

II.

1. *The view of Romans about sin.*

The well known passage in Rom 3:9-25 opens with a shockingly sweeping allegation: "I have already charged," Paul states, "that all humans, Jews as well as Greeks, are under sin" (Rom 3:9). The term "sin" is used here in the singular, implying that a single, alienating power has all humans in its grip.[5] The Revised Standard Version translation adds the word "power" to this sentence in order to make this clear: "under the power of sin." Karl Barth explained this expression with the following words: "Both Jews and Greeks, the sons of God and the natural children of the world, are . . . children of wrath. They are, without exception, in subjection to the foreign power of sin. . . . To us God is, and remains, unknown; we are, and remain, homeless in this world; sinners we are and sinners we remain."[6]

Paul had described the shape of this universal sin in the earlier chapters of his Letter to the Romans. All human beings, he argued, have an innate capacity to recognize God in the created order, but we "suppress" this truth (Rom 1:18)[7] and worship ourselves instead. One commentator suggests the vivid translation, "hold the truth imprisoned."[8] The term used here has the sense of "hold down" or "suppress,"[9] the willful effort[10] to distort reality. We exchange "the truth about God for a lie and worship and serve the creature rather than the Creator" (Rom 1:25). When this occurs, Paul contends, the human capacity to distinguish the truth is crippled. "So they are without excuse," Paul writes, "for although they knew God they did not honor him as God or give thanks to him, but they became futile in their thinking and their senseless minds were darkened. Claiming to be wise, they became fools. . . " (Rom 1:20-21).

Whenever humans place themselves rather than God at the center of the universe, they inevitably begin to lie about it, suppressing the realization of what they have done. C. K. Barrett describes the link between such suppression and a false self-image: "The immediate result of this rebellion was a state of corruption in which men were no longer capable of distinguishing between themselves and God, and accordingly fell into idolatry, which, in all its forms, lies in the last resort the idolization of the self."[11] In this way human beings come under a power so invisible, so unconscious, and yet so encompassing in its evil consequences that they cannot grasp what has gone wrong. This is how all humans fall "under the power of sin," to use the expression of our text.

2. *Salieri's Embodiment of Sin as Suppression.*

This brings us to the character of Salieri in this Milo Forman film,[12] which is much closer to the thought of Paul than Peter Shaffer's original play. Years before he met Mozart, the young Salieri as a boy had prayed to God, "Make me great. . . make me famous through the world. Make me immortal. Let everyone speak my name with love. After I die, let them repeat my name ever with love. In return, I promise you. . . my chastity . . . my industry. . . and my deep humility." Shortly after this bargain, Salieri's father died by choking on a fish bone and the lad was free to pursue his musical career. Ultimately he becomes the most famous composer in Vienna.

The conventional shape of Salieri's Christian dedication disguised what Romans refers to as "worshipping and serving the creature rather than the creator." To achieve immortality as a composer or in any other field is to become more than a creature. That every one should speak our name with love is something that only God deserves. As Samuel Terrien describes the depiction of Salieri in the play, "He sought 'to snatch the Absolute.' He knew, of course, that the Absolute belongs to God alone, but that is precisely the target of his craving, 'to blaze like a comet across the firmament of Europe.'"[13] However, the realization of the true nature of Salieri's arrogant yearning for eternal popularity was suppressed under the disguise of piety. He was caught in the net of the "tradesmen" view of "the God of Bargains" who will guarantee divine favor in return for human devotion: "You give me so—I'll give you so! No more, no less!"[14]

The entire campaign that Salieri later mounted to frustrate the career of Mozart is comprehensible in light of Paul's analysis of the "power of sin." The older composer had been deeply impressed by the originality and power of Mozart's music. When he examined some pages of Mozart's compositions, he said with amazement that they revealed "no correction of any kind. The music was already finished . . . in his head. Page after page, as if he were taking dictation! And what music, finished as no music was ever finished! Take away one note, and it would be diminished. Take away one phrase, and the structure would fall . . . . This was the very voice of God."

But Salieri found it outrageous that the uncouth Mozart should have been selected as the "instrument" capable of expressing this divine level of music. "All I ever wanted was to sing to God," Salieri complained after Mozart had humiliated him by instantly memorizing and then miraculously improving a little march he had written for the Emperor Joseph to welcome Mozart. God " . . . gave me that longing. But why impress me with the desire, like a lust in my body, and then deny me the talent?"

Later Salieri discovered that Mozart had an affair with the beautiful opera singer whom he secretly admired. "The creature has had my darling girl," he declares with bitterness. "It was incomprehensible. What was God up to?" For the first time in Salieri's life, he began to know hatred, to think "violent thoughts." After discovering the full scope of Mozart's creative power, Salieri declares war on the God who had selected this monster as his vehicle. Taking down the wooden crucifix in his chamber and placing it in the fireplace, he declares to God: "From now on we are enemies, you and I. Because you choose for your instrument a boastful, lustful, smutty, infantile boy, and you leave me only the ability to recognize your incarnation. . . you are unjust, unfair, unkind. I will block you, I swear it. I will hinder and harm your creature on earth. As far as I am able, I will ruin your incarnation."

Salieri hires a maid to serve in the Mozart's cluttered apartment so that he could spy out what his competitor was doing and discredit his compositions before they appeared. While appearing to be Mozart's friend and protector, he saw to it that his magnificent operas were given short runs in the court theater. Finally, he contrived a plan to haunt Mozart by wearing the black mask that Wolfgang's deceased father had used in an abortive mascarade party. The masked Salieri offers a large sum of money for Mozart to write a *Requium for the Dead* that Salieri could usurp and perform as his own creation at the funeral of his competitor. It was, as Salieri put it, "a way, a terrible way, in which I could triumph over God." The unfair Deity who poured his divine music into this scatological nerd, Mozart, would finally be mocked and defeated.

So it was that a person whose conventional devotion disguised the lust for immortal status ended up under the "power of sin," displaying what Paul described at the end of chapter 1 of Romans in terms of the consequences of suppressing the truth:

> And since they did not see fit to acknowledge God, God gave them up to a base mind and to improper conduct. They were filled with all manner of wickedness, evil, covetousness, malice. Full of envy, murder, strife, deceit, malignity. . . (Rom 1:28-29).

The attempt to manipulate God was really an assault on deity itself, resulting in a distortion of Salieri's humanity. In Terrien's words, "Because the religious man feels deceived, his belief turns into blasphemy. Because the moral man feels cheated, his virtue becomes the trough of malevolence."[15]

3. *Mozart's Embodiment of Sin.*

It would be tempting in the light of Salieri's sin to interpret Mozart as a genuine embodiment of human piety. There was an innocence and integrity in his music and outlook that seemed to be immune to the manipulative, conforming and suppressed sins of everyone else in the film. He did not allow the silly tastes and standards of his time to throttle the creative urge that he felt. When the Emperor Franz Josef echoes the director's complaint about *The Abduction from the Seraglio* as having "too many notes," Mozart remains true to what he has created.

> "There are just as many notes, Majesty, as are required.
> No more, no less."

The idiotic Emperor replies that Mozart should not be discouraged. His opera was "quality work, and there are simply too many notes, that's all. Just cut a few, and it will be perfect."

Mozart replies, "which few did you have in mind, Majesty?" He remains the free spirit, making music for the pure joy of the creative process, which is why Karl Barth was able to celebrate him as the purest expression of creatureliness.[16] Knowing the wide range of life's joys and sorrows, Mozart always remains within his creaturely limits. Barth writes, "Granted, darkness, chaos, death, and hell do appear, but not for a moment are they allowed to prevail. Knowing all, Mozart creates music from a mysterious center, and so knows and observes limits to the right and the left, above and below. He maintains moderation."[17] Answering why he began each morning's writing with recorded music of Mozart rather than Bach, he said that when the angels in heaven play music for worship, they use Bach, but when they play for themselves, they play Mozart.

Yet the film *Amadeus* is honest enough to portray a side of Mozart that was rather similar to Salieri. The cocky young man refuses to submit his music to the panel of judges in order to earn the lucrative position of teaching the Emperor's niece. He tells the court chamberlain that in comparison with the other composers who might apply, "They may be better qualified, but I'm the best." Having fallen prey to pride, Mozart was terribly frustrated when he failed to gain the public recognition that more conforming composers like Salieri enjoyed. He expressed his sense of being wronged by life by indulging in too much drinking and partying, falling into a dissolute life style that contributed to exhaustion and finally to his death.

In a sense, Mozart was involved in his own unique form of "worshipping and serving the creature rather than the creator," to use Paul's words (Rom 1:25). He violated his creaturely limitations.[18] For instance, he childishly hoped to retain the affection of the singer he had seduced while going ahead with the marriage to Constanza. He foolishly denied his chronic indebtedness while bounding off to yet another expensive diversion. Responding to his father's query about his financial situation, Mozart says, "It's marvelous. They love me here" in Vienna. He refused to accept any more limits to his spending, his drinking and his carousing than he did in the area of sexual fidelity. While he understood the threat such behavior posed to his life, having experienced it in the wrath of his father and embodied it in the opera, *Don Giovanni,* where exploitative behavior earns the reward of hell, Mozart failed to recognize his own condition.

In the end, Mozart was as blind in his strategies of suppressing the truth as was Salieri. And the recent investigations into the death of Mozart reveal the impact of such suppression.[19] While Maestro Salieri probably had nothing directly to do with Mozart's demise (though he felt guilty for it later), the crucial factor was Mozart's indiscretions with the wife of a well placed official who was in a position to settle scores. Mutual friends apparently arranged for a quick burial in a pauper's grave where evidence would soon be unrecoverable and a scandal avoided.[20] Whether this theory is correct or not, it remains clear that the best Mozart could achieve was to "try to suppress the truth." For him as for everyone else, the truth will finally come out, sometimes to destroy us. Could this be the deeper meaning of the hyena-like laugh that Tom Hulce affected in the film? Was it perhaps an expression of the attempt to relieve the tension between the truth one wishes to suppress and the truth that one knows will some day be revealed? However one responds to this enigma, one thing remains clear: while his music is as immortal as any ever composed, Mozart's life proved fragile indeed.

4. *The Universal Power of Sin and Its Consequences.*

The cinematic version of *Amadeus* drives us therefore to hear Romans with sharpened ears. "What then? Are we Jews any better off?" Are we law abiding, hard-working and disciplined Salieris any better off than the dissolute Mozart? Are we creative, nonconformist Mozarts really immune to the sins of the Salieris of this world? "No, not at all," says Paul with relentless logic, "for I have already charged that all humans, both Jews and Greeks, are under the power of sin" (Rom 3:9).

Each human being on this earth is similar in this regard. We react to the experience of vulnerability by pretending to be divine. From the time we were infants, we seek the secure status that only God can ever have, expressing our lust to be the big apple with countless strategies of differentiating ourselves from others. We make our bargains with a shopkeeper god, seeking for the kind of uncritical admiration and permanent achievement that humans can never finally achieve. But we suppress the truth about what we have done, and then set about to suppress competition on every hand. Blind to our condition, unconscious of our final motivations, and hence under "the power of sin," we fit the description that Paul contrived by arranging and adapting a series of citations from the Hebrew scriptures:[21]

> "There is none righteous, not one;"
> "there is not one that understands,

there is no one that seeks God.
All turn aside,
together they are corrupted;
there is no one that does what is proper,
there is not a single one."
"An open grave is their throat,
their tongues deceive."
"The poison of asps is under their lips. "
"Whose mouth is full of curses and bitterness."
"Their feet are quick to shed blood,
ruin and misery are in their paths,
"There is no fear of God before their eyes."
(Romans 3:10-18)

III.

So is there no hope for human beings? Will our suppression of the truth about God and ourselves go on until all of us are with Mozart, in an unmarked grave, or with Salieri, in the asylum? Is there no way to avoid such gruesome fates, no chance of recognition by which we can come to terms with our particular form of suppression?

The recent survey of research into the psychology of self-deception by Daniel Goleman indicates that it is a well nigh universal problem.[22] Confirmation is emerging of the essential accuracy of the Pauline perception: "The roots of self-deception seem to lie in the mind's ability to allay anxiety by distorting awareness. Denial soothes."[23] Studies of perception bring modern psychologists close to Paul's view of the power of idolatrous images to prevent a vision of the truth. Our judgment of the relevance of information is determined by what psychologists are now calling "schemas" in the human mind that lead us to suppress contrary information.[24] As we can see in the story of Salieri, some of the most powerful schemas involve our religious image of the world, of elemental justice, and of our own virtue which requires that we suppress the disclosure of details that counter this image. This leads Goleman to describe "the urgent need for compelling antidotes to self-deception," not only for individuals but also for groups. "The new research reveals a natural bent toward self-deception so great that the need for counterbalancing forces within the mind and society as a whole—forces such as insight and respect for truth—becomes more apparent than ever."[25] The problem is that psychology appears near the end of its resources in searching for truly effective counterbalances for this human habit of suppressing the truth. The great relevance of Pauline thought to this research, it seems to me, is not only its clear prescience of the basic cause of the mental dilemma but also its offer of a powerful antidote.

1. *Paul's Proclamation of Grace.*

The good news at the heart of Romans is that the grace of God conveyed in Christ is able to restore humans to righteousness, breaking the power of sin. "Since all have sinned and fall short of the glory of God, they are made righteous by his grace as a gift, through the redemption which is in Christ Jesus. . ." (Rom 3:23-24). Behind this abstract language is a powerful event of unconditional acceptance that is open to everyone.[26] Paul had discovered this in the cross of Christ. To him the cross revealed human suppression at its height and divine forgiveness at its depth. The political and religious leaders who crucified Jesus epitomized the human effort to suppress the truth about God and themselves. When people encounter what is truly good and noble, their deepest instinct is to stamp it out, to crucify him, so that they can remain alone, unchallenged at the center of the universe. Paul's persecution of the early Christians enacted his particular strategy of legalistic suppression. Not until the encounter with the resurrected Lord on the Road to Damascus did Paul grasp the shocking reality of his unconscious behavior. At the same time he discovered the unconditional acceptance of himself as a persecutor in the very process of the attempted suppression. As Paul explains in Rom 5:8, "But God shows his love for us in that while we were yet sinners Christ died for us."

The depth of love revealed in Christ is the only force capable of penetrating our strategies of suppression. It makes us know that we are acceptable to God even if we are not perfect, not godlike in our powers, not loved and not admired by the world. Christ accepts sinners precisely as we are, overcoming the bitterness and disappointment and alienation we feel because life has not bathed us in the popularity and success that we expect.

Once we begin to internalize this acceptance through faith in the grace of God, we are enabled to see for the first time the enormity of our godlike pretensions. The suppression of the truth about ourselves and God lets up for a moment, and we admit that we shall always remain vulnerable humans, and that God alone is God. In such an instant, the deepest level of forgiveness is possible, because we are confronting not the little mistakes and failures of our lives, but rather the "power of sin" to which we have given ourselves in our mad quests to stand at the center of the world. Unconditional grace enables us to experience what Paul calls the "righteousness of God, because in his divine forbearance he had passed over former sins . . ." (Rom 3:25). Forgiveness is the only power that ultimately can break the "power of sin." It subverts our strategies of suppression, rendering them unnecessary.

2. *Mozart's Conveyance of Forgiveness.*

In this connection the film *Amadeus* lives up to the implication of its title, "beloved by God."[23] The selection of Mozart's middle name as the title both of the play and the film is not explained in any of the discussions I have seen, yet it is remarkably apt as a description of the impact of the music itself. Salieri described the indelible impression made on him by the closing scene of Mozart's *The Marriage of Figaro*. Having been caught in an effort to initiate an affair, the count asks the forgiveness of his wife. The incredibly tender music Mozart wrote for this scene conveyed in Salieri's words "true forgiveness, filling the theater, conferring on all who sat there perfect absolution." The magnificent melody flowed on, "unstoppable," overwhelming every obstacle until perfect reconciliation was achieved. "It was a miracle," Salieri said with amazement. Similarly in the *Requiem* Mozart manages to convey ". . . a God who accepts and receives the sinner unconditionally. His love is absolutely different from human expectations. . . . Mozart's *Kyrie Eleison* is not. . . a somber supplication for forgiveness. The mercy has already come."[28]

3. *Salieri's Participation in Forgiveness.*

Although he was unable to understand it at the time, Salieri encountered the miracle of personal forgiveness moments before he triumphed over Mozart and Mozart's creator. While taking Mozart's final dictation of the Mass for the Dead with the diabolical intent of using it at the funeral to mock the God who placed his genius in such an unworthy vehicle, the exhausted composer stops and thanks him. "I thought you did not appreciate my music," Mozart confesses to his unacknowledged adversary. "Please, forgive me," he says. Salieri is stunned, unable to respond until long after Mozart's untimely death.

The theme of mutual forgiveness as a means of coming to terms with finitude is what holds the opening and closing of this powerful film together, it seems to me. In this regard also, the film is much more true to the Pauline vision of the human heart than was the original play by Peter Shaffer. The opening words of the film are spoken behind the closed door of Salieri's bedroom, years after the death of his adversary. "Forgive me, Mozart!" he cries. Having apparently come to terms with the error of his long and deadly thwarting of Mozart's life and music, Salieri utters these words and then tries to take his own life. He lives the rest of his years in the Asylum for the Insane in Vienna, brooding over his contest with God.

After relating his life story to the priest, the film ends with Salieri accompanying the shocked cleric to the entrance of the asylum. The elderly composer moves through the corridors filled with the mentally ill, dispensing absolution and forgiveness to all the "mediocrities" incarcerated there. Although this closing scene has elements of mockery of traditional religion,[29] it rings true to the theology of Romans. Each of us *is* mediocre when compared with truly godlike qualities; even the best of us, like Mozart, are vulnerable and flawed, likely to burn out our lives in frustration and self abuse when we seek to stand at the center of the world. The rest of us, like Salieri, disguise our frustration in envy of those more successful than ourselves, acting out scripts of mutual destruction.

4. *Conclusion.*

What the inmost soul of our generation requires is absolution. But we need it in the context of facing the truth about ourselves, our institutions, and our nation. As heirs of a long tradition of American exceptionalism, assuming our innocence in a world filled with malevolent adversaries, we desperately need to confront the shocking truth of *Amadeus* and Paul. Until the culturally encouraged strategies of suppression are exposed and acknowledged, no person or group is able to receive forgiveness at redemptive level. In fact until that happens, a theology of grace will be nothing less than corrupting, feeding our innate narcissism and sustaining our schemes of suppression. But when forgiveness, absolution—the experience of unconditional grace—is genuinely and profoundly experienced, it is capable of releasing us from the compulsion to suppress the truth about ourselves and life. Grace alone can break the "power of sin." And when it does, we are enabled to become agents of reconciliation for others, dispensing absolution to those around us, not because we have earned it or deserve it, but because we have been redeemed by grace. We are all Amadeuses, if we could only recognize it: beloved by God despite all our pretensions and disguises.

And thus it seems to me that some words written during the period depicted in the film are a fitting conclusion to our story. Charles Wesley had experienced what Paul proclaims in Romans, and wrote the well-known lines: Christ

> . . .breaks the power of cancelled sin,
> he sets the prisoner free;

his blood can make the foulest clean,
his blood avails for me.[30]

—and for you—and for Salieri.

NOTES

1. This rhetorical analysis is adapted from L. Keck, "The Function of Rom 3:10-18: Observations and Suggestions" in God's *Christ and His People: Studies in Honour of Nils Alstrup Dahl*, ed. J. Jervell and W. A. Meeks (Oslo: Universitetsforlaget, 1977) 142-46.

2. The rhetorical structure is adapted from J. Weiss, "Beiträge zur Paulinischen Rhetorik" in *Theologische Studien: FS Bernhard Weiss* (Göttingen: Vandenhoeck & Ruprecht, 1897) 214.

3. My first published effort along this line is *Jesus Against the Rapture: Seven Unexpected Prophecies* (Philadelphia: Westminster, 1979).

4. Alan Rich protests the moral stereotyping in the film as anachronistic, since Mozart's behavior would not have elicited " . . . much more in the time of *Tom Jones* or *Goetz von Verlichingen*." "Amadeus—A Fabric of Falsehoods," *Ovation* 5, Number 11 (1984) 40.

5. See E. Käsemann, *Commentary on Romans*, trans. G. W. Bromiley (Grand Rapids: Eerdmans, 1980) 86; C. E. B. Cranfield, *A Critical and Exegetical Commentary on the Epistle to the Romans* (Edinburgh: Clark, 1975) 191: "Paul thinks of sin as a power which has got control of man, and there is a marked tendency to personification in his references to it. . . ." For a critique of this view, see Günter Röhser, *Metaphorik und Personifikation der Sünde: Antike Sündenvorstellungen und paulinischen Hamartia* (Tübingen: Mohr-Siebeck, 1987).

6. K. Barth, *The Epistle to the Romans*, trans. E. C. Hoskins (Oxford: University Press, 1933) 85.

7. As Cranfield shows, however, the present participle requires the translation "try to suppresss . . . ." In *Romans*, 112 Cranfield stresses the conative force of the present participle, citing R. Funk, *Greek Grammar of the New Testament and Other Early Christian Literature: F. Blass and A. Debrunner* (Chicago: University of Chicago Press, 1961) 167 which discusses the present indicative "in [which] the durative present is bound up with the notion of incompleteness . . . "

8. C. K. Barrett, *The Epistle to the Romans* (New York: Harper & Row, 1957) 34.

9. Cranfield, *Romans*, 112.

10. See J. D. G. Dunn, *Romans 1-8* (Dallas: Word, 1988) 56.

11. Barrett, *Romans*, 37.

12. All of the subsequent quotations are from my tape recording of the film rather than from the more easily accessible play. The film is available in VHS through HBO/Cannon Video. The original play is *Peter Shaffer's Amadeus* (New York: Harper & Row, 1981).

13. S. Terrien, "*Amadeus* Revisited," *Theology Today* 42 (1986) 437.

14. *Idem*, cited again from the Peter Shaffer play rather than from the film.

15. Terrien, "*Amadeus* Revisited," 439-40.

16. K. Barth, *Wolfgang Amadeus Mozart*, trans. C. K. Pott; Foreword by J. Updike (Grand Rapids: Eerdmans, 1986) 16, 33-34.

17. *Mozart*, 53.

18. This is overlooked by Terrien in "*Amadeus* Revisited," 440-42.

19. Cf. F. Carr, "Mozart's Mysterious Death: A New Interpretation," *Ovation* 5 (1984) 19-27, providing a summary of his book dealing with the death of Mozart, *Mozart and Constanza* (New York: Watts, 1984).

20. See Carr, "Mozart's Mysterious Death," 25-26.

21. That the catena of quotations in Rom 3:10-18 was created by an early Christian scholar and quoted by Paul has been argued by O. Michel, *Der Brief an die Römer* (Göttingen: Vandenhoeck & Ruprecht, 1978) 143 and L. A. Keck, "The Function of Rom 3:10-18: Observations and Suggestions" in *God's Christ and His People: Studies in Honour of Nils Alstrup Dahl,* ed. J. Jervell and W. A. Meeks (Oslo: Universitetsforlaget, 1977) 146-147. The close links between the content of the quotations and Paul's argument suggest that Paul was either an editor of the catena or that he created it specifically for the argument in Romans. The Pauline authorship of the catena is emphasized in the most recent investigation by D.-A. Koch, *Die Schrift als Zeuge des Evangeliums* (Tübingen: Mohr-Siebeck, 1986) 179-84.

22. D. Goleman, "Insights into Self-Deception," *The New York Times Magazine* (May 12, 1985) 36-43. The article is adapted from his book *Vital Lies. Simple Truths: the Psychology of Self- Deception* (New York: Simon and Schuster, 1985).

23. "Insights into Self-Deception," 38.

24. "Insights into Self-Deception," 41-43.

25. "Insights into Self-Deception," 43, 36.

26. See Dunn, *Romans 1-8,* 179: "The gospel is that God sets to rights man's relationship with himself by an act of sheer generosity which depends on no payment man can make, which is without reference to whether any individual in particular is inside the law/covenant or outside, and which applies to all human beings without exception."

27. Terrien, "*Amadeus* Revisited," 438: ". . . a name which suggests 'the gift of God, the love of God, the one whom God loves.'"

28. Terrien, "*Amadeus* Revisited," 441.

29. Terrien quotes an editor of *The Christian Century* as charging that Shaffer's play ". . . finally insinuates a cynical view of life which is far worse than a courageously maintained nihilism." "*Amadeus* Revisited," 435.

30. Charles Wesley, "O For a Thousand Tongues to Sing," *The Methodist Hymnal: Official Hymnal of the Methodist Church* (Nashville: The Methodist Publishing House, 1964) 1, verse 4.

THE CONTRIBUTORS

DONALD E. GOWAN
Professor of Old Testament
Pittsburgh Theological Seminary
Pittsburgh, PA

JOEL B. GREEN
Academic Dean and Associate Professor of New Testament
New College for Advanced Christian Studies
Berkeley, CA

MARIANNE MEYE THOMPSON
Associate Professor of New Testament
Fuller Theological Seminary
Pasadena, CA

BEN F. MEYER
Professor of New Testament
McMaster University
Hamilton, Ontario, Canada

PAUL L. HAMMER
Professor of New Testament
Colgate Rochester Divinity School/Bexley Hall/
Crozer Theological Seminary
Rochester, NY

JONATHAN H. RAINBOW
Pastor, First Baptist Church
Porterville, CA

ALASDAIR I. C. HERON
Professor of Systematic Theology
University of Erlangen
Erlangen, Germany

JOHN WEBORG
Professor of Systematic Theology
North Park Theological Seminary
Chicago, IL

DAVID J. BOSCH
Professor of Missiology
University of South Africa
Pretoria, SA

ROBERT JEWETT
Professor of New Testament
Garrett-Evangelical Theological Seminary
Evanston, IL

PICKWICK PUBLICATIONS

4137 Timberlane Drive
Allison Park, PA 15105-2932

Critical Realism and the New Testament
By Ben F. Meyer
ISBN 0-915138-97-2 $19.95

The Epigones: A Study of the Theology of the Genevan Academy at the Time of the Synod of Dort.
By William A. McComish
ISBN 0-915138-62-X $36.00

Freedom and Civilization Among The Greeks. By A. J. Festugière
Tr. by P. T. Brannan
ISBN 0-915138-98-0 $15.00

A Gentleman in Every Slum: Church of England Missions in East London, 1837-1914
By David Brown McIlhiney
ISBN 0-915138-95-6 $15.00

The Kitchen Saint and the Heritage of Islam: Conversations, Spiritual Maxims and Letters of Brother Lawrence
Tr. by Elmer H. Douglas
ISBN 1-55635-003-1 $10.00

Luke the Theologian. Thirty-three years of Research (1950-1983)
By François Bovon
ISBN 0-915138-93-X $35.00

The Present and the Past
A Study of Anamnesis
By Richard J. Ginn
ISBN 1-55635-004-X $12.00

Searching for Lost Coins
Explorations in Christianity and Feminism
By Ann Loades
ISBN 1-55635-000-7 $12.00

Theology Beyond Christendom Essays on the Centenary of the Birth of Karl Barth
Ed. by John Thompson
ISBN 0-915138-85-9 $36.00

A Theology of Electricity
By Ernst Benz
Tr. by Dennis Stillings
ISBN 0-915138-92-1 $19.95

The Triune God. An Ecumenical Study
By E. L. Mascall
(Co-published with Churchman Publishing)
ISBN 0-915138-96-4 $12.90

The Quest for Church Unity
From John Calvin to Isaac d'Huisseau
By Richard Stauffer
ISBN 0-915138-63-8 $15.00

The Will of God and the Cross
An Historical and Theological Study of John Calvin's Doctrine of Limited Redemption
By Jonathan H. Rainbow
ISBN 1-55635-005-8 $24.00

Anselm: Fides Quaerens Intellectum
Anselm's proof of the existence of God in the context of his theological scheme.
By Karl Barth
ISBN 0-915138-75-1 $15.00